Arranging Barbershop

Volume 1: Getting Started On Your Arranging Journey

Barbershop Harmony Society

To access recordings and hyperlinks that accompany this book, go to www.halleonard.com/mylibrary and enter this code where indicated:

Enter Code
6262-9303-2743-9062

Hal Leonard Books
An Imprint of Hal Leonard LLC

Arranging Barbershop

Volume 1: Getting Started On Your Arranging Journey

Published in 2023 by Hal Leonard Books
An Imprint of Hal Leonard LLC
7777 West Bluemound Road
Milwaukee, WI 53213

Trade Book Division Editorial Offices
33 Plymouth St., Montclair, NJ 07042

Printed in the United States

Book design by the Barbershop Harmony Society

Library of Congress Cataloging-in-Publication Data submission in process

ISBN-10: 1705191797
ISBN-13/EAN: 9781705191798

www.halleonardbooks.com
www.barbershop.org

Table of Contents

Foreword

By Joe Liles

> "Let's sing a song, let's ring a song, let harmony be true. Come join the crowd, sing long and loud like good chord busters do."
>
> *From "The Chord-buster March" by W.A. Wyatt (1962)*

The glorious, ringing sound of barbershop harmony has blessed our hearts, minds, and ears for a long, long time. It was the joy of singing this harmony that brought each one of us to the feast. We quickly discovered the added benefits of creating lifelong friendships and performing for cheering audiences. Rehearsing in a chorus or quartet or woodshedding with a pickup foursome can bring thrills of delight. We are held together by the magical elixir of consonant chords voiced and sung in ways to maximize the reinforcement of overtones. I am sure each of you can give testimony as to how life-enhancing, even life-changing, your own experience has been.

I was involved in church music in my early years. I wrote my first little gospel song at age six and it was published in my teens. My first immersion into four-part barbershop harmony style happened in January of 1967. It was yet another divine experience. I was astounded by the joyful sound and the dedication of the men of the San Antonio Chordsmen Chorus. I joined them and was soon invited to be their chorus director and in-house arranger. For well over 50 years, I've enjoyed harmonizing and working with barbershop singers from all over the world. I've directed choruses, sung in quartets, taught numerous courses on barbershop craft, coached, judged contests, written and arranged music, and woodshedded with many pickup foursomes.

During this journey, the primary nourishment for our singers has become obvious to me: it's the music and how it is arranged. We all thrive on songs and tags voiced in the style of music we love, that of barbershop harmony!

This new series of books, with its associated programs and activities, is for every level of arranging interests from beginner to pro. It is dedicated to the creation and preservation processes that will continue to spread the joy of singing and bind us all together in harmony forever.

Dedication

By Steve Tramack

Figure X.1

"Shine," original verse composed and arranged by David Wright for the 1993 International Quartet Champions of the Barbershop Harmony Society (BHS), Gas House Gang, honors championship quartets that paved the way for future generations by inspiring them with their craft, musicianship, style, and excellence.

Note: "Shine," arr. David Wright, catalog no. 212661.

We, the team of contributors to the *Arranging Barbershop* project, would like to honor those who inspired, thrilled, educated, and challenged us to become arrangers and hone our craft. Many of these giants have their work featured in this project, and thanks to the online, multimedia nature of this book, you'll be able to hear their inspirations brought to life once more. Their work—still alive in iconic performances from the past, present and, quite certainly, future—serve as a perpetual power source in keeping this artform alive and thriving.

Sylvia Alsbury

Joni Bescos

Dave Briner

Floyd Connett

Renee Craig

Phil Embury

S K Grundy

Buzz Haeger

Freddie King

Walter Latzko

Joe Liles

Earl Moon

Roger Payne

Lou Perry

Molly Reagan

Ruby Rhea

Bev Sellers

Lloyd Steinkamp

Dave Stevens

Burt Szabo

Ed Waesche

So many others have also continued to keep the whole world of barbershoppers singing, ringing, and believing that, through music, barriers are broken down and that anything is possible.

Editor's Note

By Steve Tramack, Lead Editor

I walked into my first rehearsal in 1982, about the time the previous Barbershop Arrangers Manual had just been published. I was a high school sophomore who had just attended the annual show held by my dad's chorus, the Nashua NH Granite Statesmen. The show featured the quartet *The Harrington Brothers (YouTube),*[1] who were roughly my age. I also was surprised to learn that several of my high school classmates were also in the chorus. I was, in short, hooked. It could have been the harmony, which was still ringing in my ears. It could have been the songs, which told stories still rattling around in my head. It could have been the fact that singers of all ages, backgrounds, races, and creeds were equals on the risers and seemed genuinely to be having a great time. It was probably all the above; regardless, I was hooked.

During that rehearsal, I had a chance to talk with the director, Joe Kopka, not yet knowing that he would become a lifelong friend and mentor. I said, "Mr. Kopka? Um, Joe? I think I really love this barbershop thing!" After he congratulated me, I felt emboldened to ask, "Can you tell me more about what kinds of songs you sing? I happen to really love Frank Sinatra and the Rat Pack; do you sing any of those songs?"

Joe said, "Oh, no. We don't sing Rat Pack songs in barbershop."

Only slightly rebuffed, I asked, "Ok. Well, what about other Big Band songs?"

Joe said, "We only sing songs written between 1890 and 1930—and no swing songs. Only downbeat-driven songs. We only just started to hear marches." Thank you, Louisville Thoroughbreds and Ed Waesche, for opening that door with the *Mardi Gras March* (*YouTube*) at the 1981 Barbershop Harmony Society (BHS) International Convention.

That seemed specific. And arbitrary. But who was I to question? I was just a high school sophomore and Joe was a past Top 20 quartet singer and longtime barbershopper. There clearly must have been a good reason. Already knowing the answer, I asked, "So, no Broadway songs? No Elvis? No Beatles?"

Joe said, "You know what? Let's sing a tag."

"A tag? What's that?" Thirty seconds later, with the overtones still buzzing around my head, I was hooked again, now for life. I figured we could talk about Sinatra and "Fly Me to the Moon" later.

Since that time, barbershop evolved. *Michigan Jake,* the BHS 2001 International Quartet Champion, singing songs such as *Louise* (*YouTube*) and *You Make Me Feel So Young* (*YouTube*), showed the barbershop world that swing can be 'shopped exceedingly well. *OC Times*, the 2007 Quartet Champs, sang *Love Me* (*YouTube*) with harmonies and background vocals right from the King of Rock and Roll's recording and all of a sudden Elvis sure sounds like barbershop. I guess that's not too surprising, considering *Love Me Tender* features new lyrics to a song written—you guessed it—between 1890 and 1930 (*Aura Lee*). Like in every style of music and performance, performers have led the way, nourished by arrangements that and arrangers who ardently seek to find creative ways to honor both the song and the barbershop style.

[1] All YouTube links referenced throughout the book are available via www.halleonard.com/mylibrary.

Barbershop is not a genre of music. It is a style of arranging music that can be applied to songs of many different genres. The barbershop style features examples from the Tin Pan Alley era (1890–1930), Big Band era (1930s and 40s), Rat Pack era (1950s and early 60s), Motown era (1960s and 70s), selected artists from the Rock and Roll era (1950–1990), and the Broadway Musical stage (1930–present day). Country music, jazz standards, singer/songwriters, popular music and easy listening artists, disco, R&B, etc. Barbershop harmony thrives across the world, enjoying unlimited influence on the style. As links between barbershop and the expansive a cappella and choral universe continue to strengthen, new arrangers are drawn to the style, intrigued by the power and range of development options available with just four voices.

Arranging Barbershop Series Overview

The reader is about to embark on a journey: arranging music in the barbershop style. The elements of this journey are not unlike an outdoor adventure, such as hiking, mountain climbing, or skiing. For some travelers, this may be their first time venturing into this wilderness; for more experienced explorers, perhaps they're looking to build the skills to tackle new challenges or seek inspiration from expert navigators and explorers. The *Arranging Barbershop* series will serve as a guide and companion along the way, and this trail map provides an overview of the experience.

Figure X.2

Overview trail map for the Arranging Barbershop *series.*

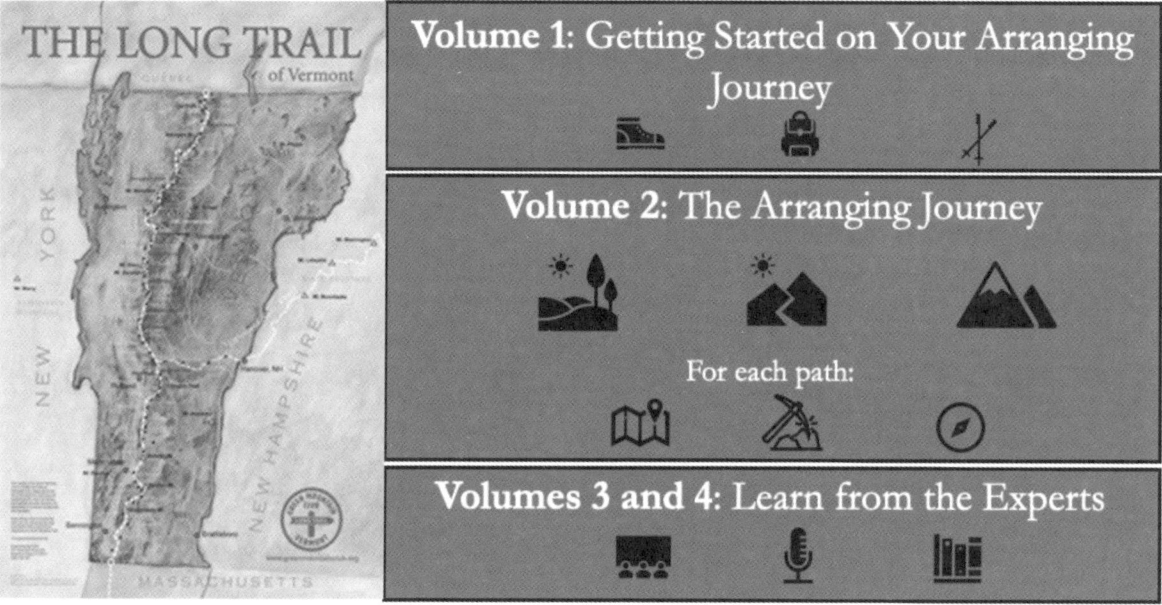

The *Arranging Barbershop* experience is broken up into four volumes: 1) *Getting Started on Your Arranging Journey*, 2) *The Arranging Adventure*, 3) *Visions of Excellence*, and 4) *Learn from the Experts*. Figure X.3 gives a maplike visual representation of the complete series. The boxes in the left column denote the various books and the boxes in the right column describe the subdivisions of the book.

Figure X.3

Arranging Barbershop *trail map.*

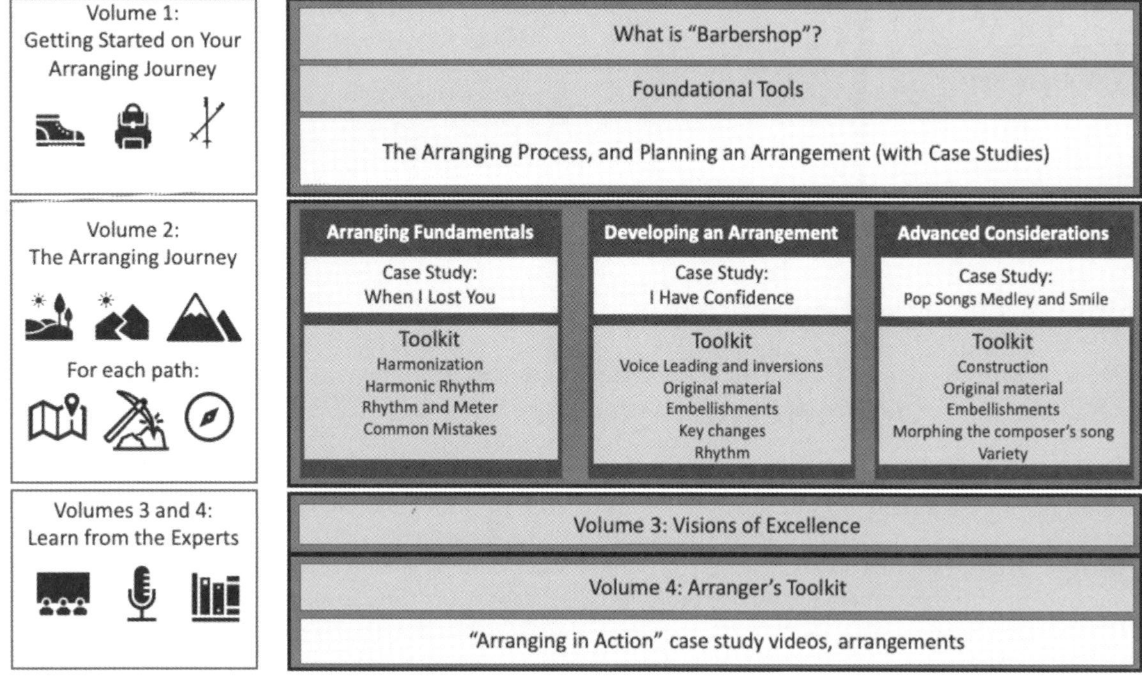

Overview of each volume

Volume 1: Before You Start Your Arranging Journey

Planning to go on a hiking adventure? Before departing, you'll need a few things to ensure your success: equipment (boots, backpack, supplies, climbing poles, etc.), a map of the area, lodging plans, and transportation to and from the hike, just to name a few. Successful planning and expertise in prerequisite skills are as important as the hike itself.

What skills and knowledge will you need along your arranging journey? This section provides a set of foundational tools and approaches that every arranging explorer will need before venturing out into the wild. This includes a glimpse into the past, a detailed overview of the style and the arranging process, a planning process roadmap, and a review of fundamental theory and musical literacy concepts that serve as a foundation for any adventure you choose. Vol. 1 includes case studies of a complete step-by-step arranging process and an example arrangement, following one arranger's process from concept to completion.

Figure X.4

Volume 1 visual description.

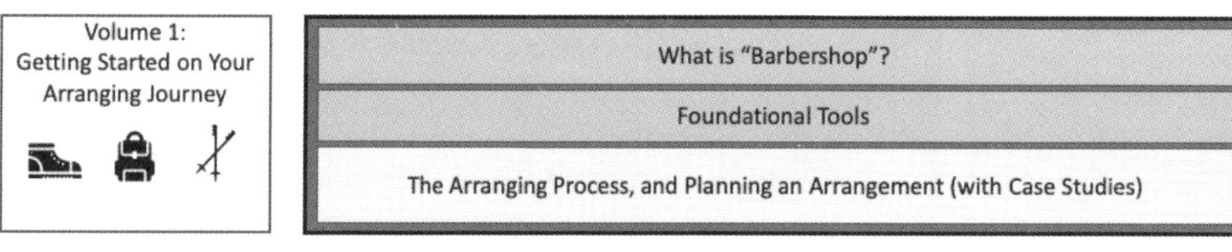

Volume 2: The Arranging Journey

The Shenandoah National Park uses a numerical rating system to determine the difficulty of a given hiking trail. Factoring elevation and distance, the hike's rating is tied to one of five descriptors: easiest, moderate, moderately strenuous, strenuous, very strenuous. There are, of course, other factors to consider, such as the steepness of a trail over a short distance, which require more expert knowledge of the trail. Note that the ratings are tied to the terrain, not the ability of the hiker. It is up to the individual to choose their own path.

Vol. 2 takes a similar approach to arranging concepts. Rather than designate sections by skill level or experience of the arranger, this volume of *Arranging Barbershop* covers different terrains of arranging concepts:

> *Arranging Fundamentals* focuses on the core set of skills required to harmonize a melody, leveraging the natural harmonic rhythms and implied chord progressions coupled with foundational arranging and theory-based skills to create a solid barbershop arrangement.
>
> *Developing an Arrangement* focuses on the skills and approaches to bring interest and contrast into an arrangement. Starting from a foundation of core harmonization, this volume explores the use of various embellishments, the development of themes (rhythm, melody, lyrics, harmony), and creating original material such as intros and tags.
>
> *Advanced Considerations* expands on these concepts, delving into a variety of challenges and choices that experienced arrangers use to create exciting musical journeys for talented performers. The case study looks at arranging for an International Champion, and how this experience follows a different trajectory than the fundamental approach.

Arrangers of all levels should find value in the case studies and toolkit associated with each stage of the arranging adventure covered in Vol. 2.

Figure X.5

Volume 2 visual description.

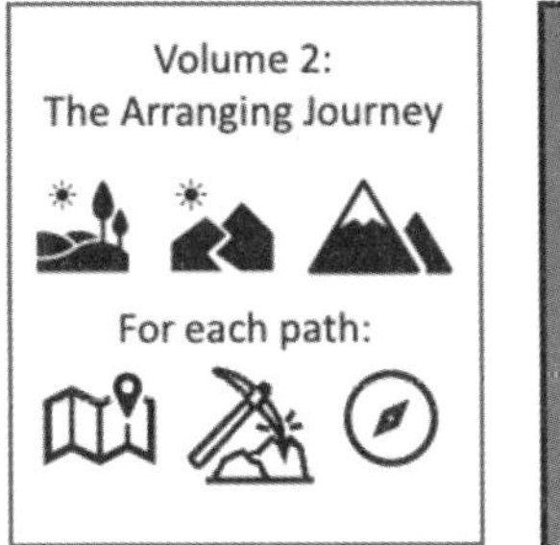

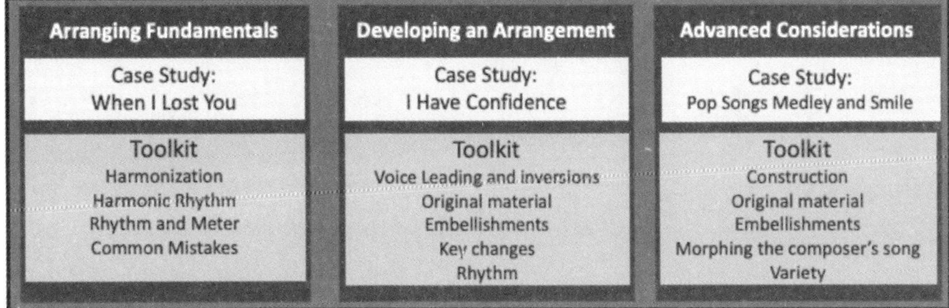

Volume 3: Visions of Excellence

Visions of Excellence is a virtual roundtable session of 38 arrangers who each answered the same 20 questions. You'll learn areas where there is broad agreement and where some might take a different approach. Example questions include:

- What methods do you consider when developing similar parts of an arrangement?
- Where do you draw inspiration when starting a new arrangement?
- What's the one thing you wish you'd learned sooner as an arranger?
- What trends might you predict happening to the barbershop art form in the future?

This is a most useful book that will be a constant source of inspiration.

Volume 4: Arrangers' Toolkit

After a long day of skiing, tackling various trails of different levels of difficulty on a given mountain, skiers gather in the lodge to break bread and share the experiences from the day. It's in these gatherings where lessons learned, best practices, and things to avoid help to expand the knowledge of the community. Vols. 3 and 4 of *Arranging Barbershop* are designed to do exactly that. Vol. 4 is divided into two parts: Arranging in Action and For Further Reference.

> In the Arranging in Action section, you'll find video and audio examples of how different arrangers approached the same problems and opportunities. Learn from iconic arrangers about iconic arrangements of memorable performances from the style. You'll see how different arrangers tackle the challenges of arranging the same song with different approaches and goals. You'll see how the same arranger developed the same song differently, once as a ballad and once as an up-tempo.
>
> In the For Further Reference section, you'll be able to explore individual topics such as *Arranging with Performance Staging in Mind* or *Arranging for Mixed Voices*, among others. Build your skills by learning from others, especially when it comes to these specialized topics.

Figure X.6

Volumes 3 and 4 visual descriptions.

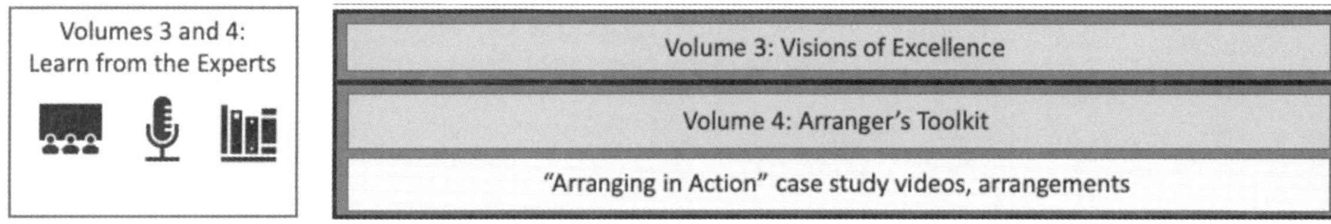

Back Matter

This guide will also contain a Back Matter section that includes the conclusion, appendix, bibliography including a detailed song list, glossary, contributor lists, sources, suggested reading, and an afterwards.

Compilation Approach

The end-to-end journey through the *Arranging Barbershop* adventure features contributions of note from nearly 40 arrangers, over 1,000 pages of content, more than 200 arrangements featured, and roughly 50 hours of video. Each volume is presented in both a printed and online version. The online version includes hyperlinks to audio and video examples throughout each volume. To get the most out of the experience, please take advantage of the multimedia clips.

This book is a *compilation* of topics, with lead contributors for different chapters providing relevant content and expertise in their own voice. The common threads, allowing for both individual voices and styles of communicating, while still feeling cohesive, will happen largely through formatting and structure of chapters:

- *Formatting* (use of bullets, paragraphs, etc.)
- *Style of sharing content* (verbiage, interspersed with examples from arrangements)
- *Chapter overall design and flow*: 1) Overview document, 2) Case study, 3) Deep dives on relevant topics

Enjoy the journey!

Who This Book is For

Arranging music is a complex, layered, rewarding musical endeavor. The arranger sits at the intersection of the creators (composer, lyricist) and performers of the music. With forethought, purpose, and sensitivity to both the original content and the performer, the arranger can help the performer successfully breathe life into the notes and words, creating a satisfying emotional journey. The arranging process includes considerations unique to the style, requiring knowledge, practice, and training to build expertise.

The *Arranging Barbershop* series of books are designed for anyone interested in arranging music in the barbershop style. No previous experience in the barbershop style is required; arrangers from other genres will find value in applying their theory and arranging expertise to the style. Experienced arrangers in the barbershop style will learn from the advanced problem-solving techniques and development approaches and may fill in gaps in knowledge in arranging and theory fundamentals that aid their journey. Novice arrangers will benefit from the journey, starting with the arranging process and definition of the style, advancing to the arranging fundamentals, and growing from there as their skills increase.

What You Need to Know Before You Start

Everything you need to know to leverage the full experience is found within the series itself. Specifically, if you are not an active arranger, and do not understand the difference between a major ninth and a dominant seventh chord, you'll find what you need in Vol. 1. Enough theory knowledge to understand triads and four-part chords, chord progressions, and melodic form are essential to taking advantage of Vol. 2 and beyond. Even if you are an experienced arranger, you'll likely find value in Vol. 1 with the arranging process and definition of the style aspects to warrant a review before jumping into Vol. 2 and beyond.

If you're new to barbershop, it is important to understand the barbershop voice parts, which differ from their classical names and ranges. The following is taken from the Barbershop Harmony Society's (BHS) website:[2]

Tenor is the highest part, harmonizing above the lead. Notated in the top stave, tenor stems always point up. Tenor singers should have a light, lyric vocal quality. Male tenors usually sing this part in falsetto and should be approximately 10% of the sound. *This is radically different than most musical performance styles because the melody is NOT in the top voice.*

Lead is the second highest part, singing the melody. Notated in the top stave, lead stems always point down. Lead singers should be prominent and have a dramatic and compelling vocal quality and should be approximately 30% of the sound. *This is different than most musical performance styles because the melody is in the second voice down. This "melody from inside" gives us the characteristic barbershop sound.*

Baritone sings above and below the lead. Notated in the bottom stave, baritone stems always point up. Baritone singers should have a lyric vocal quality and should be approximately 20% of the sound. The baritone should sing louder when below the lead, and softer when above the lead. *The unusual voice leading can be very challenging, especially to the novice barbershop baritone.*

Bass is the lowest part, singing foundational notes. Notated in the bottom stave, bass stems always point down. The bass part should be as prominent as the lead, with a big, robust vocal quality, and should be approximately 40% of the sound.

---

[2] https://www.barbershop.org/music/about-our-music

Throughout these volumes, you'll find examples written for high voices (e.g., SSAA), low voices (e.g., TTBB), and both (e.g., SATB or AATB). Regardless of individual voice ranges, voice parts are referred to as tenor, lead, bari, and bass.

Trail Markers

Along the way, you'll see these icons to delineate callouts that will help your learning journey.

Figure X.7

Definitions sidebars will highlight new vocabulary and their definitions. Example provided.

A commonly used term in barbershop is *barbershop seventh*. This is a major triad with an additional minor seventh interval. Barbershop singers love the energetic nature of this chord so much that we named it after ourselves!

Figure X.8

Notes sidebars will illuminate interesting facts about the topic being discussed.

Public domain laws vary from territory to territory. In the case of the US, songs released 96 years or more prior to the January. 1st date each year are considered in the public domain.[3] In other territories, the general rule of thumb for international public domain titles is the date of the death of the last living contributor (composer or lyricist) plus 70 years.

Figure X.9

Warnings sidebars seek to share wisdom from arrangers who identify a topic as a potential trap in the arranging process. Warnings are especially helpful for new arrangers to avoid frustration. Example provided.

Songs that feature secondary dominants that progress around the circle of fifths are well-suited to the barbershop style. Circle of fifths progressions with tritone movement in parallel half steps inherently imply dominant seventh chords, which are core to the style. Many songs, particularly those from the country, blues, and early rock genres, feature three chords: the tonic (I), the subdominant (IV) and the dominant (V). These songs move frequently from V–IV and/or IV–V, which lack the tension of the circle of fifths progressions. Three-chord songs featuring only V–IV or IV–V movement may not be best suited to the barbershop style. This Ritchie Valens song "Donna" provides an example of repeated I–IV–V7 movement.

[3] For more information on public domain laws, please visit here.

Figure X.10

The barber pole sidebar indicates how the given topic is an excellent example of good barbershop and good barbershop arranging techniques. Example provided.

The chord progression in Figure 2.10 is considered an excellent example of good barbershop arranging, as it uses eight barbershop seventh chords in a row. Note, however, that the quality of a barbershop arrangement is not determined by the sheer number of seventh chords included therein; not all melodies are well suited to this kind of harmonization.

Online Content

Barbershop is an aural artform. While looking at the examples will prove helpful for those arrangers who can hear the arrangement in their head, the artform really comes to life when you can hear and see the topic being discussed. Thus, many examples in *Arranging Barbershop*, Vol. 1 feature a corresponding audio clip. Audio clips include tone-generated examples, as well as recordings from learning track makers and, whenever possible, recordings by the original ensemble. The audio can be accessed at www.halleonard.com/mylibrary by entering the code on the back cover of this book.

The audio examples correspond with the figure names.

Figure X.11

Hal Leonard MyLibrary with audio and video examples

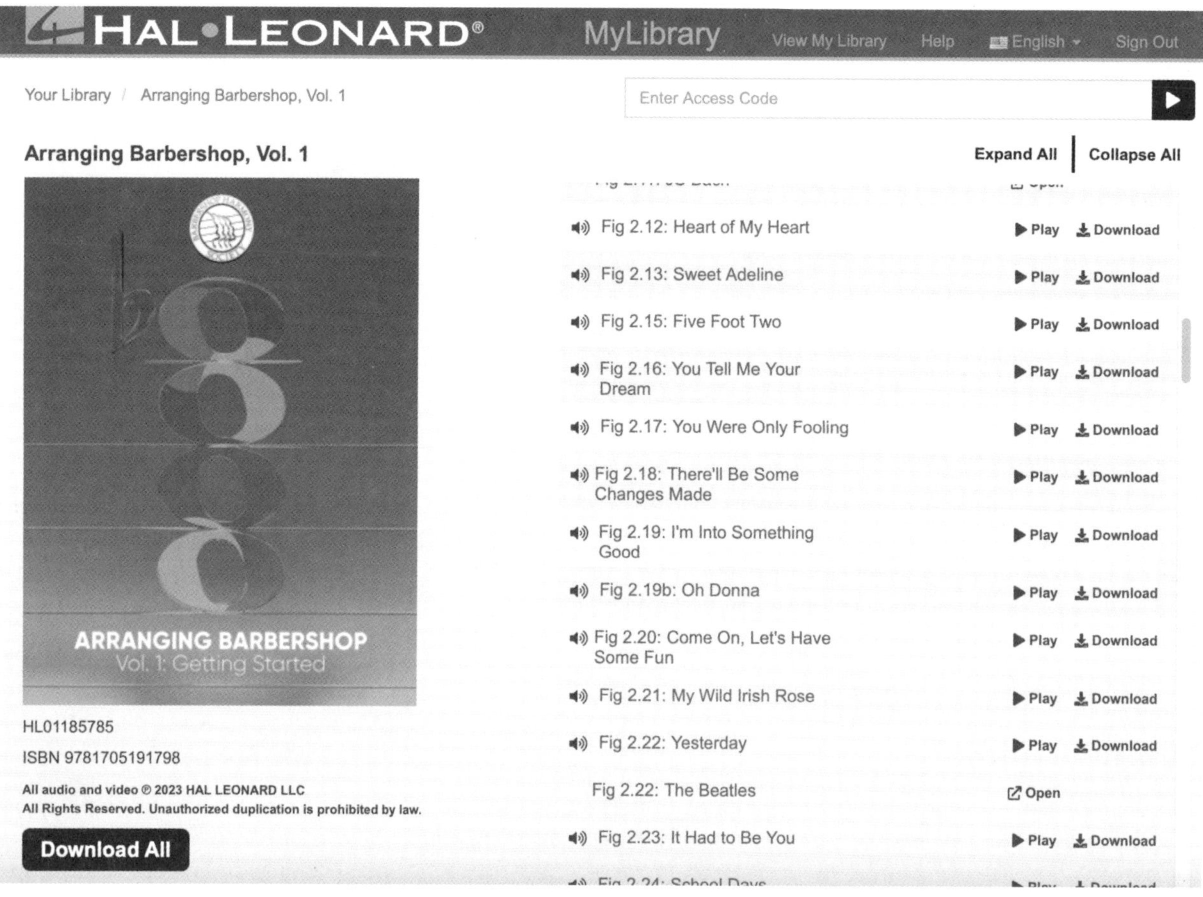

In addition to video (YouTube) content from the internet throughout the books, there is also content specific to the *Arranging Barbershop* series, such as video interviews of arrangers discussing their process in developing referenced arrangements.

Arranging Barbershop: Volume I

Getting Started On Your Arranging Journey

Contributors:

Steve Armstrong

Dylan Bell

Adam Bock

Mo Field

Tom Gentry

Clay Hine

Rafi Hasib

Kevin Keller

Joe Liles

Adam Scott

Steve Scott

Deke Sharon

Joe Stern

Steve Tramack

Andrew Wittenberg

David Wright

Intro

By Steve Tramack

Lou Perry, one of the all-time great arrangers in the four-part a cappella style known as barbershop, once said the secret to great music was "tell 'em what you're going to tell, then tell 'em, then tell 'em what you told 'em." Well, maybe Lou Perry borrowed that concept from another masterful storyteller, Aristotle, but it applies to arranging music as well. I often think of the "tell 'em what you're going to tell 'em" as the introduction or verse, "tell 'em" as the chorus, and "tell 'em what you told 'em" as the reprise and the tag.

Applying these concepts to this book, *Arranging Barbershop*, Volume 1, consider this the introduction. This volume focuses less on the how-tos of arranging, and more on whats and whys. As stated in the front matter, barbershop is not a genre of music: it is a style of arranging music that can be applied to multiple genres. This book follows the journey from the roots of the style through modern day (2023 at the time of this writing), delving into the details of what makes this style barbershop, what's needed to embark on an arranging journey, and how one might approach an arrangement. Starting with a blank sheet of staff paper, without some semblance of a plan, is akin to starting on a journey without knowing where you're going.

Figure I.1

Volume 1 trail map.

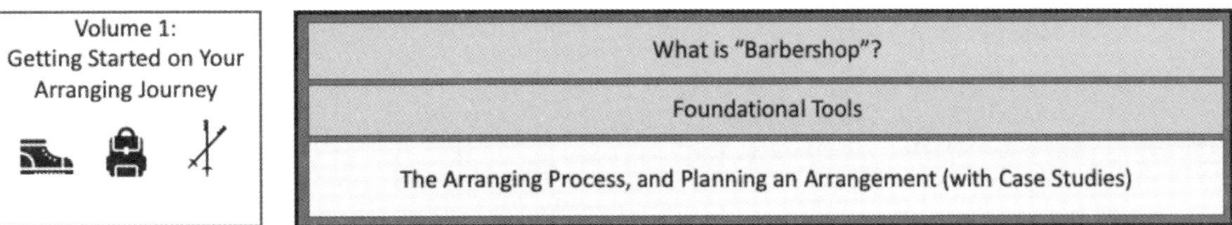

As indicated in Figure I.1 Volume 1 is segmented into three major parts:

- Part A is focused on defining the style. We begin with a historical perspective in Chapters 1 and 3, exploring both the roots of the style and a comparison of some of the earliest guidelines for arranging barbershop with today's standards. Chapter 2 is important for anyone who may be new to the style, or even for those experienced in singing but not arranging barbershop.
- Part B explores typical voice ranges, as well as reviewing music theory as applied to barbershop harmony. This includes comparing concepts (e.g., *consonance* and *dissonance*) that have stylistic implications that differ from other genres of Western music.
- Parts C through E explore the arranging process and discuss the importance of planning before embarking on an arranging journey. In addition to contributions from the barbershop world, these sections also include excerpted chapters from the book *A Cappella Arranging*, written by Deke Sharon and Dylan Bell. Just like Lou Perry borrowed a great concept from Aristotle, we borrow some great concepts from Deke and Dylan in describing the different roles and personas during the arranging process, as well as exploring different types of arrangement.
- In each volume of *Arranging Barbershop*, we include case studies to explore the concepts in action. Part E includes three such case studies, which hopefully will serve to put into practice what was covered in the first four parts of this volume.

Throughout Vol. 1, you'll find dozens of examples—many of which include audio via the Hal Leonard MyLibrary portal. You'll also find several examples which include YouTube video links. We encourage you to click, explore, and perhaps follow some of these examples and performances down a rabbit hole. You'll never know where you'll find inspiration for your next arrangement! For now, let's dive in, and enjoy the ride!

Part A: What Is Barbershop?

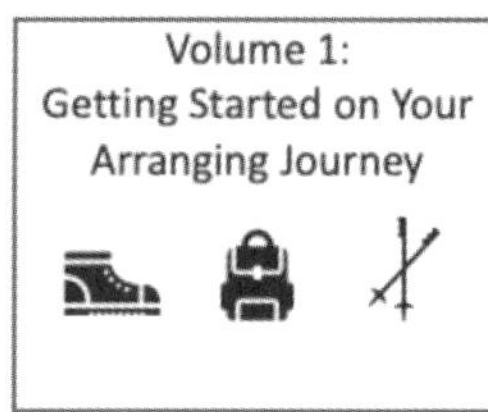

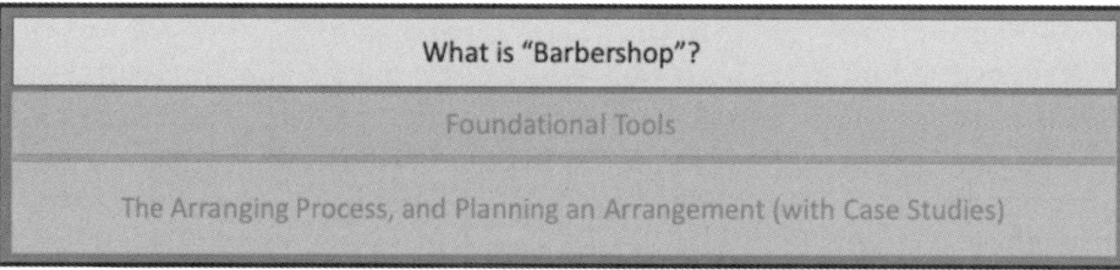

What is barbershop? Before embarking on our adventure, it will be helpful to understand a bit of historical context, as well as the broader context and landscape of this and future journeys ahead.

Chapter 1. A Historical Perspective

David Wright looks at the history of the style and how the style has evolved over the years. David explores the African American roots of the style, the popularity of quartets at the turn of the 20th century, and how these early influences were shaped and honed further with the introduction of organized societies aimed at preserving and propagating the style.

Chapter 2. The Definition of the Barbershop Style

Via contributions from Tom Gentry, Steve Tramack, Adam Bock and Mo Field, Chapter 2 examines the definition of the style (as per the Barbershop Harmony Society). The contributors explore, through examples of arrangements and arranging concepts, how the definition has both stayed true to traditional roots, as well as evolved through influences from other styles.

Chapter 3. Everything Old Is New Again

Kevin Keller examines one of the earliest documented examples of aspects of the barbershop style and associated arranging concepts—written by Joe Stern in 1941—and how those concepts apply (or not) in barbershop arranging more than 80 years later, in 2023.

Chapter 1.
Brief History of Barbershop Arranging

by David Wright

Though the precise origins of the style of harmonizing that came to be known as barbershop are buried in the murky past, we are quite certain that it is an American phenomenon, borrowing at most its name from the barber's music of Elizabethan England. While this harmony was popular in all segments of society, it was particularly so in those who led its development: the African American segment, as outlined in Lynn Abbott's 1992 article in *American Music.*[4] A plethora of references suggest the prominent, fundamental role of African Americans in the origins of the craft, expanding to other communities from there. We know that a cappella harmony became popular in the United States before the mid-1800s and that soon thereafter professional, semi-professional, and amateur quartets thrived.[5]

Early barbershop was primarily sung by males, but not exclusively, as we know of the existence of female and mixed quartets.[6] One such example, shown in Figure 1.1, was The Ranier Family, who toured America as the Tyrolese Minstrels between 1839 and 1843.

Figure 1.1

The Ranier Family premiered "Silent Night [Stille Nacht]" for American audiences.

---

[4] Abbott, L., (1992). *"Play That Barbershop Chord": A Case for the African-Amercan Origin of Barbershop Harmony,* American Music, Vol. 10 No. 3, 289–325. https://www.jstor.org/stable/3051597.

[5] Averill, G. (2003). *Four Parts, No Waiting: A Social History of American Barbershop Harmony.* Oxford University Press, 21–48.

[6] Döhl, F. (2009). "*…that old barbershop sound.*" Franz Steiner Verlag.

This music was enjoyed by amateurs not only in the barber's shop, but also in homes, on the street corner, in saloons, in colleges, and in churches. Professional quartets performed in minstrelsy, the circuit Chautauqua, and vaudeville, and as singing waiters and train porters. Starting in the 1890s, quartets were among the most popular early recording artists.

Figure 1.2

Picture in the early 1890s of the Atlanta University Quartet, including James Weldon Johnson (far right). Johnson was the Executive Secretary of the NAACP in the 1920s and wrote the lyrics to "Lift Every Voice and Sing."

It would be most enlightening to hear what a group of quartet singers would have sung, say, around 1870 as they worked out harmony by ear. What they sang is not known. Our best clues come from written descriptions of gleeful harmonic experimentation by young quartets and by the numerous recordings of professional quartets that flourished beginning around 1890.

Figure 1.3

The Unique Quartette, 1893.

Figure 1.4

The Haydn Quartet, 1894. YouTube

THE HAYDN QUARTET

Comprised of John H. Bieling, Harry MacDonough, S. H. Dudley, and William F. Hooley. Their records are now collectors' items.

Some inkling of the nature of the curbstone version of barbershop music is provided by Louis Armstrong, who sang in a quartet as a youth in New Orleans and always referred to that quartet harmony as the basis of his later cornet playing as a jazz musician.

Figure 1.5

Louis Armstrong, 1901–1971.

Many other jazz musicians of this era sang quartet harmony in their early days, which suggests that quartet harmony lent such elements as lead-ins, backtime, swipes, and stylized melodies to the jazz that sprang up in New Orleans, and that perhaps the more non-homorhythmic habits of barbershop harmony came to us primarily from African American practitioners.

In the early 20th century, quartets were highly popular in white society as well as black, with quartets seemingly ubiquitous on the streets of cities such as New York, New Orleans, Kansas City, and St. Louis. Businesses, clubs, breweries, journals, and even baseball teams had quartets under their auspices, and quartets made appearances in movies, radio programs, and commercials.

According to Gage Averill, as documented in *Four Parts, No Waiting: A Social History of American Barbershop Harmony,* professional quartets flourished with vaudeville:

> The best-known quartets were considered "big-time" acts: these included the Avon Comedy Four, the Casion Four, the Monarch Comedy Four, the Empire City Four, the Primrose Four, the Quaker City Quartet Four, and That Quartette. The spread of vaudeville into even small American cities led to a drain on big-time acts and openings for imitators and no-name quartets. Quartetting was still predominantly a male occupation, but some female harmony trios appeared in vaudeville (the Boswell Sisters, the Pickens Sisters, and the Three X Sisters, among others).[7]

Figure 1.6

The Boswell Sisters. YouTube.

[7] Averill, G. (2003). *Four Parts, No Waiting,* 58.

In the years after 1920, society became more complex; vaudeville faded, and radio became the most popular home entertainment. Consequently, professional and amateur quartet activity waned, but did not disappear. In 1938, the Society For the Preservation and Encouragement of Barber Shop Quartet Singing in America, Inc. (dba Barbershop Harmony Society [BHS]) was formed to preserve and encourage it among male singers, and in 1945, Sweet Adelines International (SAI) was formed for women. In 1959, another women's organization, Harmony, Inc., was formed, and in subsequent years numerous other organizations—male, female, and mixed—sprang up around the world.

Well before the beginning of the Barbershop Harmony Society, the style of quartet harmony known as barbershop was solidly intact and typically exuded these characteristics:

- Four parts, a cappella, with the melody carried by an inside voice, a tenor harmonizing above, a bass mostly on solid chord tones, and a baritone completing the harmony.[8]
- A chord repertoire consisting of mostly consonant chords, progressions often following the circle of fifths, with a penchant for harmonic variation richness and complete chords.
- Musical devices such as swipes, echoes, lead-ins, solos, and backtime embellishing the music.
- Primarily, but not exclusively, homorhythmic texture.

In the early days, the task of achieving consistent four-part harmony was no trivial matter. Quartets in the fields and barber shops and on street corners had woodshedding sessions during which they would experiment, arriving at their harmony by ear. This might be by following the implied harmony of a song that had it, or it might be the consequence of an exploration in harmony where singers searched and celebrated gleefully when they landed on a rich chord. As some melodic passages do not lend themselves to harmonization, quartets might have just muddled through these lines, briefly settling for non-chords or incomplete chords, heading for the destination where they could bust a good one. Even the professional studio quartets often sang rather rough harmonizations with incomplete chords.

---

[8] Many early recordings of Barbershop Harmony Society quartets featured instrumental accompaniment. In Joe Stern's 1941 letter defining the barbershop style, he wrote "No piano or other accompaniment is permissible with a barber shop quartette [sic] for the reason that a quartette [sic] should strive to smooth out the rough spots themselves, so that no accompaniment is necessary to cover them up. Besides, the accompaniment detracts from the ability of the quartette." For more insight into Stern's letter, see Chapter 3. Letter dated May 21, 1941 from Joe Stern to all national officers and directors of the Society for the Preservation and Encouragement of Barber Shop Quartet Singing, Inc.

Figure 1.7

Norfolk Jazz Quartette, 1937.

There were a few written arrangements. Going back to the 1800s, published sheet music of popular songs often had a male quartet arrangement on the back page, but these were lacking the richness and embellishment of barbershop harmony. W.C. Handy mentions writing an arrangement for his girlfriend's quartet, but it wasn't preserved. Scott Joplin incorporates one song sung by a quartet of field hands in his 1910 opera Treemonisha, and that arrangement, though simple, is very much in the mold of what we think of as barbershop today.

Figure 1.8

Excerpt from Treemonisha, an opera by Scott Joplin. "We Will Rest Awhile" is notated for "male quartet in cotton field."
YouTube

In 1925, well-known musicologist Sigmund Spaeth published *Barber Shop Ballads*, which contained several straightforward arrangements and instructions on how to sing them, as well as records in the sleeves of the book on which the arrangements were recorded by a quartet in which Spaeth sang baritone.

Figure 1.9

Barber Shop Ballads, by Sigmund Spaeth. YouTube

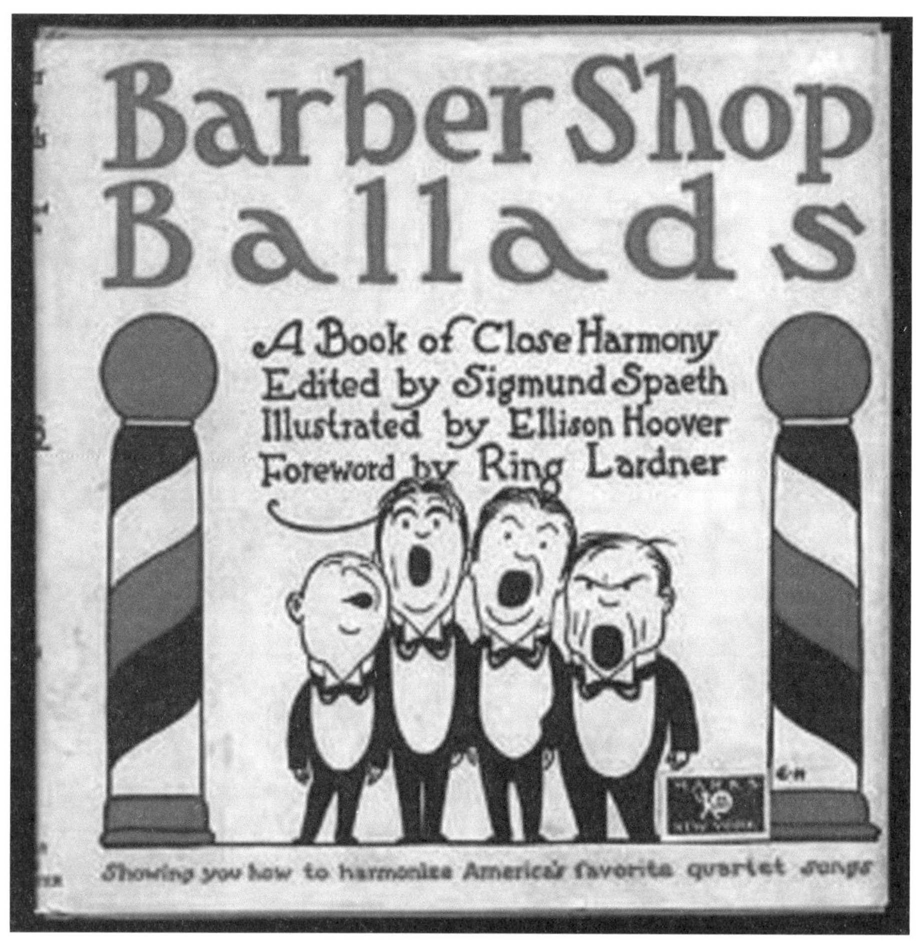

In 1936, Ed Smalle published *Close Harmony*, a collection of twenty arrangements, even better in a modern sense than Spaeth's. These two books were used as references and handbooks for barbershop quartets up through early Society days. It should be said, however, that many quartets before the Society did not use written arrangements. Some became adept at working out harmony one chord at a time, finding for each melody note a chord that contains it. Not surprisingly, this led to some awkward harmonizations, as the sequence of chords didn't necessarily follow any musical convention, but it also yielded some charming barbershop quirks that still survive.

Figure 1.10

Close Harmony, by Ed Smalle.

The craft of barbershop was greatly advanced with the advent of the organizations BHS and SAI whose local and national conventions and meetings brought quartets and harmonizers together to a degree that never existed before, thus providing a cross-pollination that accelerated listening, sharing, borrowing, and inventing that facilitated significant progress. Soon there emerged a well-developed arranger's toolkit for handling nearly any melodic passage, and, as well, for adding embellishments to provide musical interest. By the 1950s the art of harmonization, and to a lesser extent, overall construction and development, had come a long way.

Over the years these informal techniques have undergone considerable honing and evolution. In addition to harmonizations that sound natural with good voice leading and tasteful embellishments, arrangers have become more and more adept at planning a successful overall construction and contour, giving rise to performances that engage the listener from beginning to end. Modern barbershop arrangements can be marvels of elegance in the way the arranger has used techniques to create beautiful harmony, effective embellishments, and satisfying development, all the while displaying the essential singability that is characteristic of barbershop. These arrangements vary widely in complexity, range, and musical character, making it possible for any quartet or chorus to find interesting music that fits their persona and is appropriate to their level of skill.

As many performers want to sing their own music, there is always a need for more good material. Today's barbershop arranger, fortunately, does not have to reinvent the wheel, as there are so many excellent arrangements of all types from which one can learn. This book is meant to be a resource to help developing arrangers organize the learning process by better understanding the barbershop style and the various methods and techniques that can lead to the creation of a successful arrangement in that style. Its aim is to stimulate the creation of great barbershop while remaining true to the basic characteristics of the style.

Chapter 2.
Definition of the Barbershop Style

by Tom Gentry, with contributions from Adam Bock, Mo Field, Clay Hine, and Steve Tramack

The Barbershop Harmony Society has used several definitions of barbershop as the style has developed and changed over the years. The most recent update was approved by the International Board of Directors in 2018:

> Barbershop harmony is a style of unaccompanied vocal music characterized by consonant four-part chords for every melody note in a primarily homorhythmic texture. The melody is consistently sung by the lead, with the tenor harmonizing above the melody, the bass singing the lowest harmonizing notes, and the baritone completing the chord. Occasional brief passages may be sung by fewer than four voice parts.
>
> Barbershop music features songs with understandable lyrics and easily singable melodies, whose tones clearly define a tonal center and imply major and minor chords and barbershop (dominant and secondary dominant) seventh chords that often resolve around the circle of fifths, while also making use of other resolutions. Barbershop music also features a balanced and symmetrical form. The basic song and its harmonization are embellished by the arranger to provide appropriate support of the song's theme and to close the song effectively.
>
> Barbershop singers adjust pitches to achieve perfectly tuned chords in just intonation while remaining true to the established tonal center. Artistic singing in the barbershop style exhibits a fullness or expansion of sound, precise intonation, a high degree of vocal skill, and a high level of unity and consistency within the ensemble. Ideally, these elements are natural, not manufactured, and free from apparent effort.
>
> The performance of barbershop music uses appropriate musical and visual methods to convey the theme of the song and provide the audience with an emotionally satisfying and entertaining experience. The musical and visual delivery is from the heart, believable, and sensitive to the song and its arrangement throughout. The most stylistic performance artistically melds together the musical and visual aspects to create and sustain the illusions suggested by the music.[9]

This chapter explores the elements of the style, and implications on arranging barbershop, in more detail.

Definition Discussion

Barbershop harmony is a style of unaccompanied vocal music...

Occasionally, a group might be accompanied by a guitar, bass fiddle, or banjo. As explored in Chapter 1, this is rooted in the foundations and inspirations of the style. However, as covered in Chapter 2, barbershop

---

[9] BHS Contest and Judging Handbook, June 2022. Link

evolved into an a cappella style in the 1940s, and this unaccompanied aspect is now considered to be an indelible part of the style, differentiating it from other harmony-rich styles.

...characterized by consonant four-part chords for every melody note in a primarily homorhythmic texture.

Generally, all four voice parts sing the same words or word sounds simultaneously. Barbershop uses some embellishing devices that do not adhere to this pattern, which can affect the expanded sound that characterizes barbershop. These embellishments, covered in depth in Vol. 2 of *Arranging Barbershop*, are used to create interest and development in arrangements.

Figure 2.1

"Aura Lee," words and music by W. W. Fosdick and George R. Poulton. Arrangement by the Barbershop Harmony Society. An example of homorhythmic texture.

Note: The implied harmony in measure 11 is Db maj7 with the C in the melody and is generally considered dissonant.

The modified treble, or tenor, clef—featuring an 8 attached to the bottom of the clef—and bass clef staves in Figure 2.2 would typically indicate a TTTB voicing for barbershop notation. SSAA voicing would use modified bass clef—featuring an 8 attached to the top of the clef—indicating to sing the notes an octave higher than written. SATB voicing would use an unmodified treble or bass clefs. You'll find various examples of all notations throughout this chapter.

The way the term *consonant* is used in barbershop contexts is specific to the style and differs considerably from definitions in textbooks relating to classical harmony.[10] In music, the terms *consonance* and *dissonance* are relative terms used to categorize simultaneous sounds in terms of degrees of perceived pleasantness to unpleasantness. Ringing chords are a hallmark of the style; this ring is largely a function of the consonance potential of the harmony and the execution by the performers to maximize the consonance potential. Regarding the terms consonance and dissonance, in *The Craft of Musical Composition*, Paul Hindemith stated "The two concepts have never been completely explained, and for a thousand years the definitions have varied."[11]

Consonance is the pleasing sense of harmony with an absence of dissonance. As used in barbershop, chords including both a perfect fifth and a tritone interval are considered consonant based on the predominance of those chords in the style. For a complete description of the barbershop chord vocabulary, consult the *Theory of Barbershop Harmony* (chapter 5).

Part of the confusion is that the terms are used to define both acoustically objective and stylistically subjective concepts. From an acoustical perspective, the degree of consonance is determined based on the relationship between the harmonic partials of the fundamental tones in the interval or chord. The degree of coincidence of partials of the notes in the chord lend to a higher level of acoustically perceived consonance. Consider two-note intervals, the gradation of consonances include:

- Perfect consonances:
    - Unison and octaves
    - Perfect fourths and perfect fifths
- Imperfect consonances:
    - Major thirds and minor sixths
    - Major seconds and minor sevenths
    - Minor thirds and major sixths

Dissonances include tritones, minor seconds, and major sevenths. However, combine the tritone with a perfect fifth, and the result is a dominant seventh chord. Dominant seventh chords are considered consonant in the barbershop style (more on the stylistic impact in a moment), but only when all chord tones are represented; most barbershoppers would probably describe an exposed minor seventh, major second, or tritone as dissonant. However, based on the ring associated with the coincident partials based on the fifth, third, and seventh of the chord in the harmonic series, coupled with the tension demanding onward motion, the combination creates a unique harmonic texture associated with the style.

In addition to the acoustic properties contributing to a more objective sense of consonance and dissonance, the terms are often associated more subjectively with a given style or period of music. Dissonance, in this

---

[10] For further analysis of these differences, see Garnett, L. (2005). *The British barbershopper: a study in musical values* (Aldershot: Ashgate, 2005), 24–30.

[11] Hindemith, P. (1942). *The craft of musical composition*, Vol. I, translated by Arthur Mendel. New York: Associated Music Publishers.

case, would be considered a combination of sounds that do not belong to the style being considered. This is certainly the case when considering consonance as defined in the barbershop style.

The melody is consistently sung by the lead, with the tenor harmonizing above the melody, the bass singing the lowest harmonizing notes, and the baritone completing the chord.

The second highest voice, called the lead, primarily sings the melody. If an outside voice part has the melody for a significant portion of the song, it lacks an essential characteristic of the barbershop style.

Figure 2.2

"Dear Old Girl," words and music by Theodore F. Morse and Richard H. Buck. Arrangement by Tom Gentry. Example of the melody, or lead, part.

Figure 2.3

"Dear Old Girl," arrangement by Tom Gentry. Example demonstrating the tenor part harmonizing above the lead.

Figure 2.4

"Dear Old Girl," arrangement by Tom Gentry. Example demonstrates the bass part, harmonizing below all voices.

Figure 2.5

"Dear Old Girl," arrangement by Tom Gentry. Example demonstrates the baritone singing below the tenor, above the bass, and both above and below the lead.

Occasional brief passages may be sung by fewer than four voice parts.

Figure 2.6 demonstrates a solo, duet, trio and finally four-part lead-in to the phrase. Note that all chords created by this technique are consonant.

Figure 2.6

"Gimme A Little Kiss," words and music by Maceo Pinkard, Whispering Jack Smith, Roy Turk. Arrangement by Mel Knight.

Barbershop music features songs with understandable lyrics…

Barbershop music came into being in an era when song lyrics were usually quite straightforward:

> Daisy, Daisy, give me your answer, do.
>
> I'm half crazy, all for the love of you.
>
> It won't be a stylish marriage; I can't afford a carriage.
>
> But you'll look sweet upon the seat of a bicycle built for two.[12]

Barbershop songs change with the times, and now see sometimes sophisticated material:

> You're just too marvelous,
>
> Too marvelous for words
>
> Like rapturous, fabulous.

[12] "Daisy Bell," by Harry Dacre, 1892.

Your voice is tintinnabulous.[13]

Even with an obscure word, the message is clear in this song. But not every song has a recognizable meaning:

Sitting on a cornflake, waiting for the van to come.

Corporation T-shirt, stupid bloody Tuesday.

Man, you've been a naughty boy, you let your face grow long.

I am the egg man. They are the egg men.

I am the walrus. Goo goo g'joob.[14]

Some songs don't necessarily have understandable lyrics, but that doesn't always detract from their impact. An arrangement containing lyrics in a foreign language can sometimes be constructed such that the audience readily accepts what is being sung. They can follow the storyline comfortably without knowing the English meaning of every word.

Songs with lyrics that are likely to distress members of any marginalized population are not representative of barbershop. When in doubt, ask.

…and easily singable melodies…

Earlier in BHS history, easily singable melodies meant tunes that were neither too rangy nor disjunct. Today, easily singable is singer-dependent. If a melody singer or section can make the melody sound easily singable, it passes muster.

…whose tones clearly define a tonal center…

Barbershop singers perform the popular songs of the day, whether from a past era or present. Such music is almost always clearly in a given key, aiding the listener and the performer in maintaining a feeling of familiarity and security.

…and imply major and minor chords…

Major and minor triads are used extensively in barbershop with usually the root doubled to produce four-part harmonization. Major triads are especially favored since they produce bright sounds that barbershop singers enjoy. Minor triads are used when called for and some songs are in a minor mode.

The augmented triad is sometimes used, usually when demanded by the melody. Harmonic augmented fifths occur, though rarely.

---

[13] "Too Marvelous for Words," by Richard Whiting 1937.

[14] "I Am the Walrus," by John Lennon, 1967. John Lennon was said to have written this song after receiving a letter from a student at his old high school stating that a teacher had tried to analyze some Beatles' lyrics in class. Lennon thought he would give the teacher a tough one to work out. Mission accomplished!

Figure 2.7

"Shine On, Harvest Moon," words and music by Nora Bayes and Jack Norworth. Arrangement by Val Hicks and Earl Moon.

In figure 2.7, the harmonic pillar in measures 21 and 22 is G7. The G augmented chords in the first beat of each measure arise based on how we tend to harmonize a sixth above the root of a pillar harmony, which is omitting the fifth and doubling the root. Because the melody is a minor sixth above the bass, the resulting chord is an augmented triad. Note the preference for correct notation with respect to each individual singing part rather than spelling the chord correctly. In a specific voice part, notes are generally written with respect to whether the line is ascending or descending. Thus, in measure 21 the lead has an E♭, rather than a D♯, because the next note is down a half step. The E♭ is enharmonically equal to D♯, the augmented fifth.

Figure 2.8

"If I Had My Way," words and music by James Kendis and Lou Klein. Arrangement by Tom Gentry.

Note: The harmonic augmented fifth, as shown in the tenor part in measure 4, is rare but not unheard of.

The diminished triad is thought to have a weak sonority and it therefore rarely used. It can be found in unaccented spots of songs with quicker tempos. Figure 2.9 shows an example of the diminished triad in the second chord in the first measure of the barbershop classic "Lida Rose."

Figure 2.9

"Lida Rose" words and music by Meredith Wilson. Arrangement by Mo Rector and Joni Bescos.

It would be poor voice leading for the tenor or bass to sing a D in the first measure on the second syllable of the word "Lida" just to make this a fully diminished seventh chord. This chord lasts only one-half of one beat, so the hollow nature of the diminished triad does not cause a distraction.

… and barbershop (dominant and secondary dominant) seventh chords…

Major-minor (or dominant) seventh chords are four-part chords with dominant seventh functionality and are found extensively in barbershop arrangements.

A commonly used term in barbershop is *barbershop seventh*, which theorists would call a dominant (or major-minor) seventh. This is a major triad with an additional minor seventh interval. Barbershop singers love the energetic nature of this chord so much that we named it after ourselves!

Figure 2.10

"Where the Southern Roses Grow," words and music by Richard Henry Buck and Theodore F. Morse. Arrangement by Dave Stevens.

The chord progression in Figure 2.10 is considered an excellent example of good barbershop arranging, as it uses eight barbershop seventh chords in a row. Note, however, that the quality of a barbershop arrangement is not determined by the sheer number of seventh chords included therein; not all melodies are well suited to this kind of harmonization.

Most barbershop authorities would agree that a good barbershop arrangement needs to have a predominance of consonant chords, including the dominant (major-minor) 7th chord.

As discussed earlier, here is the gradation of consonance to dissonance for two-note intervals in barbershop:

- Unison and octaves
- Perfect fourths and perfect fifths
- Major and minor thirds and sixths
- Major seconds and minor sevenths

Dissonances include tritones, minor seconds, and major sevenths. However, the combination of a perfect fifth (e.g., C and G) and a tritone (e.g., E and B) creates the dominant seventh. The combination of the perfect consonance and the dissonant intervals within the chord add tension demanding onward motion to a stable chord. That sense of tension demanding motion is an essential part of the style.

Because barbershop seventh chords and major triads are considered more consonant, at least in the barbershop style, arrangements that feature these chords tend to sound the most stylistic.

In addition to the major triad and major-minor seventh, referred to as dominant sevenths, barbershop harmony uses the following chords:

- minor triads
- incomplete dominant sevenths with added ninth
- ninths
- minor-minor sevenths
- major sixths (major triad with added sixth)
- minor sixths (minor triad with added sixth)
- half-diminished sevenths

The half-diminished seventh, minor sixth and incomplete dominant seventh with added ninth all include the same four notes in the chord (for example, C–E♭–G–A). Labeling the chord is dependent on its contextual harmonic function.

- diminished sevenths
- major sevenths
- major chords with added ninth
- augmented triads
- augmented dominant sevenths
- diminished triads
- dominant sevenths with flatted fifth[15]

The tritone between the third and seventh of a dominant seventh chord gives it its characteristic sound and implies subsequent harmonic movement around the circle of fifths. The strength of this implication relies heavily on the listener's familiarity with Western classical traditions, but an experienced listener will find the resolution of V7 to tonic somewhat obligatory. This resolution, in the Western classical tradition, commonly involves the third and seventh of a V7 chord moving by step in contrary motion to reach the subsequent the tonic chord's root and third. The final cadence in the following example from Bach illustrates traditional tritone resolution.

Figure 2.11

J.S. Bach BWV 425: "Was Willst Du Dich, O Meine Seele."

Note: While there are several other tritones in the example, not all of them are resolved by step in contrary motion. Music theory is meant to be descriptive, not prescriptive.

[15] For more information on these chords, and to hear what they sound like, please visit http://www.musictheory.net/exercises/ear-chord.

In barbershop arranging, traditional tritone resolution is often eschewed in favor of a series of tritones moving in parallel motion. This is an effect that would sound extremely unusual in a Bach chorale but is very common in barbershop. The first phrase of the Barberpole Cat song "Heart of My Heart" ends with an example of parallel tritones (between the tenor and lead in mm. 3–4), as shown in Figure 2.12.

Figure 2.12

Parallel tritone movement in "The Story of the Rose (Heart of My Heart)," words and music by Andrew Mack and Alice. Arrangement by the Barbershop Harmony Society.

The above is also a prime example of a secondary dominant; the chord on "love" is B♭7, which a classical musician would probably define as V7/V in the key of A♭ major. And in classical literature, V7/V would traditionally move on to V (E♭, in this case). B♭7 is the dominant in the local key of E♭, but as we are not in E♭, this dominant relationship is referred to as secondary.

However, instead of moving on to E♭, "Heart of My Heart" moves directly to another dominant seventh, E♭7. This necessitates two consecutive tritones and, with the simplest possible voice leading, they move in parallel motion.

It would be incorrect in either the classical or barbershop idiom to refer to this movement as a resolution. The instability of the tritone is what gives it its harmonic energy and its apparent need to resolve; a chord that involves a tritone is inherently unresolved.

The parallel tritone, facilitated by a series of consecutive chords that all possess a traditionally dominant function, is one of the hallmarks of the barbershop style. "Sweet Adeline," shown in Figure 2.13, is perhaps the most well-known barbershop song and is characterized by the repeated use of parallel tritones.

Figure 2.13

"Sweet Adeline," words and music by Richard Husch Gerard and Harry Armstrong. Arrangement by the Barbershop Harmony Society. Includes several examples of parallel tritone movement. YouTube

Here we see parallel tritone movement in all four echoing phrases: bari and bass in the first, tenor and bari in the second, tenor and lead (facilitated by a quick dip to G# in the lead) in the third, and again between the tenor and bari in the fourth phrase. Note that while the first several instances of parallel tritone movement occur in descending half steps, the third and fourth phrases feature it in ascending half steps. This movement of a fully diminished seventh chord to a dominant seventh chord built on the same root (Fdim7–F7, in both cases) is an effect that is arguably just as idiomatic to barbershop as the secondary dominant.

…that often move toward the tonic around the circle of fifths…

The implied movement of the barbershop seventh generally follows a root movement of a descending fifth. This is commonly called moving around the circle of fifths.

The circle of fifths is an easy way of graphically organizing and showing the relationship of interval movements of a perfect fifth.

Figure 2.14

The circle of fifths.

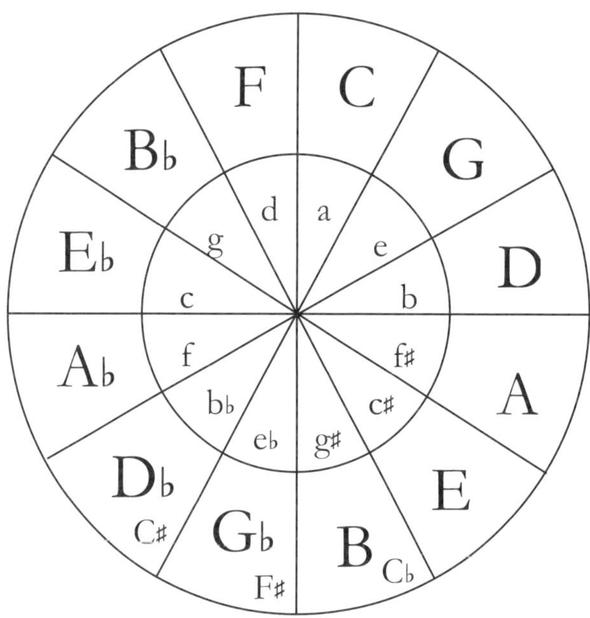

The circle of fifths is an essential concept in western music theory, identifying the number of sharps (moving clockwise from C) or flats (moving counterclockwise from C) in each key signature. The circle also indicates implied movement from chord to chord. Adding a minor seventh interval to a major triad traditionally implies subsequent movement of that chord root to the next chord root a perfect fifth below. Root movement down a perfect fifth is seen by going counterclockwise on the circle in Figure 2.14.

It is handy to note that every V7 chord pulls itself toward resolving down a fifth, or up a fourth. This makes resolution and root movement easier to instinctively feel.

This also creates leading tone tension and resolution opportunities in two unique ways:

- the 7th of the V7 wants to resolve down to the 3rd of the I chord
- the 3rd of the V7 wants to resolve up to the root of the I chord.

Following the logic of chord resolutions around the circle of fifths, a chord built on C will resolve to F, and F resolves to B♭, and so forth. Once implied harmony leaves the tonic chord, referred to by the Roman numeral I, the harmony tends to return or progress back to the tonic by descending fifths root movement.

A classic example of this kind of harmonic progression is found in the song "Five Foot Two, Eyes of Blue." When the harmony leaves the I chord, it goes out to an altered chord built on the third degree of the scale, III7 (or V7/vi). The featured occurrence of secondary dominants, with raised third, is an essential part of the barbershop style, and is discussed in more detail in chapter 5. The dissonant tension in the tritone intervals between the 3rd and flat 7th within the secondary dominant promotes root movement chord progressions by intervals of a perfect fifth downward. Note that a root, a perfect fourth above, is the same root as a perfect fifth below.

Figure 2.15

"Five Foot Two," words and music by Ray Henderson, Sam M. Lewis and Joseph Widow Young. Arrangement by Joe Liles.

Note: Observe also that all the chords underlying the melodic movement are barbershop sevenths.

Classic barbershop arrangements will feature this type of chord progression around the circle of fifths.

What other styles might consider dissonance related to a dominant seventh chord, the barbershop style would consider musical tension. Circle of fifths progressions that are core to the style are closely aligned to "the long tradition of thinking of a musical phrase as consisting of a cadence and a passage of gradually accumulating tension leading up to it."[16]

…while also making use of other progressions…

Chords move in many other ways than around the circle of fifths. Examples include:

- Half steps (see Figures 2.16 and 2.17)
- Major seconds (see Figures 2.18 and 2.19)
- Thirds (see Figures 2.17 and 2.20)

16 Parncutt, R. and Graham H. (2011). "Consonance and Dissonance in Music Theory and Psychology: Disentangling Dissonant Dichotomies," *Journal of Interdisciplinary Music Studies* 5, no. 2 (Fall): 119–66.

Figure 2.16

"You Tell Me Your Dream," words and music by Albert H. Brown, Charles N. Daniels, Seymour Rice. Arrangement by Phil Embury.

Note: This classic barbershop song has root movement down and then up by half steps.

Figure 2.17

"You Were Only Fooling (While I Was Falling in Love)," words and music by Larry Fotine, Ben Gordon, and Billy Faber. Arrangement by Steve Tramack.

Note: The III7 leads up a half step to IV7. This example also contains a IV7–I chord progression. This is commonly referred to as a plagal resolution. Voice leading plays a role in this subdominant-to-tonic resolution, with the fifth of the IV7 (the F in the baritone part) representing a common tone with the root of the I. Voice leading is covered in more detail in chapter 5, as well as Vol. 2.

Figure 2.18

"There'll Be Some Changes Made," words and music by Benton Overstreet and Billy Higgins. Arrangement by Tom Gentry.

Note: Chords can progress by root movement up a major second, such as the progressions from measure 6 (II7 pillar) to measure 7 (III7 pillar), and measure 10 (V7) to measure 11 (VI7). This ascending movement by major seconds is unusual; it is specifically dictated by the harmony of the original song, and not standard harmonic practice.

Figure 2.19

"I'm Into Something Good," words and music by Gerry Goffin and Carole King. Arrangement by John Fortino.

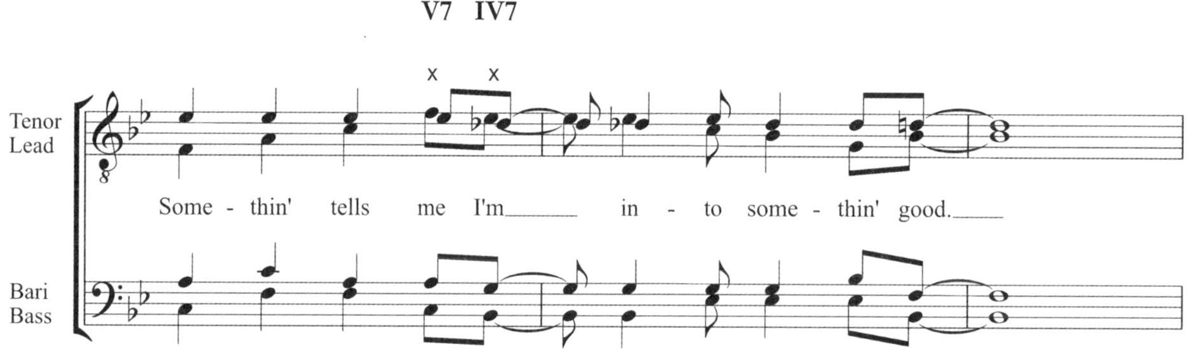

Note the chord movement down a major second (V7 to IV7). This type of descending second motion is used primarily in two circumstances:

1. Using a plagal resolution (IV7 to I) rather than a strong perfect authentic cadence, such as in Figure 2.23.
2. Sometimes a song will skip a stop on the circle of fifths, moving from VI7 to V7, omitting the II7.

Songs that feature secondary dominants that progress around the circle of fifths are well-suited to the barbershop style. Circle of fifths progressions with tritone movement in parallel half steps inherently imply dominant seventh chords, which are core to the style. Many songs, particularly those from the country, blues, and early rock genres, feature three chords: the tonic (I), the subdominant (IV) and the dominant (V). These songs move frequently from V–IV and/or IV–V, which lacks the tension of the circle of fifths progressions. Three-chord songs featuring only V–IV or IV–V movement may not be best suited to the barbershop style. This Ritchie Valens song, "Donna," provides an example of repeated I–IV–V7 movement.

Figure 2.20

"Come On, Let's Have Some Fun," tag written and arranged by Tom Gentry.

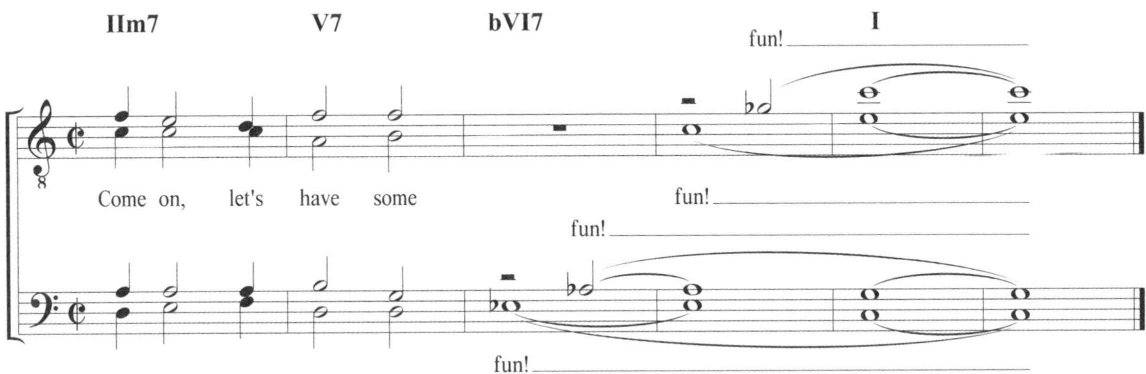

Note: This excerpt showcases root movement of a major third. Root motion by a major third creates interest for the singer and listener, allowing for voices moving in contrary motion by a semitone, quickly and smoothly moving to a new and unexpected dominant 7th chord.

There are plenty of other ways chords can move, but this should give you some idea of the possibilities for non-circle root movement. Even when considering circa-2023 BHS contest rules, where featured occurrences of secondary dominants and circle of fifths progressions are part of the contest rules, non-circle root movement and resolutions are part of the style. More examples are featured throughout this book.

Barbershop music also features a balanced and symmetrical form.

Form refers to the horizontal structure of a given section of a song, usually a division of musical material into phrases. The most familiar part of almost any song is the chorus. Balanced and symmetrical means a number of bars in each section of form that is divisible by four, and an even number of sections of form within a chorus.

Choruses

Choruses of most popular songs are 32 measures long. This length has been popular since the turn of the last century and many still write in this same pattern. Choruses can be further subdivided into groupings of four or eight measures.

Figure 2.21

"My Wild Irish Rose," words and music by Chauncey Olcott.

Note: It is common for a chorus to consist of four phrases.

Measures 1–8 of "My Wild Irish Rose" are referred to as the A section. Measures 9–16 contain melodically and rhythmically different material, and so this is called the B section. Note that measures 17–24 are musically identical to 1–8 and therefore are also labeled A. The last phrase is like the B section, but not the same and so it is called B prime, written B'. Thus, the form of "My Wild Irish Rose" is ABAB', sometimes simplified to just ABAB.

There are examples of songs whose forms are unbalanced, but still feel like they could be adapted to the style. The Beatles' "Yesterday" is a good example of this. The first two phrases are exactly alike musically (labeled A). Both are seven measures in length. The third phrase, eight measures in length, is quite different, thus is called B. And the last phrase is just like the first two, making the form of this song AABA.

Figure 2.22

"Yesterday," words and music by John Lennon and Paul McCartney. YouTube

The AABA form is quite common in popular music: "Over the Rainbow," "Blue Skies," "Can't Help Falling in Love" and countless other songs. The B section in this form is often referred to as the *bridge*. The Beatles liked to call it the *middle eight*. Even the lyrics of the bridge are usually different from those of A sections.

Another common form is ABAC, the last phrase being clearly unlike the other three. "It Had to Be You" is one song that takes this form.

Figure 2.23

"It Had to Be You," words and music by Isham Jones and Gus Kahn.

Songs that have the form ABCD are called through-composed. While some such songs are fine artistically—for example, "School Days" contains enough musical sequences to render it satisfying to the ear—others come across as weak or disjointed.

Figure 2.24

"School Days," words and music by Will Cobb and Gus Edwards.

On the other end of the spectrum are songs with a form of AAAA that have no contrasting phrases and no verse. This type of song is called *stanzaic* or *strophic* and is characterized by having several short refrains. "When the Saints Go Marching In" is a familiar example of this sort of piece.

Figure 2.25

"When the Saints Go Marching In," traditional. YouTube

There are songs that do not adhere to the patterns we have been examining. One of these is Cole Porter's "Night and Day," which has six phrases in the following configuration: ABABCB'.

Figure 2.26

"Night and Day," words and music by Cole Porter. YouTube

Some songs with an unusual form adapt very well to the barbershop style. Figure 2.27 showcases an AABA'C form.

Figure 2.27

"You Make Me Feel So Young," words and music by Mack Gordon, Josef Myrow. Arrangement by Mark Hale. YouTube

You Make Me Feel So Young
3
B
You, you and, you and I
You and I are just like a cou-ple of tots,
You, you and, you and I
I
run-ning a-cross a mea-dow pick-ing up lots of for - get - me - nots.
A''
young, so young and you
You make me feel so young and you make me feel there are
young, so young and you
You
flung,
songs to be sung, bells to be rung, and a won - der - ful fling to be flung.
flung,

Notes: Note that the chorus is composed of five eight-measures phrases (40 measures).

Verses

A verse typically functions as the composer's introduction to the chorus, the familiar focal point of a song. Verses come in varying lengths, though most modern verses are a multiple of eight measures. Many songs have either a 16-measure or 32-measure verse, introducing a 32-measure chorus. Take, for example, the Rodgers and Hart song "Manhattan." Figure 2.28 features an arrangement of this song by Adam Bock, showcasing the 16-measure verse and 32-measure chorus.

Figure 2.28

"Manhattan," words and music by Lorenz Hart and Richard Rodgers. Arranged by Adam Bock.

MANHATTAN

for Flatiron Four

Words and Music by
LORENZ HART and
RICHARD RODGERS

Arrangement by
ADAM BOCK 6/13

Freely

A

Tenor
Lead

Bari
Bass

Ooh Ah

Sum - mer jour - neys to Ni - a - gra and to oth - er pla - ces ag - gra -

Ooh Ah

Ooh Ah

5

Ooh

vate all our cares; we'll save our fares.

Ooh

Ooh

9

I've a co - zy lit - tle flat in what was known as old Man - hat - tan;

13

we'll set - tle down right here in town.

We'll

2 MANHATTAN

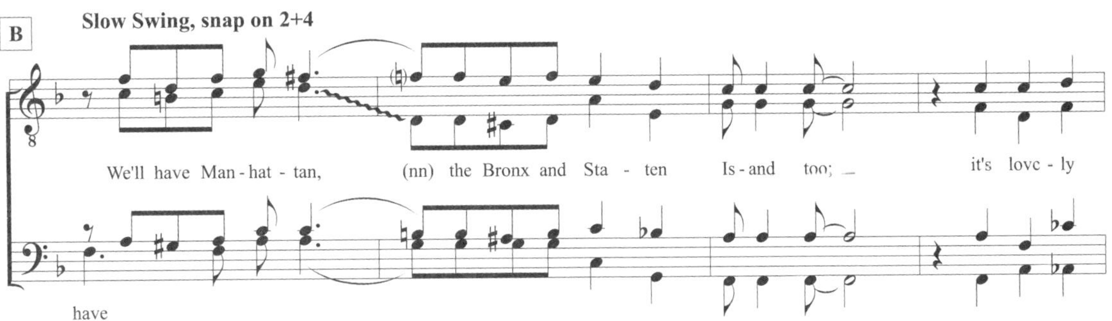
B
Slow Swing, snap on 2+4
We'll have Man - hat - tan, (nn) the Bronx and Sta - ten Is - and too; it's love - ly
have

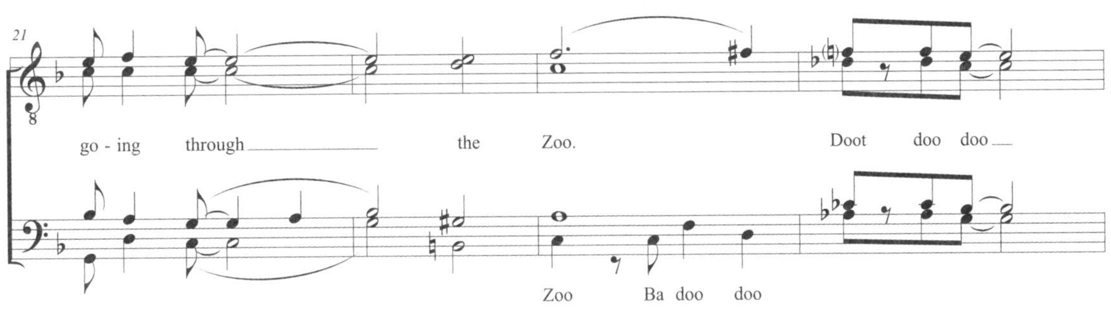
21
go - ing through the Zoo. Doot doo doo
Zoo Ba doo doo

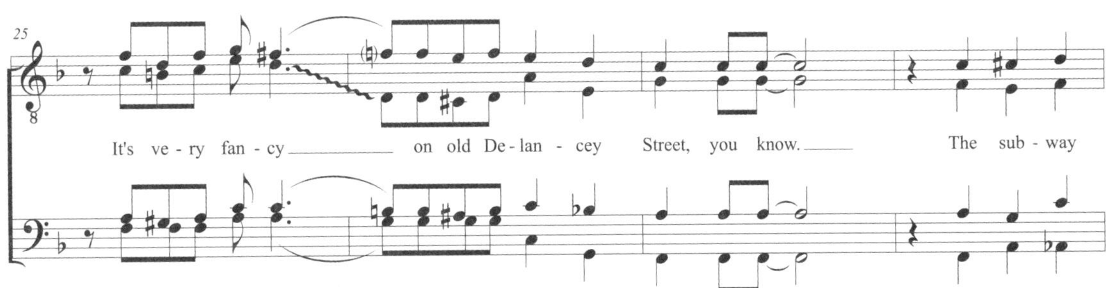
25
It's ve - ry fan - cy on old De - lan - cey Street, you know. The sub - way

29
charms us so when bal - my bree - zes blow to and fro.

MANHATTAN 3

33
And tell me what street compares with Mott Street in Ju - ly, sweet push carts

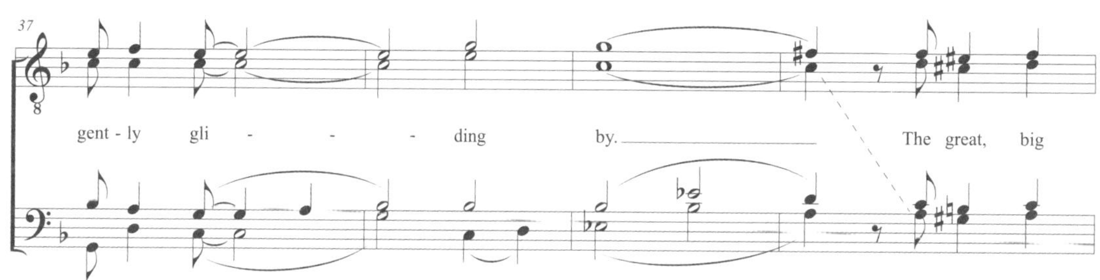
37
gent - ly gli - - - ding by. The great, big

41
ci - ty's a won-drous toy just made for a girl and boy. Babe,

45
accel, snap ends
we'll turn Man - hat - tan (nn) in - to an isle of joy! Yeah, I'd
We'll join the hoi - pol - loi

Occasionally, songs contain a verse that is longer than the chorus. "When You and I Were Young, Maggie" features a verse that is 16 measures and a chorus that is only eight measures long.[17]

Figure 2.29

"When You and I Were Young, Maggie," words and music by George Johnson and James Butterfield. YouTube

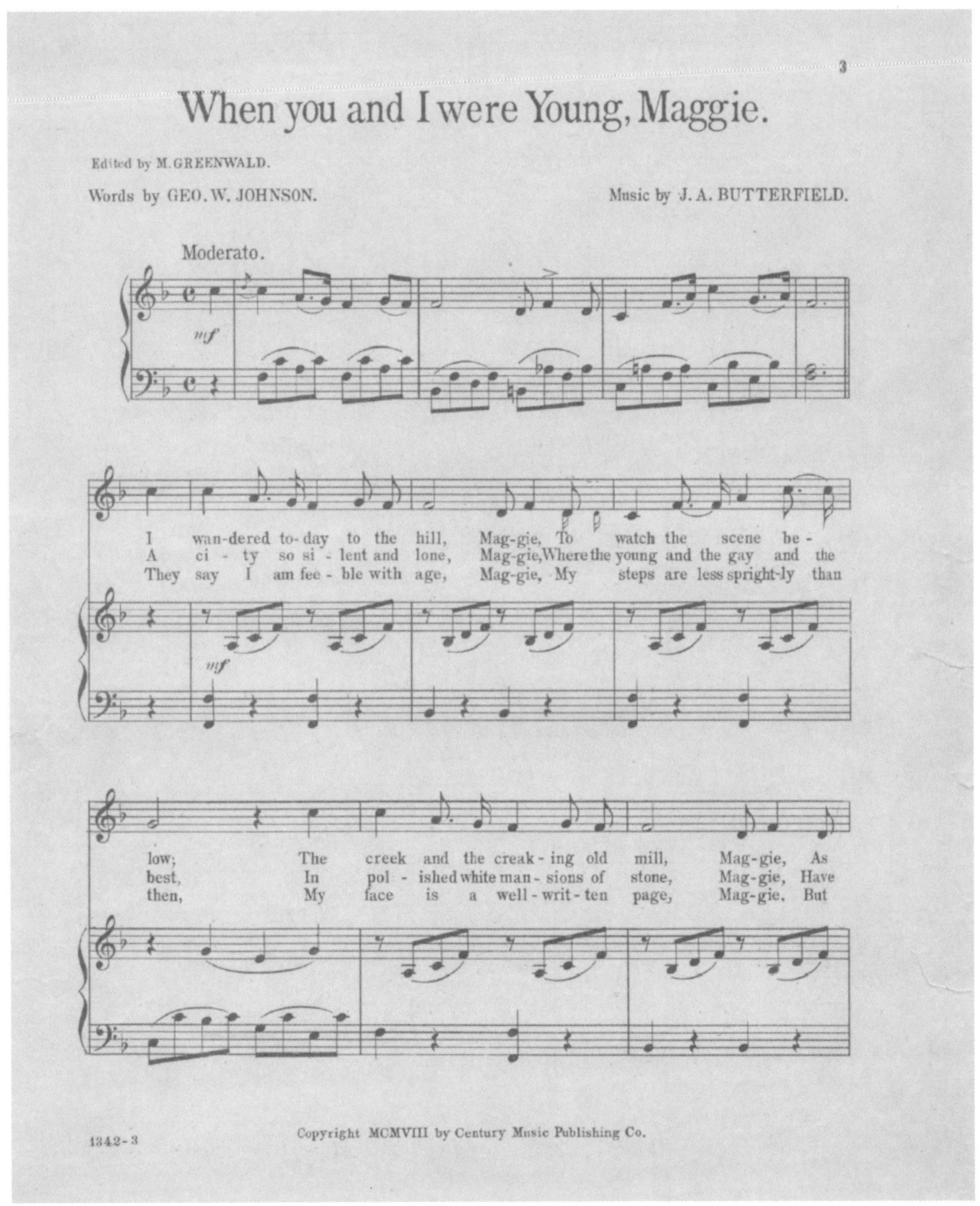

[17] "After the Ball," which sold over two million copies of sheet music in 1892 and thus has been described as America's first popular song, has a verse twice as long as its chorus, 64 measures versus 32.

4
we used to long a - - go. The green grove is gone from the
each found a place of rest, Is built where the birds used to
time a - lone was the pen. They say we are a - ged and
f
hill, Mag-gie, Where first the dai - sies sprung; The
play, Mag-gie, And join in the songs that were sung: For we
gray, Mag-gie, As sprays by the white breakers flung; But to
creak-ing old mill is still, Mag-gie, Since you and I were young.
sang as gay as they, Mag-gie, When you and I were young.
me you're as fair as you were, Mag-gie, When you and I were young.
mf
1342-3

5
CHORUS.
Sop.
And now we are a-ged and gray, Mag-gie. And the tri - als of life near-ly
Alto.
Tenor.
And now we are a-ged and gray, Mag-gie, And the tri - als of life near-ly
Bass.
mf
done; Let us sing of the days that are gone, Maggie, When you and I were young.
rit.
done; Let us sing of the days that are gone, Maggie, When you and I were young.
Let us sing,
rit.
rit.
1342-3

Related to form is the structure, or construction, of an arrangement. Structure refers to the larger sections of a piece: intro, verses, choruses, reprise, interlude, interpolation, bridge, medley, tag. The judicious inclusion and placement of these segments is vital in constructing a musical whole that is satisfying to performer and listener alike.

Good barbershop arrangements exhibit a pleasing balance of unity and contrast, or theme and variation.

The basic song and its harmonization are embellished by the arranger to provide appropriate support of the song's theme and to close the song effectively.

A comprehensive list of the embellishments most frequently used in barbershop arranging, including examples, is found in *Arranging Barbershop*: Vol. 2, Part B, Chapter 23.

Barbershop singers adjust pitches to achieve perfectly tuned chords in just intonation while remaining true to the established tonal center.

Just intonation: a system of tuning simultaneously produced notes to achieve the fewest number of beats, or the clashing of sound waves, which the human ear interprets as dissonance. This results in frequency ratios that perfectly mirror the integer proportions found in the harmonic series.[18]

Instruments such as the violin, double bass, trombone, and the human voice can make minute adjustments in pitch. This is not possible for fixed-pitch instruments like the piano or guitar.

Whether consciously or not, barbershop singers—considered to be great ear singers—seek to sing chords justly in tune, tuning to the harmonic series, while harmonizing with the melody and striving to maintain the tonal center. Higher degrees of just intonation lead to increased agreement in tuning of coincident partials, which is an important aspect of the style.

The degree of consonance of intervals and chords are related to the coincidence of partials, with higher degrees of consonance equating to a greater coincidence of partials. To understand this further, let us consider the *harmonic overtone series* associated with a given fundamental note.

---

[18] https://en.wikipedia.org/wiki/Harmonic_series_(music)

Figure 2.30

The harmonic series.

Harmonic	Freq. Hz	Note	Comment
1	131	C3	Fundamental pitch (first harmonic)
2	262	C4	1st overtone, 1 octave above than the fundamental
3	393	G4	2nd overtone, 1 octave and a 5th (justly tuned) above the fundamental
4	524	C5	3rd overtone, 2 octaves above the fundamental
5	655	E5	4th overtone, 2 octaves and a 3rd (justly tuned) above the fundamental
6	786	G5	5th overtone, 2 octaves and a 5th (justly tuned) above the fundamental
7	917	B♭5	6th overtone, 2 octaves and a flatted 7th (justly tuned) above the fundamental. And note that the overtone series of the fundamental creates a barbershop 7th chord.

Observe that the 4th through 7th harmonics form a barbershop seventh chord, associated with every fundamental tone. These harmonics are frequency ratios, associated with nodes of a vibrating string (figure 2.31).

Figure 2.31

Harmonics shown as nodes in a vibrating string.

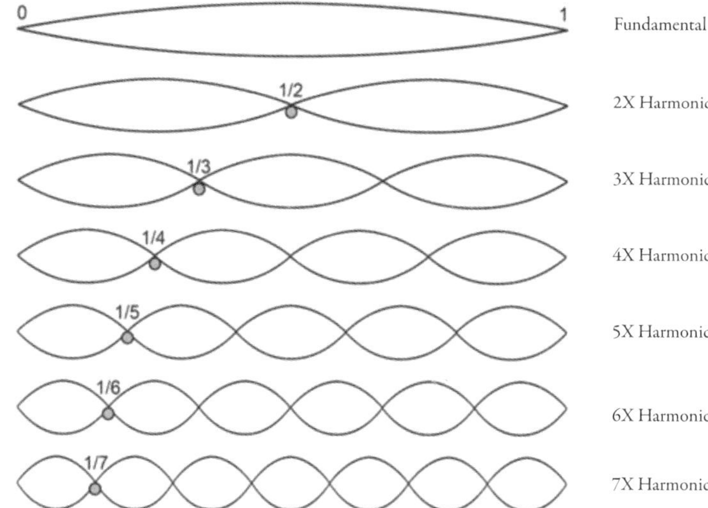

The fundamental tone is the first harmonic; subsequent harmonics are known as *higher harmonics*. These harmonics, produced from typical SATB voice ranges, are well within audible ranges for most humans. Consider now an octave interval, frequently sung between a bass and one of the upper parts, and why this is the most perfect of consonant intervals:

Figure 2.32

Harmonics and coincident partials of an octave.

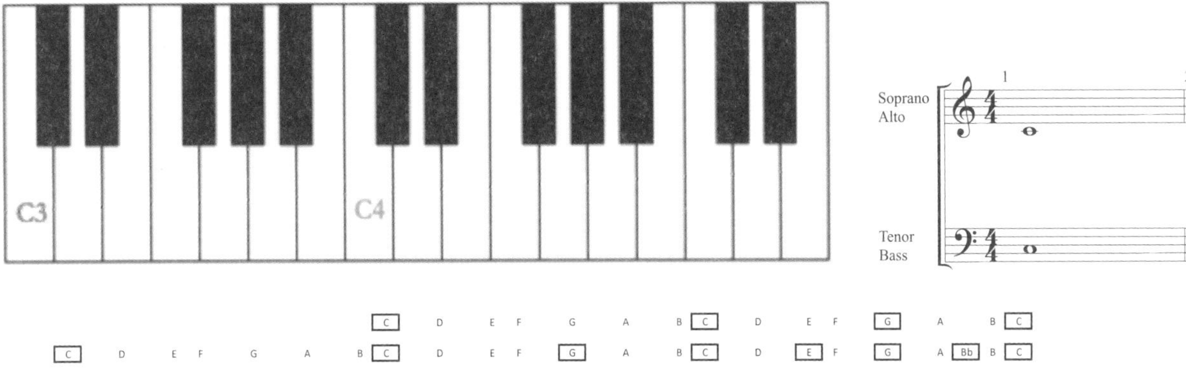

The aligned harmonics from the C3 and C4 fundamentals are called *coincident partials*, frequencies from two different fundamentals that have the same frequencies. Barbershoppers strive to tune these coincident partials to limit the beats that come from mismatched frequencies.

Observe the number of coincident partials starting with the fundamental sung by the upper octave matching the second harmonic of the lower octave. When barbershoppers tune this octave by tuning the partials, beats (dissonance) are eliminated, and the result of the coincident partials at higher frequencies create the ring in the voices and chords. Figure 2.33 shows the mapping of coincident partials associated with adding the perfect fifth in between the octaves (a typical voicing for major triads in the barbershop style):

Figure 2.33

Harmonics and coincident partials associated with an octave and a perfect fifth.

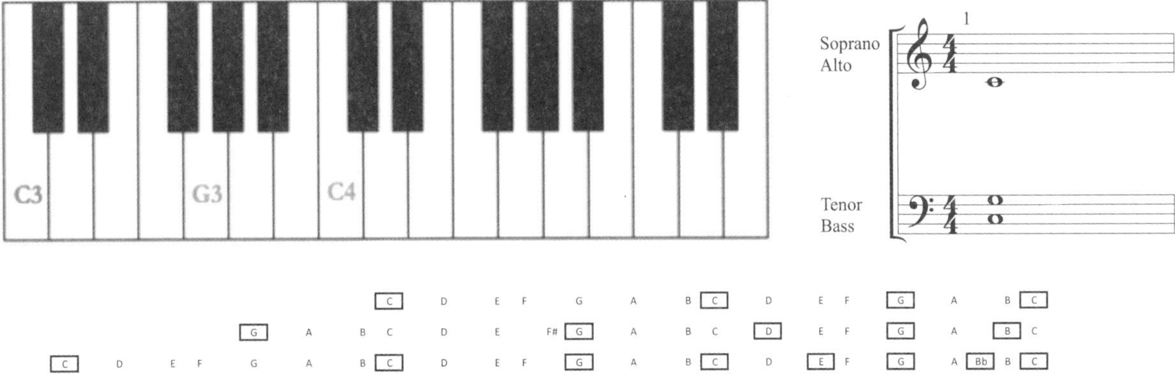

Note the additional reinforcement, in the lower portion of the harmonic stack, between the root position tonic (third harmonic) and the perfect fifth (second harmonic), and the coincident partials an octave higher from all three voices. The perception of the ring and consonance from well-tuned intervals overshadows the dissonance associated with the major second interval between the F and G. Even these perfect intervals, when combined in a chord, include a certain degree of dissonance (semitones between the B♭5, B5, and C6 higher in the harmonic series). However, higher harmonics are typically less loud and the overall perception is one of a high degree of consonance when well-tuned and balanced.

Now, let's look at a dominant seventh chord.

Figure 2.34

Harmonics and coincident partials associated with a root position dominant seventh.

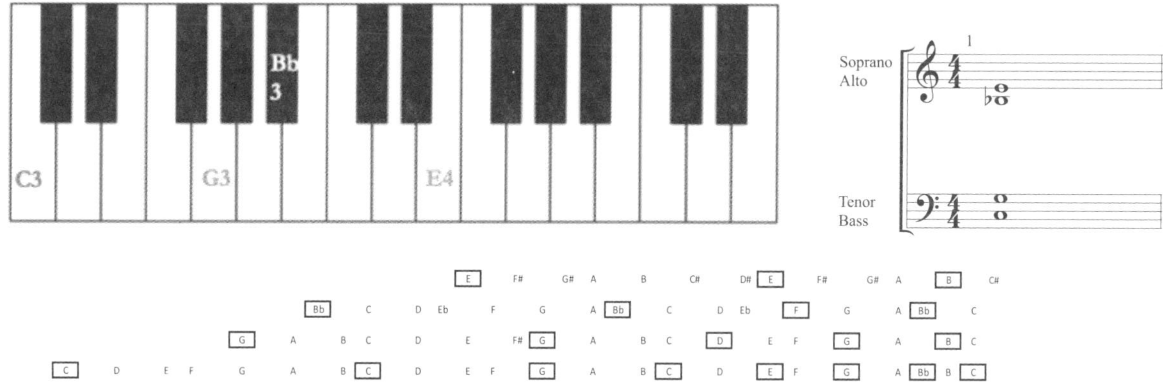

The harmonic energy in the dominant seventh comes from well-tuned coincident partials between the root and the fifth at G4 and G5, as well as coincident partials between the root and the third at E5. As seen in figure 2.34, there is dissonance created by the semitone interval of the partials at E5 and F5, as well as a pair of coincident partials a semitone apart at B♭5 and B5. This helps to create the tension of movement that is inherent in the style. Dominant seventh chords are considered consonant in the barbershop style (more on the stylistic impact in a moment), but only when all chord tones are represented; most barbershoppers would probably describe an exposed minor seventh, major second, or tritone as dissonant. However, based on the harmonic energy associated with the coincident partials based on the fifth, third, and seventh of the chord in the harmonic series, coupled with the tension demanding onward motion, the combination creates a unique harmonic texture associated with the style.

Artistic singing in the barbershop style exhibits a fullness or expansion of sound, precise intonation, a high degree of vocal skill, and a high level of unity and consistency within the ensemble. Ideally, these elements are natural, not manufactured, and free from apparent effort.

What can an arranger do to facilitate artistic singing? Plenty. For example, effective arrangements designed for a specific quartet should feature melody lines that can be easily rendered by the lead singer. Arrangers can contribute to the artistic success of a given ensemble when that arrangement plays to the performers' strengths.

The performance of barbershop music uses appropriate musical and visual methods to convey the theme of the song and provide the audience with an emotionally satisfying and entertaining experience. The musical and visual delivery is from the heart, believable, and sensitive to the song and its arrangement throughout. The most stylistic artistic performance artistically melds together the musical and visual aspects to create and sustain the illusions suggested by the music.

Performers of any contemporary musical form, including barbershop, strive to create an emotionally satisfying experience. That effect is what keeps the audience engaged and connected to the performer. For the audience, it could invoke emotions, alter their sense of time, or create moments that are remembered or talked about after the performance has concluded. Utilizing this kind of audience-focused approach can be a significant component of the barbershop style; it allows the performer to explore various degrees or styles of communication and expression to deliver honest emotion. This should exist in both the vocal and visual components of the performance; all aspects must be considered for the effect to be maximized.

The arranger is the first interpreter of the composer's song. Decisions that an arranger makes will inform the ensemble and can help contribute directly to that emotionally satisfying experience. Some questions to keep in mind:

- Does the song need an intro, or is the composer's verse sufficient to start things off?
- Would the piece benefit from a key change? If so, where, and how far up or sometimes even down?
- What sort of tag will finish things off just right?
- Which embellishments sound better in a given spot?
- What sort of voicing will translate to memorable moments in a performance?

Summary

Barbershop is a style of arranging four-part, a cappella music. Unlike other styles, barbershop features primarily homorhythmic texture, melody on an inside voice, and featured instances of secondary dominants that move around the circle of fifths. The best examples of the style feature the concepts of unity and contrast, thematic development, and high levels of inherent consonance potential based on the voicings, textures, and vocabulary of chords chosen.

There are no barbershop songs; songs from multiple genres can be arranged in the barbershop style. The best examples include naturally occurring secondary dominants (e.g., D7 or A7 in the key of C) that progress around the circle of fifths toward the tonic. Lyrically featured songs with balanced form, including contrasting segments such as bridges or interludes to offset verses and choruses, often adapt well to the style.

Barbershop is not simply a style defined on the page. When arrangements of songs that inherently imply the aspects of the style are artistically rendered by performers who are sensitive to thematic material, the audience is rewarded with an emotionally satisfying and entertaining experience. As the style has evolved over the course of time, allowing for a broader range of source material from the 20th and 21st century, so has the opportunity to connect via multiple thematic elements: lyrics, melody, rhythm, and, of course, harmony.

But is this really evolution of the style, or a return to its roots? In the next chapter, Kevin Keller compares and contrasts the key elements of barbershop harmony circa 1941 with the state of the style in 2022.

Chapter 3.
Everything Old Is New Again

by Joe Stern and Kevin Keller

The Society for the Preservation and Encouragement of Barber Shop Quartet Singing in America was formed in 1938 and hosted its first convention in 1939, yet it wasn't until 1941 when the Society board of directors recognized that the barbershop style was not defined. They turned to Joe Stern, a barbershop pioneer, to define it. He had been singing barbershop in Sedalia MO long before the Society began.

Figure 3.1

Joe Stern's 1941 letter defining the barbershop style.

THE SOCIETY FOR THE
PRESERVATION AND ENCOURAGEMENT
OF BARBER SHOP QUARTET SINGING IN AMERICA

JOE STERN

Kansas City, Mo., May 21, 1941

TO ALL NATIONAL OFFICERS AND DIRECTORS:

Since the rise and growth of our Society, I note there is some misunderstanding, and some variance of opinion as to what kind of harmony constitutes barber shop harmony. I was raised on it, but I find it difficult to put my conception of barber shop harmony into words. However, I want to set forth, what seems to me to be a few fundamentals of this kind of harmony.

1. Real barber shop harmony contemplates four part harmony, that is to say chords with four different notes, as far as possible.

2. There should be a minimum of doubling. By doubling I mean where two of the parts are on identical notes, or an octave apart on identical notes.

3. High bass is preferable at all times. Low bass (sometimes called "church bass") is not conducive to close harmony and should be discouraged. Some times the bass can take his note exactly one octave below the normal range for the note, however, the note at the high end of this octave is best for close harmony.

4. Lead, tenor and barytone, never double with each other at any time, that is to say, at no time do any of these three parts ever duplicate or sing on the same note. Every single chord struck by these three parts should consist of three different tones, and there are no exceptions to this rule.

5. The bass at times will double with each of these three other parts, usually an octave below the part which he is doubling with. However, such doubling should be kept to a minimum at all times. Four part harmony is preferable, whenever possible.

6. Close harmony chords are best. A chord with an extremely high tenor, and a very low bass, produces a long range chord, and while this sort of chord may be alright for an orchestra or piano, it is not good in a barber shop quartette of four male voices, because such a chord is difficult for the listener to comprehend, and it does not carry the punch and drama of close harmony chord.

7. It is permissible, in fact, sometimes expedient, to change the lead melody in order to improve the harmony.

8. PITCH - If a song is pitched too low, the harmony will sound "muddy". If pitched too high, it may cause the singers to show evidence of straining. A medium high pitch will cause the harmony to "ring clear" and this kind of a pitch is best - just high enough so that no one has to strain.

9. No piano or other accompaniment is permissible with a barber shop quartette, for the reason that a quartette should strive to smooth out the rough spots themselves, so that no accompaniment is necessary to cover them up. Besides, the accompaniment detracts from the ability of the quartette.

10. In judging a barber shop quartette contest, while showmanship should be taken into account, I believe that a small ratio of points is sufficient for this, and that major emphasis should be placed on the quality of good old fashioned barber shop harmony.

11. Generally speaking, if you can distinguish which individual is singing bass, barytone, lead or tenor, when a quartette is singing at a distance of about fifty feet, then it is an indication that the blending of voices is not good. In other words, at this distance it should be impossible to pick out who is singing what part. In a top-notch quartette it is impossible to pick them out even if placed much closer than fifty feet.

I am sending this to all the National Officers and Directors. Maybe some of you can define barber shop harmony better, I shall appreciate hearing from some of you and look forward with lots of pleasure to seeing you in St. Louis.

Sincerely yours,

Jos. E. Stern, Pres. Kansas City Chapter
200 Temple Building, Kansas City, Missouri.

It is interesting to note what has changed over the years since Joe wrote this. The following paragraphs are transcripts of Joe's letters—marked with [JS]—with a 21st century commentary—marked with [KK].

Old vs. New

[JS] Since the rise and growth of our Society, I note there is some misunderstanding, and some variance of opinion as to what kind of harmony constitutes barber shop harmony. I was raised on it, but I find it difficult to put my conception of barber shop [sic] harmony into words. However, I want to set forth what seems to me to be the fundamentals of this kind of harmony.

> [JS] 1. Real barber shop harmony contemplates four-part harmony, that is to say chords with four different notes, as far as possible.
>
> > [KK] This is still relevant to a large degree with "contemplates" being the keyword. Today, arrangers use far more embellishments and will purposefully use chords and textures with less than four parts. However, each chord could accommodate four different notes.
>
> [JS] 2. There should be a minimum of doubling. By doubling I mean where two of the parts are on identical notes, or an octave apart on identical notes.
>
> > [KK] Today: Overall, this is still relevant. It is important to add: on major and minor triads, typically the root of the chord is doubled with the bass singing the lower root and doubling with one of the top three parts. There is the occasion that the baritone and bass might double and then quickly move away.
>
> [JS] 3. High bass is preferable at all times. Low bass (sometimes called "church bass") is not conducive to close harmony and should be discouraged. Some times [sic] the bass can take his note exactly one octave below the normal range for the note, however, the note at the high end of this octave is best for close harmony.
>
> > [KK] Today, this point is one of the major distinguishing features between barbershop and gospel music. Gospel music will feature a low bass. In barbershop, voicings with a *divorced bass* can make the harmony seem muddy while voicings featuring higher bass notes—and thus closer harmony—will be cleaner and sing better. In the 40s there would be occasions where the lead would be the lowest note in the chord and the bass would go above. Today, the bass will almost always be the lowest note. Several notable basses can sing very low and create expansion, but by and large most of our singers and arrangements follow Joe's advice. It is not discouraged; our culture and practices keep it high.

A *divorced, low bass part* is defined as the bass part being at least an octave away from the next highest voice part.

> [JS] 4. Lead, tenor and barytone [sic], never double with each other at any time, that is to say, at no time do any of these three parts ever duplicate or sing on the same note. Every single chord struck by these three parts should consist of three different tones, and there are no exceptions to this rule.
>
> > [KK] Examinations of printed arrangements from the 1940s note violations of this principle from time to time. Today, it is the rarest exception that the tenor, lead, and baritone ever

double in arrangements from skilled arrangers and it would only be done for a specific reason.

[JS] 5. The bass at times will double with each of these three other parts, usually an octave below the part which he is doubling with. However, such doubling should be kept to a minimum at all times. Four-part harmony is preferable, whenever possible.

> [KK] Beyond triads (major and minor), where the bass will double another part, this is true today. In the 1940s there were empty chords where a third, fifth, or seventh would be omitted. Today, any skilled arranger will follow the principle of writing complete chords.

[JS] 6. Close harmony chords are the best. A chord with an extremely high tenor and a very low bass, produces a long range chord, and while this sort of chord may be alright for an orchestra or piano, it is not good in a barber shop [sic] quartette [sic] of four male voices, because such a chord is difficult for the listener to comprehend, and it does not carry the punch and drama of close harmony chord.

> [KK] Although in principle true, widely spread chords are acceptable if the singers can execute them well. Although the majority are close harmony chords as Joe defines, divorced chords are used periodically.

[JS] 7. It is permissible, in fact, sometimes expedient, to change the lead melody in order to improve the harmony.

> [KK] The pendulum has swung a bit on this over time. Only a few years after this original letter was published, the pendulum had swung to avoid altering the melody much. Over time, arrangers gradually began taking liberties. In 1971, as part of the definition of the new Arrangement (ARR) category, it was mandated, "absolutely no melodic alteration," with some extremely limited exceptions. The BHS Musicality category, as of the 2023 category school review of stylistic practices for contestable arrangements, has relaxed that policy. As long as it isn't jarring to the listener's familiarity with the piece and/or the melodic alteration is the only way the secondary dominant seventh requirement is achieved, melodic alteration is permissible.

[JS] 8. PITCH – If a song is pitched too low, the harmony will sound "muddy." If pitched too high, it may cause the singers to show evidence of straining. A medium high pitch will cause the harmony to "ring clear" and this kind of a pitch is best— just high enough so that no one has to strain.

> [KK] This still holds true today. Vocal Spectrum would likely pitch a song higher than The Boston Common! If it sings well for the group, it's the right key.

[JS] 9. No piano or other accompaniment is permissible with a barber shop [sic] quartette [sic] for the reason that a quartette [sic] should strive to smooth out the rough spots themselves, so that no accompaniment is necessary to cover them up. Besides, the accompaniment detracts from the ability of the quartette.

> [KK] There was a lot of controversy over this. Although it is believed that in 1939 and 1940 no one competed with instruments, most recorded barbershop harmonies of the 1930s were all accompanied. There were lots of disagreements in the BHS magazine *The Harmonizer* about whether barbershop should be a cappella or could be accompanied. Over time, fewer and fewer groups used instruments. Joe's point was not to say barbershop couldn't be accompanied, but it was a rule for contest. Arrangement swipes and echoes are what Joe refers to about smoothing over the rough spots. As well as the ability to hear the harmonies uninterrupted.

[JS] 10. In judging a barber shop [sic] quartette [sic] contest, while showmanship should be taken into account, I believe that a small ratio of points is sufficient for this, and that major emphasis should be placed on the quality of good old fashioned barber shop [sic] harmony.

> [KK] Ironically, the Board of Directors first chose 25% for showmanship in 1941. After the backlash from the membership, it was reduced to 10%. Over time it has increased. Today's Performance category does not specifically judge showmanship. As of 2022, Performance judges adjudicate entertainment value, audience rapport, expressiveness, visual/vocal agreement, and believability. Performance accounts for one-third of the overall score for an ensemble.

[JS] Generally speaking, if you can distinguish which individual is singing bass, barytone [sic], lead or tenor, when a quartette [sic] is singing at a distance of about fifty feet, then it is an indication that the blending of voices is not good. In other words, at this distance it should be impossible to pick out who is singing what part. In a top-notch quartette [sic] it is impossible to pick them out even if placed much closer than fifty feet.

> [KK] For many years, there was a push to get singers to match the timbre of the lead singer. Only in the past 25 years is there less emphasis on this. In addition, prior to the 1970s singers stood in almost a random order. Coaching from the 1970s put the lead and bass in the center predominantly. More embellishments in the arrangements allow an audience to quickly identify who is singing what. But Joe's overall point is relevant in that quartets that are executing at a high level from a distance will sound homogeneous.

[JS] I am sending this to all the National Officers and Directors. Maybe some of you can define barber shop [sic] harmony better.

> [KK] Today's description, circa 2023, is a bit more prescriptive, but Joe did a great job early in our Society. The Board of Directors took his 11 points word for word in the 1941 Rules for the National Contest and they were in place for a couple of years. One interesting omission on Joe's part is that there is no mention of the melody being below the tenor and being an inside voice. This was added a few years later. However, it was the practice at the time, and discussed in future issues of *The Harmonizer*.

Part B: Foundational Tools

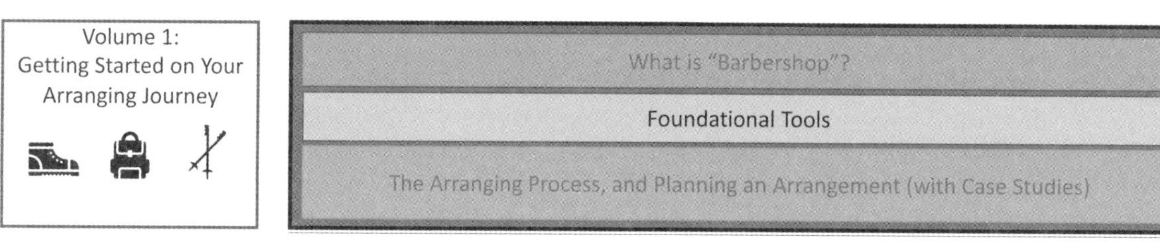

Now that we've defined the style, explored the historical perspective, and delved into the definition, we're just about ready to embark on our own arranging journey, which is detailed in Vol. 2. However, any journey requires the acquisition of some prerequisite knowledge and tools. Traveling abroad? You'll need a passport. Hiking through the wilderness? Better wear a good set of hiking shoes and bring a compass. This part of *Arranging Barbershop* Vol. 1 highlights some of the key tools and concepts needed for arrangers to engage in any of the journeys along this trail.

Chapter 4: Ranges for Arranging

Steve Scott provides an overview of voice ranges typically leveraged in arranging for different types of barbershop ensembles, including those for changes voices.

Chapter 5: Theory of Barbershop Harmony

In 2010 BHS staff member Adam Scott wrote a music theory manual to match the curriculum found at Harmony University. It is now updated for this book by Rafi Hasib and Andrew Wittenberg. The chapter on the Theory of Barbershop Harmony highlights theory and musical literacy concepts specifically through the lens of the barbershop arranger.

Chapter 4. Ranges for Arranging

By Steve Scott

Intro

The most successful ensembles performing barbershop arrangements sing repertoire that fits their voices. An effective arranger understands the range and *tessituras* of the singers who will perform the arrangement. When ranges are unknown or when arranging a song for general use and publication, the arranger is aided by a general understanding of voice ranges.

	*Tessitura* refers to the general range of pitches where the vocal line lies.

Barbershop is sung by people of all voice types. This book will use SSAA to describe a traditional all-female ensemble composition, TTBB to describe a traditional all-male ensemble composition, and SATB for an ensemble that is of mixed composition. It is understood that humans can sing any one of these parts (SATB) and a voice part shouldn't be associated with gender.

Overview

From highest to lowest, the voice parts in barbershop are tenor, lead, baritone, and bass. Figures 4.1 and 4.2 indicate the common vocal ranges by voice parts used in barbershop arrangements.

Figure 4.1

Traditional TTBB barbershop voice ranges.

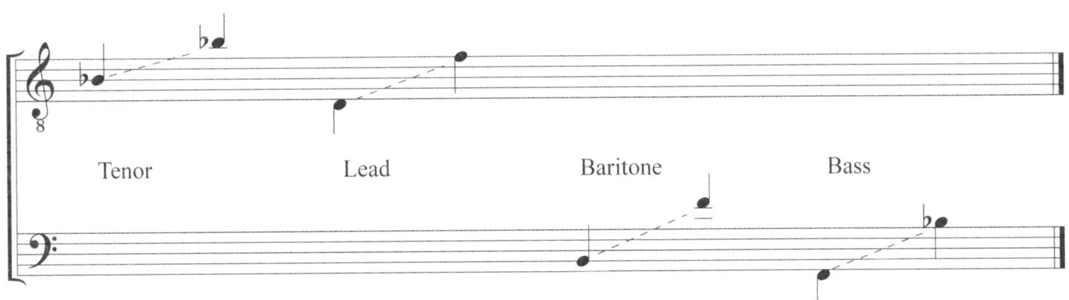

Note the subscript 8 under the treble clef to indicate that it sounds an octave lower than written.

Figure 4.2

Traditional SSAA barbershop voice ranges.

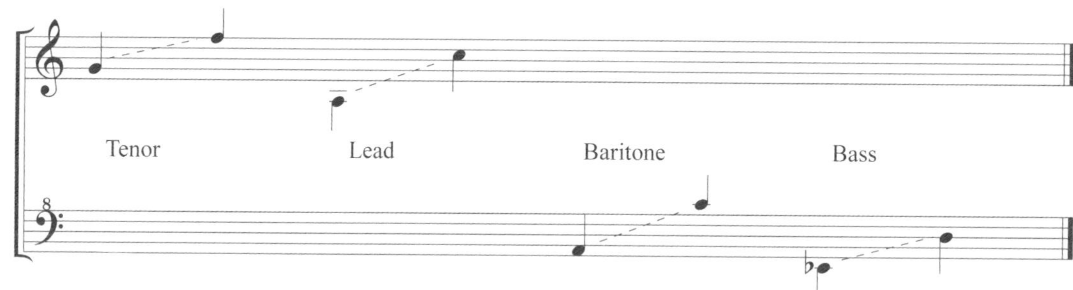

Note the superscript 8 over the bass clef to indicate that it sounds an octave higher than written.

Note that this section of *Arranging Barbershop* does not include a graphic for SATB or mixed/treble clef/bass clef barbershop ranges. This is because there isn't really a standard voicing for SATB barbershop. Know the voices for whom you arrange before picking a key.

Changing Voices

The present information uses a summary of the research for changing male voices (Cooksey) and female/treble voices (Gackle). Note that even changed voices are not fully mature and vocal health needs to be the primary concern. In all young singers, be aware of extraneous vocal tension.[19]

This text uses terms *male* and *female* when describing differences in changing voice.[20]

The *adolescent unchanged male* has an approximate comfortable singing range of A3 to F5. The entirety of the TTBB barbershop tenor range is included in this range.

---

[19] Thurman, L. and Welch, G. (2000). *Bodymind & voice: foundations of voice education*, Vol. 3, Collegeville, MN: VoiceCare Network.

[20] See Jackson Hearns, L. and Kremer, B. (2018). *The singing teacher's guide to transgender voices,* San Diego, CA: Plural Publishing. The authors of this book note that the term *sex* is biological and refers to chromosomal, hormonal, and primary and secondary sex characteristics, while the term *gender* is behavioral or social. The more accurate term for male is *male-assigned*; the more accurate term for female is *female-assigned*. Further, the authors note that some humans are intersex, which describes a person whose chromosomal and anatomical characteristics differ from traditional male or female. For simplicity, *male* and *female* are used in this text.

Figure 4.3

Unchanged male voice range compared with traditional TTBB barbershop tenor range.

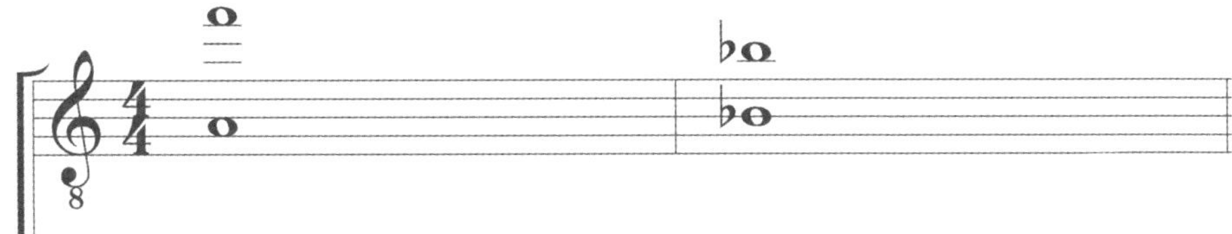

unchanged male voice TTBB barbershop tenor range

The *adolescent changing male* has an approximate comfortable singing range of F3 to A4 in Midvoice II and D3 to F4 in Midvoice IIa.[21] TTBB barbershop lead range will fit into Midvoice IIa stage range.[22]

Figure 4.4

Adolescent changing male voice (MVII and MVIIa) range compared with traditional TTBB barbershop lead range.

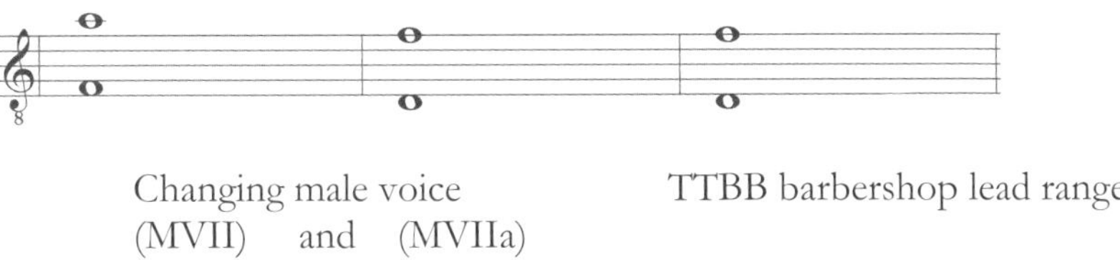

Changing male voice (MVII) and (MVIIa) TTBB barbershop lead range

Note the subscript 8 under the treble clef.

The *adolescent changed male*, including new baritone and emerging adult bass, has an approximate comfortable singing range B2 to D♯4 and G2 to D4, respectively: TTBB barbershop baritone and bass will accommodate these voice parts, depending on the individual voice.

Figure 4.5

Adolescent changed male voice (new baritone) range compared with traditional TTBB baritone and bass ranges.

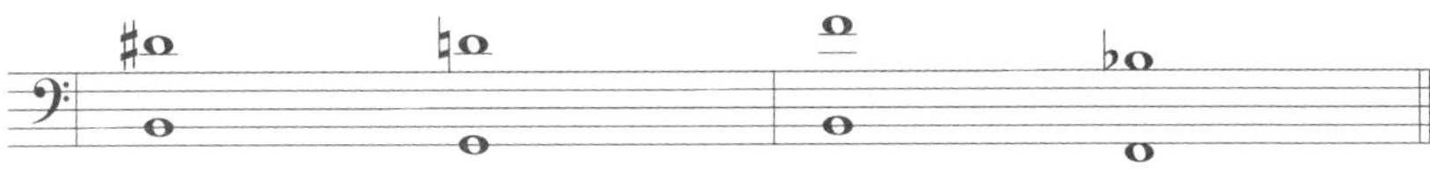

New baritone TTBB barbershop baritone and bass

[21] See the Cooksey findings in Thurman and Welch. Note that the male changing voice will have periods of restricted range, sometimes as little as a fifth. The voice change is a brief occurrence.

[22] The highest and lowest notes of male barbershop lead should be approached with care. Numerous arrangements are available in the Barbershop Harmony Marketplace that will accommodate the range of changing voices. One advantage of singing unaccompanied is the ability to transpose songs to a more comfortable key, provided the other parts are still within comfortable ranges.

Changed male voices have several options in barbershop. The TTBB barbershop baritone and lead ranges could be compared to singing in the same range as a choral tenor II in SATB part writing. Choral bass I may be more comfortable singing TTBB barbershop bass or baritone. Choral tenor I will likely be comfortable singing TTBB barbershop lead or barbershop tenor.

The *adolescent unchanged female* has an approximate comfortable singing range of B♭3 to F5. SSAA barbershop tenor encompasses the entirety of the range of the unchanged female voice.

Figure 4.6

Unchanged female voice range compared with SSAA barbershop tenor range.

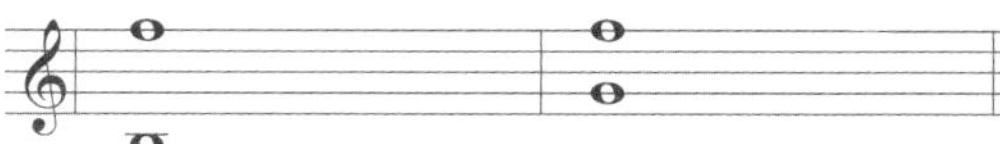

Unchanged female voice SSAA barbershop tenor

The *adolescent changing female* has an approximate comfortable singing range of A3 to F♯5. SSAA barbershop tenor, lead, and baritone encompasses the entirety of the range of the changing female voice.

Figure 4.7

Changing female voice range compared with SSAA barbershop lead and baritone

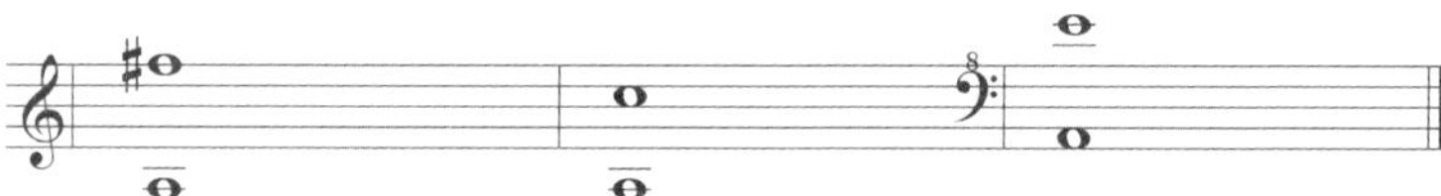

Changing female voice SSAA barbershop lead and baritone

Note the superscript 8 over the bass clef to indicate that it sounds an octave higher than written.

The *changed female* has an approximate comfortable singing range of A3 to A5. SSAA barbershop tenor, lead, and baritone encompasses the entirety of the range of the changed female voice.

Figure 4.8

Changed female voice range.

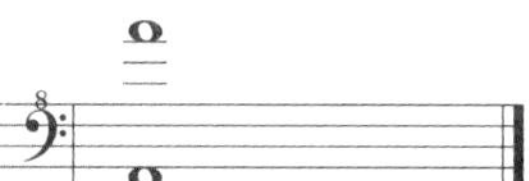

Changed female voices have several options in barbershop. The SSAA barbershop tenor range could be compared to singing in the same range as a choral soprano I or II in SATB part writing. SSAA barbershop baritone and lead range could be compared to singing in the same range as a choral alto I. Incorporating the comfortable speaking pitch of F♯3, the changed female voice shares six pitches with SSAA barbershop bass and is analogous to singing alto II.

Of interest to arrangers is the treatment of SSAA barbershop tenor. The range in which a SSAA barbershop tenor sings is, classically speaking, often the most powerful part of the singer's range. Chord balancing may require a soprano singing SSAA barbershop tenor to sing quieter, but this should be done with care.

Chapter 5. Theory of Barbershop Harmony

By Rafi Hasib and Adam Scott, with contributions from Steve Tramack and Andrew Wittenberg

Introduction

The understanding of the theory of barbershop harmony benefits from familiarity with three areas as they relate to barbershop: (1) music fundamentals,[23] (2) chord vocabulary, and (3) stylistic conventions. Most introductory music theory courses cover music fundamentals used in barbershop arranging. Experienced barbershop singers may recognize conventions of the style but benefit from covering the vocabulary used to describe them. Furthermore, arrangers and composers familiar with the 20th century harmony associated with American popular music may already understand concepts from classical and popular music but benefit from learning the conventions specific to the style.

This chapter of the book assumes basic music literacy, such as recognition of notes, rhythms, clefs, keys, and other common symbols found in Western music. It also assumes a familiarity with basic music theory, such as intervals, triads, seventh chords, and root identification. A comprehensive knowledge of music theory is not necessary to begin arranging, though strong familiarity will help. Many ideas described here standardize terms and theory used throughout the book.

Music Fundamentals

This section reviews music theory fundamentals within a barbershop context, whose motivation and notation derive largely from classical, jazz, and popular American music.[24] Much of the material covered here overlaps with an introductory music theory course, and most aspiring arrangers or trained musicians can proceed to the next section.

Keys

In music, a group of sequentially named pitches define a scale or key, with a central note, the tonic, providing a subjective sense of departure and arrival. Keys may be in major mode or minor mode, with the tonic indicated alongside the mode, e.g., C major or C minor, though major is assumed when the mode is not specified, e.g., key of C.[25]

---

[23] Different cultures have schemes to describe and present music. Music fundamentals, in this context, refer to conventions embraced in the European common practice period that covers the mid-Baroque period through Classical, Romantic, and Impressionist music, from the mid 1600s to the early 1900s, with further influence on popular music and jazz. For simplicity, this will be referred to as *classical music*.

[24] See the section on "A Historical Perspective" for more context.

[25] Other sequentially organized scales exist in Western classical music called modes. These modes have scale degrees that vary from major and minor scales and are, therefore, rarely used in barbershop.

Major keys are constructed as a pattern of whole steps (W) and half steps (H), where a half step, e.g., E to F, is half the size of a whole step, e.g., F to G. Minor keys are constructed with a different pattern of whole steps and half steps. Some keys share the same notes, e.g., C major and A minor; they are treated as different keys, different tonic, but share the same key signature, indicating which notes are sharp or flat.

Figure 5.1

Major and minor keys with their associated half- and whole-step intervallic relationships.

Scale Degrees

For a given key, we assign scale degrees, based on their distance from the tonic, which is called 1. This allows for analysis without tying relationships to tones or keys.[26] For simplicity, we identify scale degrees by Arabic numbers, e.g., write 5 but say "five," and chords built atop them by their corresponding Roman numeral, e.g., write V but say "five chord," allowing discussion without tying it directly to the named key.

Figure 5.2

Scale degrees in C major.

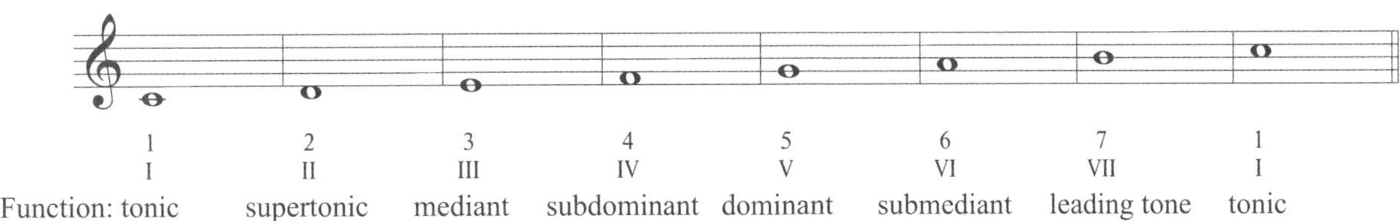

Another convention is referring to scale degrees by their solfège syllable, e.g do, re, mi sol, etc. Still yet another convention is referring to scale degrees by their function, tonic (I), subdominant (IV), and dominant (V) functions. Figure 5.2 displays all of these conventions.

Intervals

Intervals describe the vertical distance between notes and help define note relationships. Notes found within a given key are diatonic and require no additional accidentals. Diatonic intervals are either major or minor (seconds, thirds, sixths, and sevenths), or perfect (unison, fourth, fifth, octave). Adjacent notes outside the key are considered non-diatonic and become important when chromatically altering them for a more characteristic barbershop sound.

---

[26] Note that this is a different system than that used in some European and South American countries, e.g. Spain, that tie solfège names to specific pitches: F is Fa, A♭ is La bemol, etc.

When altering an interval:

- Diminished intervals are one half-step smaller than perfect or minor intervals.
- Augmented intervals are one half-step larger than perfect or major intervals.

Figure 5.3

Perfect intervals and diminished and augmented variations.

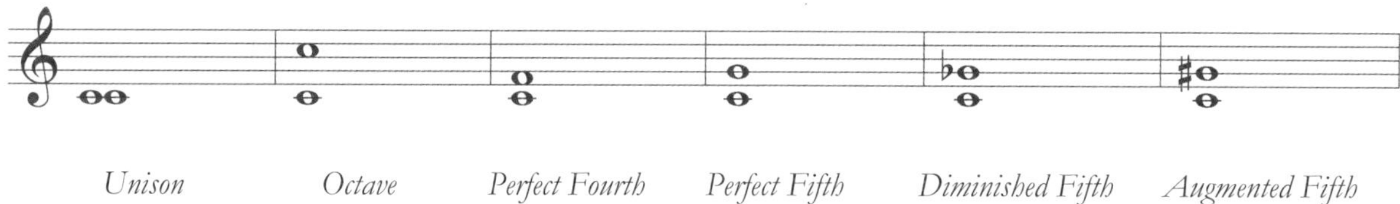

The interval of a diminished fifth or augmented fourth is also known as a *tritone.* The unstable energy of this interval has a pull, either inward or outward, toward a consonant interval, making it integral to the forward motion of the barbershop style. Tritones are notated as an either a *diminished fifth* or an *augmented fourth.* These intervals have the same sound, but are notated differently, an example of enharmonic spelling. The spelling of the chord determines its context and function. See figure 5.4 for examples.

Figure 5.4

Tritones with their enharmonic spellings.

All other intervals—including seconds, thirds, sixths, and sevenths—are imperfect.

- Minor intervals are one-half step smaller than major intervals. For example, a minor third interval consists of three half-steps.
- Major intervals are thus one-half step larger than minor intervals. For example, a major third interval consists of four half-steps.
- Diminished intervals are one-half step smaller than minor intervals.
- Augmented intervals are one-half step larger than major intervals.

Figure 5.5

Examples of imperfect intervals.

Note that some intervals share the same sonority but use a different enharmonic spelling, e.g. diminished 7th and major 6th; minor 7th and augmented 6th. The spelling helps in identifying related notes and describing the overall sound.

To summarize chromatic alterations of intervals by half step:

- perfect interval (unison, fourth, fifth, octave)
  diminished ← perfect → augmented
- imperfect interval (second, third, sixth, seventh)
  diminished ← minor ↔ major → augmented
- tritone
  perfect fourth ← tritone → perfect fifth

Chords

Chords form when at least three pitches (built from two intervals) occur simultaneously. The interval that broadly classifies chords is the third. Chords with thirds appears in two qualities, the major or minor third.

Figure 5.6

Major and minor intervals.

The type of third in a chord is particularly important as it determines its overall quality. In barbershop, we expect chords to contain a third above the root, even when other chord members are absent.

Figure 5.7

Stacked triads.

Stacking two intervals of thirds creates a triad, where the upper two notes lie a third and fifth above the lowest tone. The lowest tone is often called the root and can be thought of as the root of a chord. The middle note in a triad is referred to as the third of the chord and the top note is referred to as the fifth of the chord. In major and minor triads, the interval of the fifth is a perfect fifth, consisting of seven half steps—3 and ½ steps—between the root and fifth of the chord. This unique, open sound is significant in anchoring and tuning barbershop chords.

Placing an additional interval of a third above a triad introduces a seventh above the root, referred to as the seventh of the chord. The pattern can continue with a ninth and so on.

Stacking thirds is an important concept in barbershop music theory.

- Its harmony yields a satisfying sound for our ears, conditioned from performing and hearing tonal music.
- The respelling or rearrangement of any given chord in terms of its closest form of stacked thirds helps in the identification of the chord.
- Physical properties of the relationship reinforce the broader overtone series, which itself motivates the microtuning of barbershop chords.

Chord Qualities

The choice of third and fifth in a triad leads to different sonorities.

Figure 5.8

Examples of triads.

The basic triads are:

- The major triad: root, major 3rd, perfect 5th
- The minor triad: root, minor 3rd, perfect 5th
- The augmented triad: root, major 3rd, augmented 5th

[27] For chords with more than four distinct notes, such as ninth or thirteenth chords, certain notes are omitted to retain four-part harmony. This is discussed in a later section.

- The diminished triad:[28] root, minor 3rd, diminished 5th

The choice of triad and seventh leads to different sonorities.

Figure 5.9

Examples of how stacked thirds of different qualities change sonority of seventh chords.

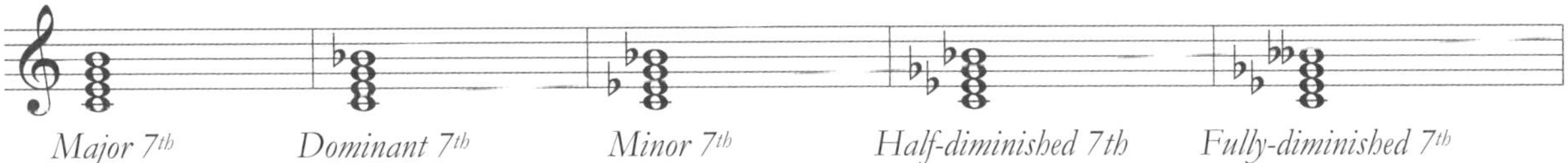

The common seventh chords are:

- Major seventh: major triad + major 7th (major-major seventh chord)
- Dominant seventh: major triad + minor 7th (major-minor seventh chord)
- Minor seventh: minor triad + minor 7th (minor-minor seventh chord)
- Half-diminished seventh: diminished triad + minor 7th (half-diminished seventh chord)
- Diminished seventh:[29] diminished triad + diminished 7th (fully diminished seventh chord)

The chord comprised of a major triad and a minor seventh is traditionally called a dominant seventh, as it is the diatonic seventh chord based on the fifth scale degree, or the dominant, of the major scale. This is also called a major-minor seventh chord, which barbershoppers call the *barbershop 7th*. It is one of the principal sonorities of barbershop harmony.

Chord Inversions

When a note other than the root of a chord appears in the lowest voice, the chord is inverted.

- Root position: the root is the lowest voice
- First inversion: the third of the chord is the lowest voice
- Second inversion: the fifth of the chord is the lowest voice
- Third inversion: the seventh of the chord is the lowest voice

---

[28] This explanation is included for completeness. However, examples of good barbershop arrangements favor the fully diminished seventh chord over the triad as it offers four distinct notes and a richer, fuller chord than the hollower sounding diminished triad.

[29] The diminished seventh interval is enharmonically a major sixth but correctly spelled as a doubly-lowered seventh. When notating the chord in arrangements, the chord may be respelled for more intuitive reading.

Figure 5.10

Examples of chord inversions.

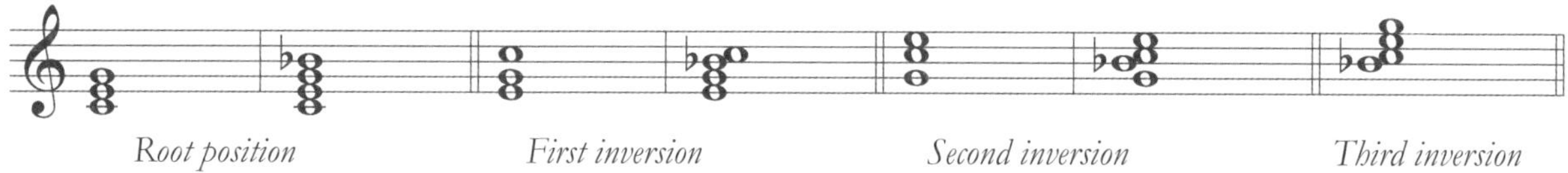

The root position for triads and root position and second inversions for seventh chords are considered more stable and easier to tune than the others, motivating bass parts to sing the roots and fifths of chords. However, unstable inversions—first and third—occasionally appear, usually to accommodate voice leading, provide variety, support the subtextual tension of the line, or to swipe from unstable to stable chords.

Note that the first, second, and third inversions of the major seventh chord are not found in barbershop arrangements, though root position major seventh chord are found, typically when implied by the melody.

Related Keys

The term *related key* denotes a relationship between keys that share similar characteristics to the original key. Figure 5.11 shows examples of related keys.

- The relative key: shares tones but uses a different tonic, such as A minor for C major.
- The parallel key: shares the tonic but uses different tones, such as C minor for C major.
- Closely related keys: share several scalar tones, such as G major or F major for C major. Closely related keys are only different by one sharp or one flat.

Other closely related keys exist, though ones rooted a fifth above or below are the most like the original key.

Figure 5.11

Keys related to C major.

Barbershop arrangements often establish a key, leap to a distant chord, and gradually return to the home key or modulate to another. When using a chord from a related key, this is called *borrowing*.

Circle of Fifths

The circle of fifths is a way of organizing the chromatic pitches as a sequence of perfect fifths, listed clockwise around a circle. Musicians often use this to describe the relationships between pitches and keys. It also helps with composition, harmonization, and modulations.

The circle of fifths represents different information, but principally it is a map of keys.

Figure 5.12

The circle of fifths.

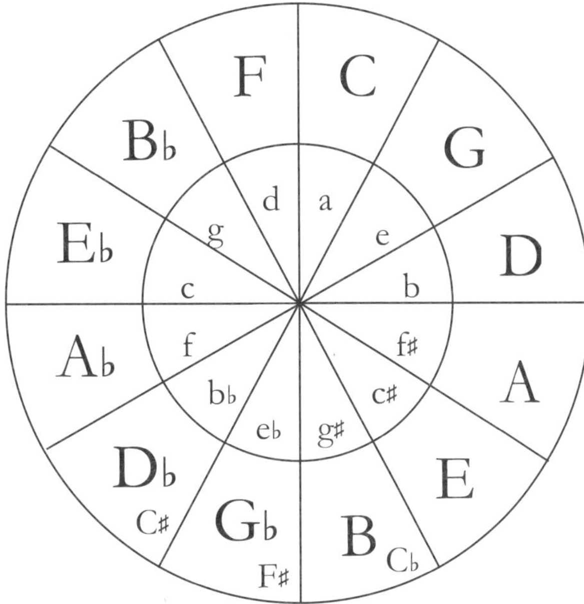

The outer ring lists the major keys (shown in capital letters), and the inner ring lists minor keys (shown in lowercase letters). Each wedge pairs relative keys that share the same key signature (flats or sharps). Adjacent slices associate closely related keys with similar key signatures (a difference of one flat or sharp).

The book will cover the circle of fifths later in greater detail as the arranging process unfolds.

Roman Numeral Analysis

As a standard, chords with a major quality—triads, sevenths, etc.—are spelled with uppercase Roman numerals, e.g. I, IV, V. Chords with a minor quality are commonly spelled with lowercase Roman numerals, e.g., ii, iii, vi, though they may also be spelled with the uppercase Roman numeral and a qualifier *m* or *min*, e.g., IIm, VIm; IImin, VImin.

Using the diatonic notes in C major yield the following triads naturally without any alteration as shown in Figure 5.13.

Figure 5.13

Example of Roman Numeral Analysis.

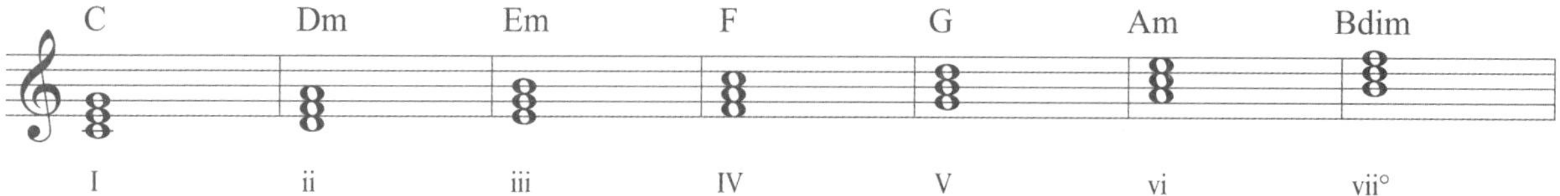

Alterations to a chord's quality recast the chord based on its root and new quality, e.g., i, II, III, iv. Chromatic alterations to the root—raising or lowering it by a half step—add a corresponding accidental to the left of the Roman Numeral, e.g., ♭II, ♯IV, ♭VI.

Figure 5.14

Examples of chromatic alterations to diatonic chords and their associated Roman numerals.

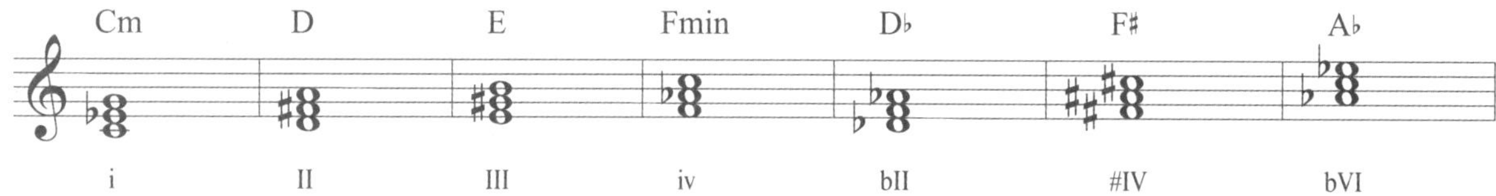

Seventh chords have different qualifiers, discussed in the next section. The added note is effectively an alteration of the triad, so the modifier identifying the type of seventh is specified to the right, e.g., M7, 7, ø7.

Figure 5.15

Examples of combining Roman numerals and associated qualifiers.

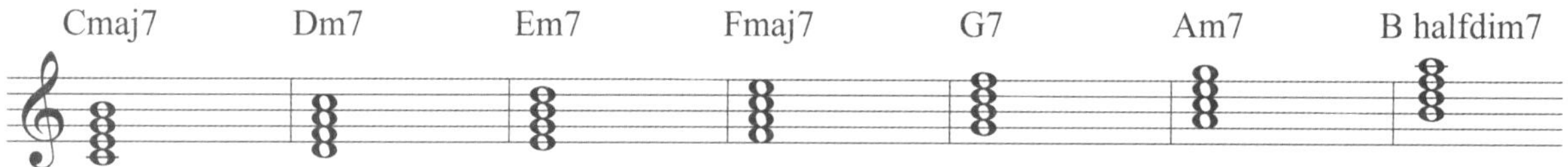

Chord Vocabulary

The characteristic sound of the barbershop style is just as much the texture—four-part, primarily homorhythmic, inner-voice melody—as it is the choice of harmonies supporting it. Certain chords and contexts lend themselves to stable, effective chord progressions and substitutions.

Before exploring effective chord progressions, it is important to understand the chords preferred in the barbershop style. The context of the underlying harmony determines their root, name, and relationship, which in turn affect the implications and treatment of the chord.

Triads

In four-part harmony, the root of a triad is usually doubled in another voice. The appearance of pure triads in barbershop harmonization is commonly observed on I and IV, and to a lesser extent on vi, though we also see examples of triads on other scale tones often preceding a swipe to the seventh chord.

Figure 5.16

Examples of triads.

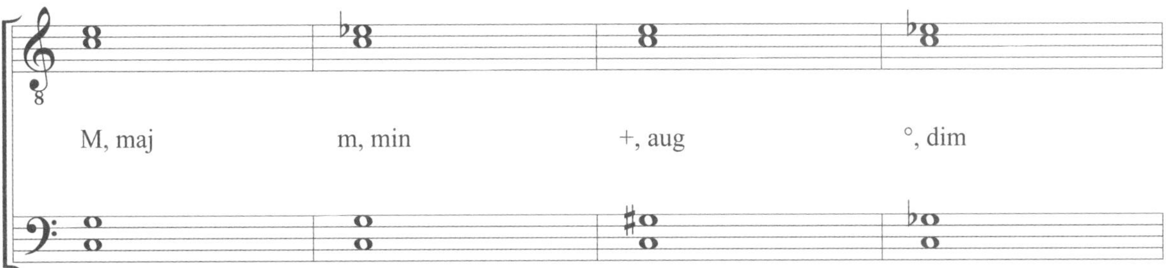

Figure 5.16 shows major triads, indicated with *M* or *maj*, and minor triads, indicated with a lowercase *m* or *min*, are common when defined by the key, supporting embellishments, or borrowing from a related key.

The augmented triad, indicated with + or *aug*, is a symmetric chord that may appear to provide color or when the melody is on the raised chordal fifth, though it is often harmonized with a seventh chord.

The diminished triad, indicated by *o* or *dim*, is rarely used, as it lacks the fullness offered by the fully diminished seventh chord and is discouraged for use in barbershop contest arrangements.

Seventh Chords

Stacking a third on a triad produces a four-part seventh chord. Combining different triads—major, minor, diminished, augmented—with different seventh intervals—major, minor, diminished—yields different chords.

Figure 5.17

Examples of how different triads and associated sevenths are noted.

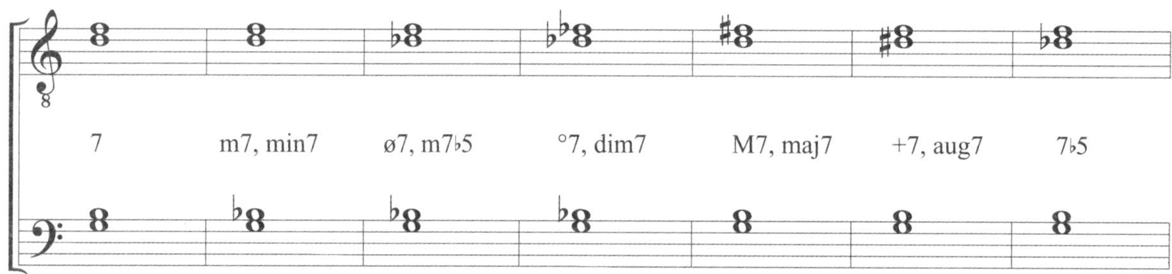

Figure 5.17 shows the dominant 7th chord (the barbershop 7th), indicated with *7*, which is the hallmark of the style. It contains two overlapping intervals: the perfect fifth—between the root and fifth—and the tritone—between the third and seventh—that offers both structure and tension with a pull toward resolution.

The minor 7th chord (sometimes called the minor-minor 7th), indicated with *m7* or *min7*, is less common in the style. The chord's two stable fifths a minor third apart lack any *tendency tones* wanting to resolve by a half step. It is often used to set a mood and may occur as a passing chord or when remaining true to a song with minor 7ths, such as when the melody features notes which are a minor third above the root of the pillar harmony.

Tendency tones are pitches that are harmonically or melodically unstable and tend to move toward another pitch, resolving itself either upward or downward by a semitone.

The half-diminished 7th chord (sometimes called the diminished-minor 7th), indicated with *ø7*, frequently occurs—sometimes as often as the barbershop 7th. Similar to the barbershop 7th, it contains a tritone and perfect fifth. It often appears as an embellishment, substitution, linking, or passing chord.

The diminished 7th, indicated with *o7* or *dim7*, is a symmetric chord with four evenly spaced notes. Like the half-diminished chord, it often embellishes or substitutes for another chord, though it may also anticipate, extend, or imply other harmonies.

The major 7th chord (sometimes called the major-major 7th), indicated with *M7*, naturally occurs on I and IV and is featured when the melody has the major seventh degree or the chord is characteristic of the song.

The augmented 7th chord (sometimes called the augmented-minor 7th), indicated with *+7*, may harmonize a melody tone on the augmented fifth. It is a rare chord and should be used sparingly and only when implied by the melody.[30]

[30] If the prevailing harmony within a measure is a dominant 7th chord and the melody lands on an augmented fifth above the pillar root, an augmented 7th chord may be appropriate. Another option would be to move the 7th of the chord to double with the root, creating an augmented triad. The question about which is more appropriate is up to the arranger, based on the subtext of the chord and lyric.

The dominant 7th with lowered 5th chord, indicated with *7b5*, may occur when the melody is on the lowered fifth or when harmonizing with this chromatic motion or color in mind. It is a rare chord and discouraged in barbershop contests due to the degree of dissonance.[31]

Sixths

Given a major or minor triad, adding a tone a whole step above a fifth (an interval of a major sixth) produces a triad with an added sixth, or simply a sixth chord.

Sixth chords most often appear when the melody note contains a sixth and the underlying harmony is a triad. They usually occur on a I or IV chord.

As shown in Figure 5.18, major sixth chords may appear either complete with all four notes, or incomplete with the fifth omitted and root doubled. For clarity, one can refer to these as *add 6* or *sub 6*, respectively. Note that the incomplete sixth chord is enharmonically a revoiced minor triad. The complete sixth chord is a revoiced minor seventh chord. As always, the context determines the root and whether the chord substitutes for a major triad, or if it is an inversion of a minor chord.

Figure 5.18

Examples of sixth chords.

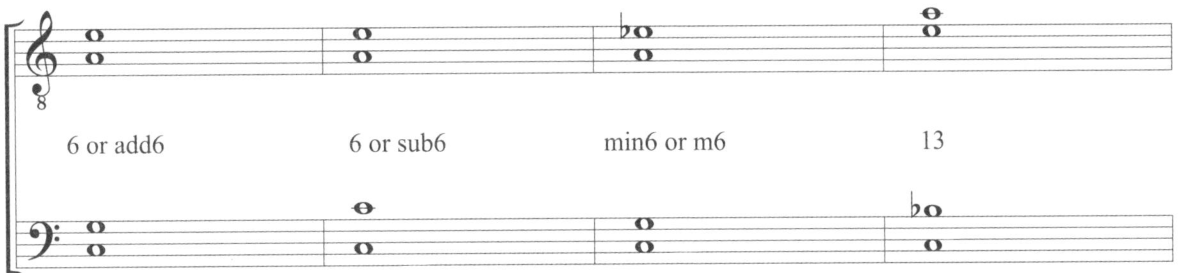

Adding a major sixth interval to a minor triad yields a minor 6th chord. This is a revoiced half-diminished 7th that substitutes for a minor triad. It often occurs as the penultimate chord. While the complete minor 6th is frequently used in style, the incomplete minor sub6 is not often used in barbershop arranging.

When a sixth chord sonority substitutes for a seventh chord, it is instead referred to as *thirteenth chord*,[32] e.g., the dominant V13, shown above in the final chord in 5.18. Although it shares the same notes as another sixth chord, doubled root, third, and sixth, we hear it in the context of a seventh chord. In contrast, a sixth chord is understood to substitute for an underlying triadic harmony, e.g., the I6 in C, shown in the first chord in Figure 5.18.

---

[31] In common practice music, this is an augmented 6th chord called a French 6th without the classical treatment, which may be unintuitive in discussion. This chord consists purely of whole tones, which gives it a unique, unstable tonality.
[32] This name derives from stacked thirds. Consider a seventh chord with a root, call it *1*, containing the required third, *3*, fifth, *5*, and a seventh, *b7*. A complete 13th chord includes a ninth, degree 2, eleventh, degree 4, and thirteenth, degree 6. Removing the dissonant notes and retaining the characteristic thirteenth sound reduces it to 1–3–6, for which we double the root to accommodate four voices.

Ninths

Ninth chords are flavors of harmony that include the major ninth above the root, usually when the melody is on the ninth.

Figure 5.19

Examples of ninth chords.

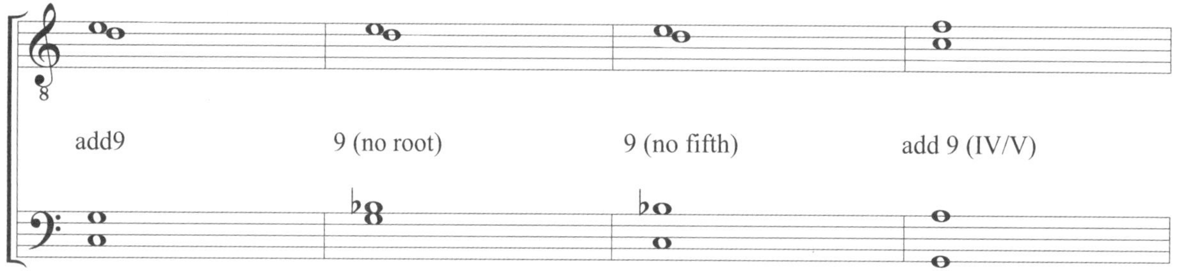

Figure 5.19 shows the add 9 chord[33] as a major triad with a ninth, often when the melody is on the ninth and the underlying harmony is a triad.

The dominant or barbershop 9th chord, indicated by *9*, is an extension of the barbershop 7th chord with another stacked third. To reduce this five-note chord to four parts, there are two options shown in Figure 5.19: omitting the root and omitting the fifth. In either case, we hear the root, even when absent from the chord. The rootless barbershop 9th is a revoiced half-diminished chord.

Although rare, it is possible to invert the add 9 chord with the ninth in the bass. This usage has the effect of IV/V, called four over five or subdominant over the dominant. Spelled as if a barbershop 9th with a suspended 4th, *9sus4*, this chord is discouraged in barbershop contests.

Non-Vocabulary Chords

In rare cases, chords outside of the barbershop vocabulary appear incidentally in arrangements. These chords are typically discouraged because of their degree of dissonance and difficulty in tuning properly, reducing the overall consonance in the resulting arrangement. However, they can have great impact when used carefully and sparingly by experienced arrangers for specific coloring of a lyric.

Figure 5.20 shows common non-vocabulary chords found rarely in barbershop arrangements.

---

[33] Some text improperly refers to the *add 9* as a *major 9th* chord, which is widely accepted as the major 7th chord with the added 9th. As a triad with a ninth, the add 9 is the most popular and intuitive.

Figure 5.20

Examples of non-vocabulary chords.

A rare, dissonant chord in barbershop is one that has a minor seventh and a high major sixth with the bass on the root below the seventh. This chord is called the *Waesche 13th* in honor of Ed Waesche, a prolific barbershop arranger who featured this chord in the tag of "Jeanie With the Light Brown Hair." See measure 26, baritone note on beat 2 in Figure 5.21.

The minor-major seventh chord, the second chord in Figure 5.20, is a rare chord with a minor triad and a major seventh. The minor 9th chord, the third chord in Figure 5.20, is a rare chord with the major ninth and a minor triad, resulting in a dissonance between the major second (ninth) and minor third.

Suspensions are discouraged in barbershop, as they lack a third, which we expect in barbershop chords. These rare chords can appear as triad with the perfect fourth or triad with a major second. They may also appear with minor seventh chords in place of the second root, for a seventh with a perfect fourth or seventh with a major second.

Proceed with caution when using dissonant chords outside the primary vocabulary. Egregious or improper usage could result in a holistically lower Musicality score in a barbershop contest due to reduction of consonance in a barbershop contest.

Figure 5.21

"Jeanie With the Light Brown Hair," words and music by Stephen Foster. Arrangement by Ed Waesche. YouTube

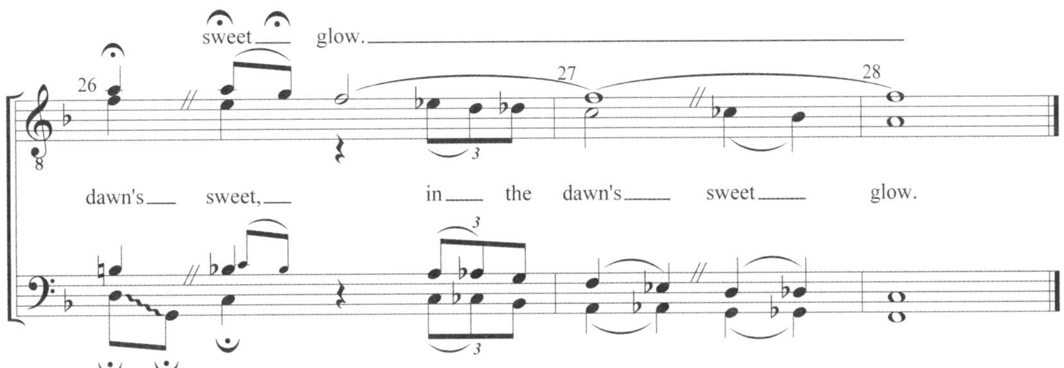

Stylistic Conventions

Beyond music fundamentals and chord vocabulary, barbershop also handles musical concepts in ways that blend elements of classical, folk, jazz, and other popular genres. This section highlights several conventions and trends that influence the treatment.

Voice Leading

Part writing in counterpoint examples from classical music supports an upper-voice melody with independent voices—often in counterpoint—discouraging parallel fifths and preferring smooth voice leading that may sacrifice four-part chords and allow dissonant passing tones. Barbershop, instead, focuses on consonant, four-part chords for every inner-voice melody note in a primarily homorhythmic texture. Its unaccompanied style allows singers to adjust pitches to precisely tuned chords, with attention to horizontal gaps in the melody normally supplemented by an accompaniment.

The consequences of this treatment include:

- an emphasis on dependent voices, built on the inner-voice melody and anchored bass
- an upper (tenor) part continuously harmonizing above the melody
- the baritone part abandoning traditional voice leading in favor of four-part chords
- the (infrequent) appearance of parallel fifths or octaves, especially for effect
- treating passing and neighboring tones as chord tones, vertically harmonized to reduce dissonance
- the use of embellishments to continually converge to homorhythmic chords

Although the melody lies primarily in an inner voice, arrangers should strive for ease of voice leading so that other voice parts remain melodic and singable. Here are a few guidelines for writing easily singable parts. Note that these guidelines are subservient to the primary aim of writing complete, consonant triads and seventh chords.

- Common tones should be retained whenever possible
- Move by least motion whenever possible
- Avoid dissonant leaps whenever possible
- Resolve tendency tones appropriately, especially leading tones in dominant seventh chords

The tritonal energy of dominant-functioning barbershop seventh chords demands resolution. The two chord tones that compose the tritone interval, the third and the seventh of the chord, are called tendency tones because of their strong pull towards resolution. Appropriate resolution of these tendency tones is vital for a satisfactory sense of resolution. In classical part-writing, the seventh of a dominant seventh chord nearly always resolves down by step. In barbershop arranging, this rule is loosened somewhat to accommodate the melody and complete harmonies. However, it is still best practice to resolve the seventh of a dominant seventh chord within those constraints if possible. The other tendency tone in a dominant seventh chord is the third of the chord, called the leading tone. Leading tones should resolve up by half-step to the root of the chord of resolution. Figure 5.22 demonstrates this type of movement of the tendency tones from measure 4 to 5.

Figure 5.22

Traditional resolution of tendency tones. "My Wild Irish Rose," arranged by Floyd Connett.

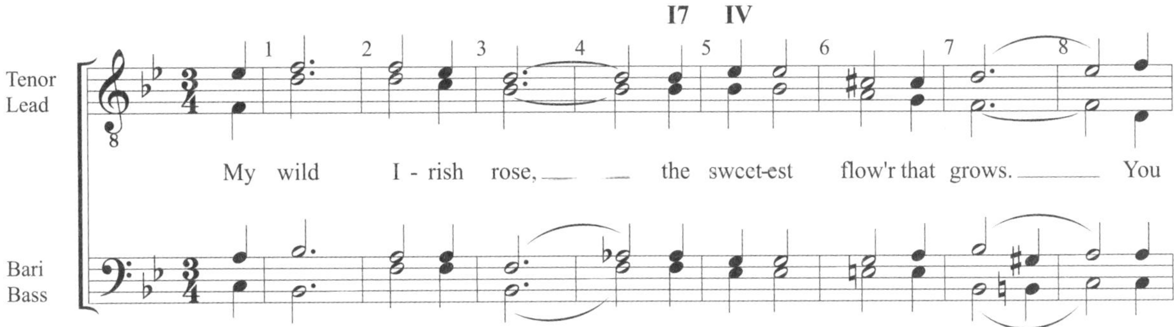

The rule regarding dominant seventh resolution should be followed as a best practice, with two exceptions: first, the leading tone may resolve down to the fifth of the chord of resolution if it appears in an inner voice (lead or baritone), as shown in Figure 5.23

Figure 5.23

Leading tone resolving down to the fifth of the chord. "Oh, How I Miss You Tonight," words and music by Benny Davis, Joe Burke, and Mark Fisher. Arranged by Renee Craig and Bill Wyatt.

The other exception is if a dominant seventh chord is a secondary dominant resolving to another dominant seventh by fifth motion, both the seventh and third (leading tone) of the chord should resolve down by half-step, resulting in parallel tritones. Note the tenor and baritone movement in measures 5 and 6 in Figure 5.24.

Figure 5.24

Parallel tritone movement. "My Mother's Eyes," words and music by Abel Baer and L. Wolfe Gilbert. Arranged by Renee Craig.

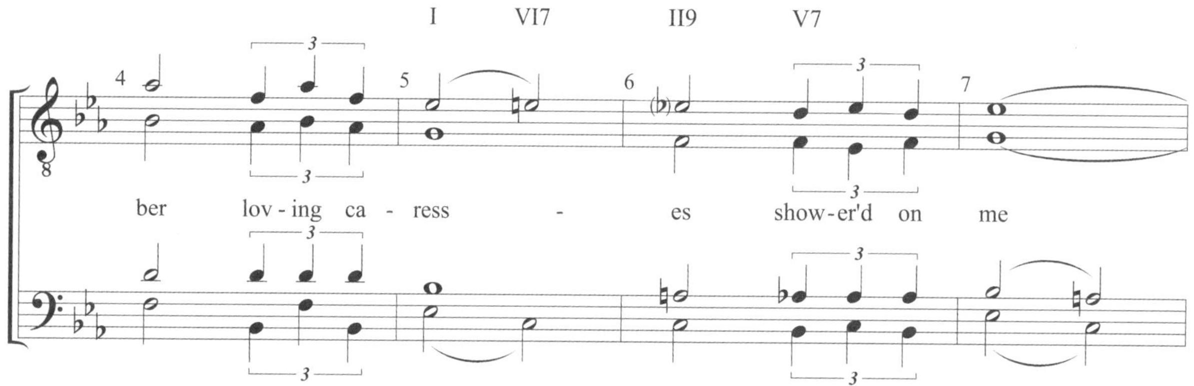

Related to voice leading, the choice of chord inversion affects overall consonance. Arrangements favor stable inversions, such as the root position and the second inversion of triads and seventh chords. The major seventh chord only appears in root position. Other inversions of triads and sevenths occasionally appear, usually to accommodate voice leading, provide variety, support the subtextual tension of the line, or swipe from unstable to stable chords.

Chord Notation

While barbershop chord analysis borrows heavily from the analysis practices found in classical music that uses Roman Numerals, some elements reflect chord structures found in more contemporary styles. Seventh chords on all scale degrees are frequently altered to produce barbershop 7th chords. For simplicity, these secondary dominant chords are named directly in terms of their root with respect to the key. For example, if built on scale degree 2, call it II7, rather than using the secondary dominant notation of function/target, e.g., V7/V. In this way, the name of the versatile barbershop 7th broadens the application of the popular dominant 7th, which frequently subverts the implied dominant relationship with the target chord.

Figure 5.25

Examples of dominant seventh chords. Note the dominant (G7) seventh is the only unaltered seventh within a major key.

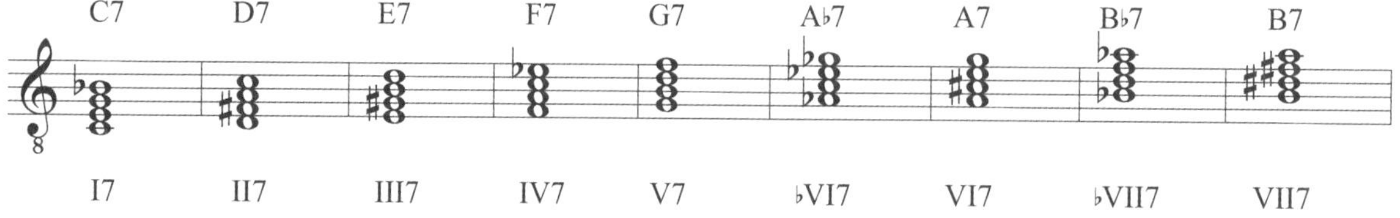

With the frequent use of stable, easily tuned, root position and second inversion chords, specifying the inversion is not critical to discussion. Consequently, classical figured bass notation is neglected in favor of the simplicity of the root alone.[34] This also avoids confusion when referring to Roman Numerals with additional numbers, e.g., the 6 in a IV6 chord.[35]

Chord Progressions

Before arranging in the barbershop style, it is important to remember three basic principles:

1. *Barbershop, as a style, is often applied to existing songs with a natural, implied chord progression.* To remain true to the original song, one should take care to embellish the existing chords, substituting when necessary. Certain songs and chord progressions—especially those with fifths movement—lend themselves better to the barbershop style.
2. *Music theory follows practice, not the other way around.* With such a detailed-oriented musical style, it is easy to fall into the trap of applying the theory to analyze every chord. Instead, it benefits to gain an understanding of the theory and use it to influence the musical moments between chords.
3. *At its core, barbershop harmonizing is based on ear singing, preferring intuitive chords that easily tune.* Shoehorning complex chord progressions that obscure the underlying harmony leads to arranging and performance challenges. However, the balanced and symmetric form of the music offers the arranger many opportunities to start simple and develop the song's theme and ideas, providing an emotionally satisfying and entertaining experience.

As with classical music, most music begins on a tonic chord, increasing the tension through a progression of chords, before releasing upon arrival at a tonic chord. The tonic and subdominant (I and IV) chords tend to freely progress to any other chord. Other chords, including the barbershop minor, and major 7th, tend to naturally pull toward a chord rooted a fifth below the present chord, often another 7th or 9th chord. When harmonizing a tone, certain chords can effectively substitute for others, providing variety and allowing preferred chords within the vocabulary.

A series of chords progressing toward the tonic to chords rooted a fifth below yield a circle of fifths progression. Barbershop songs tend to feature barbershop sevenths and ninths that progress around this circle of fifths, while making use of other progressions.

Circle of Fifths, Revisited

With an understanding of the chord vocabulary, circle of fifths movement, and conventions of the style, this gives new context to the circle of fifths.

---

[34] This includes inversion indicators such as ^{3} indicating root position, ^{6} indicating first inversion, $^{6/4}$ indicating second inversion, $^{4/3}$ indicating third inversion, and $^{4/2}$ indicating fourth inversion.
[35] Barbershop borrows from popular and classical music. However, in popular music and in barbershop, the IV6 is the sixth chord on IV. In classical music, IV^{6} reads as a IV triad in the first inversion.

Figure 5.26

The circle of fifths with Roman Numerals instead of traditional key signatures.

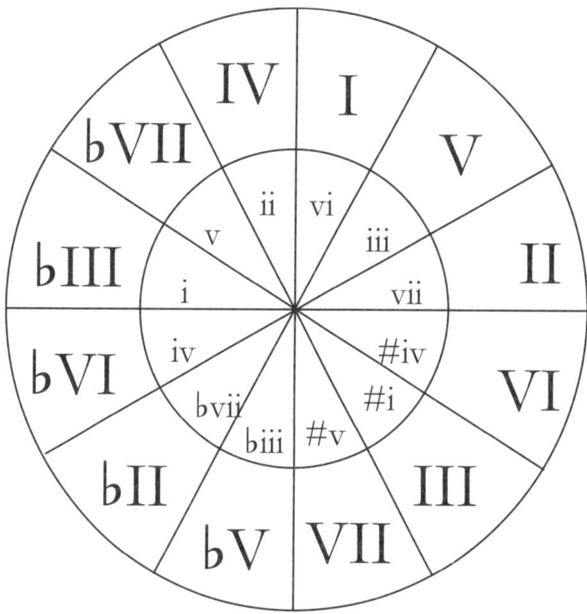

Consider the same circle discussed earlier, now treating the key of C as scale degree I. By substituting Roman Numerals, this removes key relationships, and the diagram reduces to a generalized circle of fifths where we can treat the scale degrees as chord roots.

With all twelve semitones present, this circle of chord roots can be related to a clock, or, more accurately, an analog timer, where counterclockwise movement reflects a circle of fifths progression.

A progression typically starts on tonic, i.e., the I triad, before leaping to a faraway chord on the circle, usually a 7th or 9th, e.g., III7, rooted on a different scale degree. It then relaxes counterclockwise through a series of chords, usually 7ths or 9ths, eventually arriving at the I triad, e.g. I → III7 → VI7 → II7 → V7 → I. This approach applies to the broad chord progressions, but it also applies locally to chords in tags, swipes, and between phrases.

A popular example of this progression can be found in the song, “Five Foot Two”.

Figure 5.27

"Five Foot Two," arrangement by Joe Liles.

Note the prevailing harmony stays constant throughout a measure, most often moving at the downbeat of the next measure. The rate of movement of harmonic pillars is called harmonic rhythm, a concept discussed more fully in *Arranging Barbershop*, Vol. 2.

Later chapters will cover the use and applications of the circle. However, the foundation presented thus far provides a fundamental understanding of the chords, stylistic conventions, and theory of barbershop harmony to help you dive into your first barbershop arrangement.

Part C: Arranging Process and Roles

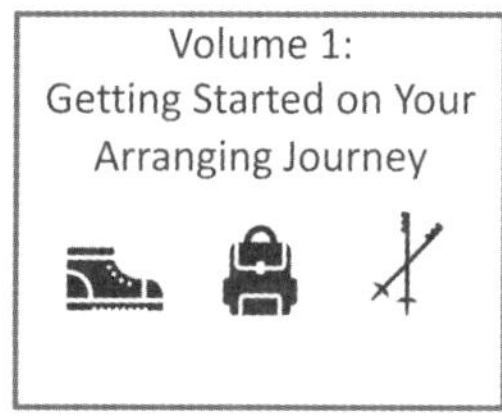

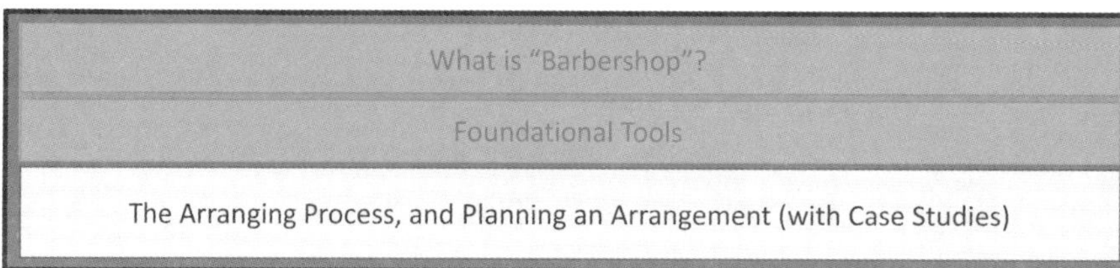

What is "Barbershop"?
Foundational Tools
The Arranging Process, and Planning an Arrangement (with Case Studies)

Very few journeys are successful if the traveler doesn't prepare. Different skills and personae are required at different stages of the journey. The same is true for arranging; one must implement some degree of process to navigate from start to finish, and recognize different skills and perspectives are required at different stages. Every arranger develops their own arranging process, and that process likely evolves and changes over time. Even though there is no single process that works for every arranger, developing a process that works for you is an important stage in the arranger's journey.

Chapter 6: The Arranging Process: Key Elements

There are certain key components of the arranging process that seem ubiquitous. Steve Tramack examines the Arranging Process and key components from a high level, highlighting those key elements which bear consideration.

Chapter 7: The Dreamer, the Editor, and the Critic: Discovering Your Toolkit

From the great book, *A Cappella Arranging,*[36] authors Deke Sharon and Dylan Bell share the distinctly different characters or archetypes one embodies throughout the arranging process.

[36] Copyright © 2012 by Deke Sharon and Dylan Bell. Published by Hal Leonard Books.

Chapter 6.
The Arranging Process: Key Elements

By Steve Tramack

So, you've decided you want to embark on the barbershop arranging journey. Much like a traveler embarking on a mountain climbing expedition, multiple factors come into play when considering all the different elements of the journey. Some of these are art and some are science; striking the right balance often yields the best results. Prerequisites such as choosing a song, identifying the foundational harmonization highway, and developing the construction of the chart apply to every journey. Other choices may be different every single time you embark on the journey. These choices may be driven by the performer, the delivery approach, the voice leadings, and the arranger's disposition and influences at the time of arranging.

Even if you aren't a detailed planner who maps every stage, mile, and hour of a journey, a certain amount of preparation is required. You need to know where you're going, even if that answer is, "I don't quite know where I'm going yet, but I'll figure it out on the way." For the purposes of this book, this is defined as the *arranging process*. Ask 100 arrangers about their process, and you're likely to get 100 different answers. Many will say their process is constantly changing.

Over forty arrangers were interviewed about their arranging process for *Arranging Barbershop*, documented in Vol. 3 of the series, Visions of Excellence. While no two processes were the same, there was a high degree of agreement on a few key concepts:

1. Arrangers identify a song to arrange and allow time for inspiration—allowing the song to become a part of their head and heart—before beginning the process of capturing the arrangement in notation.
2. As part of this inspiration stage, many arrangers listen to various recorded versions of the song, and/or repeatedly listen to a source version.
3. Prior to actively notating the arranging, most arrangers develop some sort of blueprint, consisting of a high-level form and construction mapping of the chart. This would include mapping verses, choruses, key changes, and original material such as introductions and tags.
4. Once starting the notation of the arrangement, most arrangers begin with the melody, following the construction outlined in the blueprint. The bass line—laying the harmonic pillar foundations—is next.

Chapter 7 is a deep dive into the arranging process, including looking at some of the roles that each of us as arrangers play at different stages during that process. This concept—*The Dreamer, the Editor and the Critic*—is excerpted from the book *A Cappella Arranging* by Deke Sharon and Dylan Bell. It provides insight into how our role changes as the process evolves.

Chapter 7.
The Dreamer, the Editor, and the Critic: Discovering Your Toolkit and Developing Your "Inner Ear"

By Deke Sharon and Dylan Bell

Excerpted from *A Cappella Arranging, Copyright 2012 by Deke Sharon and Dylan Bell.*

It's nearly impossible to describe the creative process in any meaningful terms, but, foolishly enough, we're going to try anyway.

We can talk all we want about quantifiable skills such as theoretical knowledge, or the ability to voice lead or transcribe—all necessary skills—but if that were enough, we'd be able to write computer programs that followed rules to create great art.

There are other, "fuzzier" skills that we all possess and develop over time which lie somewhere between the art and the science of arranging (or any creative process, for that matter). Rather than describe them as specific skills, we prefer to think of them as three distinct characters or archetypes. They're present in all of us, and if we can help them to get along, there's no limit to what they can do together.

Enter the Dreamer, the Editor; and the Critic.

If you studied twentieth-century psychology, this might remind you of the id, the ego, and the superego. Or, if you prefer, try Jung's archetypes.

The Dreamer

The Dreamer is raw, unpolished creativity. The Dreamer is the part of you that generates ideas, simple or crazy. The Dreamer isn't practical: he's not the type to figure out how to make things work. Someone else can do that.

The Dreamer needs a lot of space and time to do his thing. He doesn't understand time or deadlines: sometimes he only works when he feels like it. And the Dreamer is a sensitive soul. Interrupt him, analyze his work, or criticize him, and he'll run out of the room and disappear for a while. And you don't want that: without the Dreamer, you have nothing to work with. He can create something from nothing, and that is his greatest power.

The Editor

We all know the Editor well. She gets things done and makes things go. She's practical and logical (if a little stodgy and boring sometimes). The Editor loves to tinker and execute, and this is her big skill. The Editor has an eye for the big picture and is excellent at assimilating different ideas and making them work together.

But the Editor is useless without something to work on. And she's not the one who creates it: that's the Dreamer's job. Sometimes the Editor is a little myopic: she can't see beyond what's in front of her; She needs help on either side to make things go: raw material to work with as well as someone to look it over and help make it better.

The Critic

The Critic looks for faults. Like a detective with a magnifying glass, or a tax auditor, he's looking for things that aren't right. He's looking for weakness, and if it's there, he'll find it.

Sounds like a nasty character. Why include him at all?

At first glance, the Critic seems like a negative type—but really, he's not. His end goal is the same as the Dreamer's and the Editor's: he wants to make the best arrangement possible. He just has a very specialized tool set, useful at very specific times. Unlike the Editor, who's simply working with what she has, the critic can see what's missing and thus help to find it. But he's like a guy with a chainsaw, so you want to be careful about letting him loose.

Making Them Work Together

All these characters are essential to the creative process; the trick is to know when and where to let them play. We imagine the creative process as being a room where two people can work together (occasionally three, but it tends to get crowded). Different people will come in and out at different stages of the game.

Let the Dreamer Start

Let the Dreamer into the room first. Tell the Editor and the Critic to come back later. When? When the Dreamer says so, and no sooner (unless you're on a deadline). Give the Dreamer plenty of time and space to create. For you, this means wild, vague brainstorming. Write all your ideas down (mostly in word form only, since you're not getting specific yet) on a piece of paper or some kind of portable recorder. Don't worry if the ideas are incomplete, don't try to make the ideas fit together, and most important, *don't judge them.* These steps happen later. Go crazy, try stupid things., and give yourself permission to come up with lousy ideas. *Do not let the Critic into the room.* Although both essential to the process, the Dreamer and the Critic are essentially at odds with each other. If you let the Critic in, you will immediately start judging your half-formed ideas, extinguishing them before they have a chance to grow. This is probably the single most common cause of creative blocks and the reason so many people feel as though they've been stopped before they even start. We'll talk about strategies for dealing with this later.

Eventually the Dreamer will get tired, and the raw ideas will stop flowing. If all is well, you've got a bunch of vague, unconnected scribblings. This is the stuff that art is made from, and now it's time to let the Editor in to turn them into something tangible.

Let the Editor In

You've got your creative mess: now let's make something of it. The Editor in you can take a look at the raw material, make connections, and decide which pieces can work together well and which pieces should be left behind. The Dreamer can stay on, occasionally explaining what he was trying to do or why he came up with the idea. This is important for the Editor: even if an idea isn't used, the artistic impulse that generated the idea might show its face in another way.

> *The Dreamer*: I want something sparkly-sounding. I know—an angel choir!
>
> *The Editor*: No angel choir...we don't have enough parts. But you want sparkly, right? Let's borrow the sopranos for a bar to do something sparkly. The tenors can take over during this section to fill it out.

Much of the actual writing of parts happens at this point, and this process will take a while. But this is where you'll feel a lot of progress as scribblings become actual notes on paper.

Invite the Critic

Once you've got a section mostly done, it's time to let the Critic in. Now you can look it over with an eagle eye and spot weaknesses, such as bad voice leading or a lack of movement and energy, or a dull passage that should be cut. At this point, most of the dialogue happens between the Critic and the Editor.

> *The Critic:* This section has your sopranos too high for too long. It's going to sound shrill.
>
> *The Editor*: OK, then I'm going to revoice them lower.

There will be times when the Editor and the Critic are at an impasse: the Critic sees a weakness, and the Editor can't figure out a solution. What to do? Ask the Dreamer. Be prepared to go in a completely new direction:

> *The Critic:* This section is too repetitive. It sounds like the last section. Do something new.
>
> *The Editor*: I can't keep it continuous-sounding AND do something new. I don't know how!
>
> *The Critic and the Editor sit glumly, staring at each other.*
>
> *The Dreamer*: Those guys are always singing guitar parts, right? What about a new sound…like strings or something?
>
> *The Editor*: I suppose I could turn this section into a vocal "string quartet" instead. Let's see what happens.

You'll probably identify with each character to some extent, and you may find you lean more toward one than another. This is very helpful to know and shows a strong sense of creative self-awareness. Do you come up with a dozen ideas effortlessly but find it hard to actually get anything finished? You have a strong Dreamer.

Are you great at working with ideas but can't get started easily? You probably have a strong Editor tendency. Can you see/hear the "improvables" in any chart right away but tend to shoot down your own work? You have a good Critic. Keep in mind that no one of these archetypes is better than either of the others: they're all valuable, all essential to the creative process.

All this talk about fictional characters may seem a little goofy to some. But trust us—it really helps to separate the different personalities that come into play in the creative process. If you distinguish them this way, you'll have more control over each aspect and a stronger ability to call upon the different strengths of each *when you need it.* And this is the key to a successful creative process.

>>*Deke says: Even though I've done over two thousand arrangements, I still like to try something new in every arrangement, especially when I'll be the one teaching it, since I can quickly make changes as needed. I usually describe this to others as, "I'm taking a risk here" or "the bridge of this song is risky." I almost always have an easy, risk-free fallback position should the risk not pay off, but sometimes the risk results in the best passage in the arrangement. Using the above terminology, sometimes you have to hold off the Editor and Critic and try an idea the Dreamer has dreamed up, however loudly the other two complain.*

Part D: Planning an Arrangement

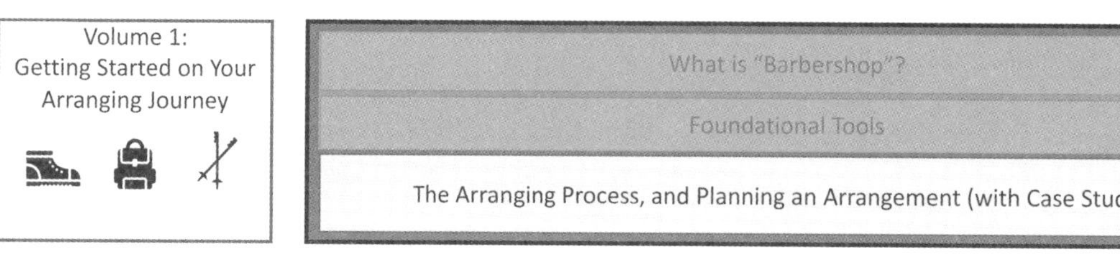

Successful planning leads to successful arrangements and more efficient time spent when actually arranging. Aspects of planning include the approach when considering source material, determining a blueprint for the arrangement, consideration of the performer, and how to get started.

Chapter 8: The Arranging Spectrum

Also excerpted from *A Cappella Arranging* book, Deke Sharon and Dylan Bell discuss different arranging styles as points on a spectrum.

Chapter 9: Arrangement Planning Overview

Steve Tramack explores some of the basic elements in planning for a successful arranging journey.

Chapter 8.
The Arranging Spectrum

By Deke Sharon and Dylan Bell

Excerpted from *A Cappella Arranging, Copyright 2012 by Deke Sharon and Dylan Bell.*

The term "arranging" in music has a definition so vague as to be almost useless. Technically speaking, you can put a couple of people in a room with a lead sheet, shout "1, 2, 3, 4!," and whatever comes out of their mouths is an arrangement. But it's doubtful anyone would refer to it as such.

Arranging is a creative process and an organizational process; but, simply put, it's about making choices—dozens and dozens of choices, both artistic and logistical. Because there are so many ways to arrange and so many different arranging styles, it's helpful to define them a little. For the purposes of discussion, we're defining the different styles of arranging by the kinds of choices and decisions made during the process. If pushed, though, we'll be the first to admit that any delineation is somewhat arbitrary, with demarcation lines more properly considered gray areas.

In other words, in line with the "no rules, no rigid structures" philosophy of this book, we present these arranging "styles" not as hard-and-fast categories, but rather as points on a spectrum. And like colors on a spectrum, different arranging styles can be mixed and blended, even within a single work. Here are some points on our arranging Spectrum in order of the fewest to the greatest number of decisions.

Transcription

Transcription (known colloquially as *lifting*) is the process of listening to music and writing all the parts down, note for note, as accurately as possible. Truthfully speaking, transcription is not actually arranging. The transcriber is not making any choices, just writing down what he or she hears.

So why include it at all?

Even though it's not arranging in and of itself, transcription is an essential tool for the arranger. You can't arrange without being able to lift the melody, or the bass line, or that cool synth hook in the chorus. Moreover, transcription is the single second-greatest way to learn how to arrange (next to this book, of course!). Transcription allows you to peek under the hood of a great chart, get your hands dirty, and really see how it works. It allows you to step into the shoes of the masters, learn what they do, and even gain insight on their own decision-making process. More on this later.

Caveat: it is extremely unusual simply to transcribe and not make a single decision at all. When listening to a recording, unless you can pick out each individual voice from start to finish, you'll be making decisions about which voice or vocal part will be singing which of the notes you hear, who will cover vocal splits, how to handle doublings, and so on. This is still transcription: almost all decisions are already made for you, leaving just a couple of notational and divisional choices for you to make.

Adaptation

We define "adaptation" as the act of taking something already written primarily for voices and altering its format. Examples could include:

- Taking a TTBB (all male voices) chart and writing it for SATB (mixed voices)
- Taking a voices-and-rhythm section chart and "a cappella-fying" the rhythm section (for instance, an electric bass line would be sung an octave higher in most cases, and vocal percussion would be simplified to something that can be done by a single voice rather than an entire drum kit)
- Adjusting someone else's arrangement to suit your group (your tenors are a bit weak in their upper range so you split your altos and give them the first tenor notes, you remove the final chorus because their version is too long for your purposes, and so on)
- Condensing a multipart arrangement into fewer parts (for smaller groups who write arrangements in the studio and want to perform them live, this is an essential skill).

When adapting, decisions are usually more logistical than creative. Nothing or very little new is added or changed: the form, tempo, harmonic information, and overall vibe remain the same. Decisions and changes might include such things as transposing the key or swapping a few vocal lines from one part to another for better voice allocation. Put it this way. if you can play the two arrangements one after the other and say, "They're basically the same thing," that's adaptation. It may not really feel like arranging to some since it doesn't involve much of a creative element, but it requires many of the same practical, logistical techniques found in any arranging style.

Translation

This is what we often think of when talking about a cappella arranging, particularly in the contemporary genre: taking a song written for a band and arranging it for voices. Often the idea behind this arranging style is to replicate the feel and style of the original piece as closely as possible, so that the novelty for the listener lies in hearing something familiar recreated with voices.

Some may consider this style of arranging to lack creativity, but we disagree. Truth be told, it can lack creativity, but it also can be very creative and fun. No one criticized the Kronos Quartet when they arranged and performed Jimi Hendrix's "Purple Haze" as an encore, and that was pure translation.

There are countless decisions to be made. Which instruments do you replicate and which do you leave behind? What sounds and syllables do you use? How do you keep the energy moving forward? How on earth will my singers replicate that crazy sound effect in the bridge? There's a pretty wide spectrum here for creative work, and although throughout the book we'll be showing you some tricks to keep it interesting, at best we'll be scratching the surface. The best contemporary a cappella arrangements often drive off-road and return with a sound or choice no one has used before.

A good, simple guide to writing an interesting translational arrangement is this: instead of focusing on the original piece and how to push that onto voices, focus on your group sound and imagine what sounds you want to pull from the original into your sound. Even if you think you're just translating, using this approach will drive your creative decision making, and you and your group will define the final sound.

> *>> Deke says: When working on The Sing-Off I often find myself telling a group "Don't go to the song, bring the song to you!" In other words, rather than going out of your way to use your voices to sound exactly like the original recording, rely on your group's core sound and style, and make arranging choices based on your strengths so in the end you'll be performing your version of a song rather than trying to imitate someone else's.*

Transformation

Transformation or "compositional" arranging is the term we use for taking a piece of music and substantially changing how it sounds. This may come from adding new elements, significantly changing the harmonies or form, or other large-scale changes. Often it is achieved through deconstruction and reconstruction: breaking the song down to its basic elements of melody and lyrics (you'll notice that the bass line and chords are not included here) and rebuilding it into something new or considerably different. With this approach, depending on how far away from the original style the arranger goes, he or she can almost feel like the piece's second composer. If you get comments like, "I love what you did with that song," it usually means someone heard something new, and your arrangement probably contains transformative elements. A really good transformational arrangement may even sound better to some than the original!

Mixing the Elements

Most arrangements land somewhere in the middle of the spectrum, written with a combination of translational and transformational approaches. They may start by keeping the "bones" of the song the same (translation, but then add a few completely new elements, or they might take a rock song and treat the voices more like a string quartet (transformation). There is plenty of room for all types of arranging even in a single chart.

Often arrangers will change their approach over time. They start out transcribing arrangements by their favorite a cappella artists, then they start tweaking those arrangements to fit their own group. Then they start writing their own charts, intending them to sound like the original. As they get more comfortable with their skill set, they start adding and changing the pieces, melding their creativity with that of the original artist. As they develop their own signature sound, their arrangements will feel more and more like creative works in their own right. This is why being a vocal arranger is so rewarding once you've developed your craft well enough, your arrangement may become one of the best-known or best-loved versions of a song.

It's easy to ascribe a value judgment to this: more creativity = "good" arrangement, less = "bad." But not only is this not valid, it doesn't even make any sense. Music is subjective, and in some cases a very transcriptive, straightforward arrangement will result in a very powerful performance, whereas a very clever, unusual arrangement will fall flat.

Remember that the success of your arrangement will not be judged by how complicated it is or how far you've taken it from the original, it will be judged by how well it allows a group to make music that's powerful, moving, and exciting. It doesn't matter how creative a football coach is in his drills and plays; it only matters whether the team wins the game. Bringing an audience to its feet is winning the game. People want to hear some songs or styles sound close to the way they remember them; twist the song into something unrecognizable and they won't be happy.

And it's important to make sure the creative elements of the arrangement serve the song, rather than the song serving your need to show off your arranging chops or creative masterwork. If all you want is a platform for your own creative skills, take the leap, go all the way, and write your own music!

*>> Dylan says: I sing in an a cappella group devoted to music of the 1980s, and the big kick for the audience and for us) is hearing all the guitar and synth bits that are the signatures of the songs reproduced vocally, note for note. Most of my arrangements for this group are pretty translational; but I'll use some of the *transformational" vocabulary to add some extra sparkle, remove a passage that seems dull, or come up with a crazy new way of representing a guitar solo. The result is a chart that satisfies both the audience's desire to hear what they know and my desire to create something interesting, different, and new.*

Chapter 9.
Arrangement Planning Overview

By Steve Tramack

Introduction

Akin to the tailor's adage—measure twice, cut once—time spent planning an arrangement before writing chords can lead to a more successful, efficient journey. The high-level steps of this process are:

1. Find the right song to arrange.
2. Consider the performer for whom you're arranging.[37]
3. Plan the journey by building a blueprint.
4. Embark on the journey by laying down the melody and begin developing the arrangement.

Find a Song

Some songs work better than others when considering arranging in the barbershop style. You'll also find certain songs or artists or genres will resonate more with you at different stages of your arranging journey. Taking both into account sets you up for success before ever writing a note. Additionally, you'll need to consider the form, inherent harmonies, and the lyrics.

Find a Song That Speaks to You

Have you ever been in the audience of a musical or at a concert and you find an arrangement forming in your head in real time? Have you listened to a song on the SiriusXM Sinatra channel, and suddenly you ask yourself why you haven't heard this song in the barbershop style? Find a song that connects with your inner arranger—particularly your creative dreamer role, as outlined in chapter 5.

Assuming you've identified a song you want to arrange; how do you start to find the arrangement inside the song? First, consider listening repeatedly to several different versions of the song. Figure out what you like from each version. Are there harmonies, rhythmic textures and grooves, treatments of the lyric and melody, different tempos, etc., which resonate with you? Decide if one or more of these versions is going to be the inspiration for some or all the song or if you're going to take a completely new and different approach.

Will It 'Shop?

As a quick summary, there are a handful of core elements of the barbershop style. These fundamental tenets of the style, as of 2023, are codified in the BHS contest rules.[38] Arrangements featuring these aspects—the

---

[37] Many arrangers consider this the first step and perhaps the most important consideration. The individual singers / sections within an ensemble, and their strengths and weaknesses, will have a significant impact on the arranger's choices.
[38] https://files.barbershop.org/PDFs/Contests-Judging/CJ_Handbook.ver_13.2_Jun_2020.pdf, 3–29.

immutable laws of barbershop—are easily recognizable by fans of the style, even if they lack the music theory understanding.[39]

- *Always*: 1) Four-part a cappella texture; 2) Featured characteristic chord progressions
- *Most of the time*: 1) Melody in an inside voice, meaning harmony above and below the melody; 2) Lyrics sung by all four parts as opposed to solo plus neutral syllables.
- *Other arrangement choices*: 1) Expanded sound enabled by choice of voicing, inversions, chord vocabulary and homorhythmic textures; 2) Balanced form; 3) Embellishments; 4) Construction (e.g., tags).

Expanded sound is a frequently used term in barbershop circles. Essentially, expanded sound is the perception of pitches beyond the four being sung. Expanded sound is achieved when 1) sung pitches are mathematically proportional (in tune) with each other, and 2) vowels are tuned, meaning the shape of the vocal tract (formants) of each singer aligns in such a way that the overtones being produced by the individual singer are proportional with the overtones being produced by other voice parts. Essentially, the vowels match.

Expanded sound is a hallmark of barbershop singing and should be something for which ensembles strive. This term is used interchangeably with *ring* and, in fact, more accurate to the style than the colloquial—especially among barbershoppers—*ring* is.

Does the song you're considering easily support these fundamental elements? Will it support a four-part a cappella texture? Can you hear harmonies above and below the melody, and a texture where all four parts are singing lyrics most of the time, as opposed to a solo with background voices and instruments? Does the melody naturally support the variety of harmony and kinds of chord progressions that are inherent to the barbershop style?

If you're inspired by an iconic performance of a given song, chances are that audience members will be as well. The closer the arrangement adheres to the original performance from the harmonic and form perspectives, the better the synergies between what the listener hears in their head—the original performance—and what they hear in their ears—the performance of your arrangement. Finding material that inherently exhibits the strongest elements of the style gives you as an arranger the best chance of creating something that honors both the original song and the style.

Get the sheet music.

Get a version of the sheet music which matches (or at least comes close to) an iconic performance of the song. Sheet music sites such as sheetmusicdirect.com, sheetmusicplus.com and musicnotes.com are great online sources for published music. ArrangeMe.com is an excellent source for self-publishing copyrighted, public domain, or original works via Hal Leonard. IMSLP.org (worldwide) and PDinfo (US-specific) provide a list of public domain songs.

[39] The definition of immutable (unchanging over time) seems appropriate when describing those fundamental pillars of the style.

Public domain laws vary from territory to territory. In the case of the US, songs released 96 years or more prior to the Jan 1st date each year are considered in the public domain.[40] In other territories, the general rule of thumb for International public domain titles is the date of the death of the last living contributor (composer or lyricist) plus 70 years.

Consider Form

Take a close look at the sheet music, and consider some of the following aspects of your song candidate: is the form balanced, with a variety of sections of form? Forms most often found in the barbershop style are AABA or ABAC. Songs featuring multiple verses and choruses that also include a bridge work well in the style, providing sufficient variety and development opportunities. This topic is covered in more depth in chapters 10, 11, and 12 of this book. Bridges, verses, and varying sections of form (e.g., ABAC) inherently provide interest in the source material.

Strophic form songs which follow a repeated verse structure (e.g., AAA) present some challenges for the arranger to create interest. Figure 9.1 provides an example of a popular strophic form folk song (*You Are My Sunshine*), and features several creative ways in which the arranger, Vicki Uhr, created artistic interest. Of note:

- **Chorus 1** (pickup measure through measure 16): Vicki uses a layered entrance (solo, then duet with the tenor, then baritone embellishment, then finally four parts), which highlights the traditional harmonies of the song. The homorhythmic texture which follows highlights both the lyrics and inherently supports expansion of sound.
- **Verse** (measures 17 through 32): This begins with a tertian movement key change (E♭ to G), which creates a sense of heightened urgency and emotion. The contrast with the bass and tenor melody sections creates both a sense of emotional change, before and after the key event, and addresses melodic range issues. The harmonic choices in measures 26, 28, and 30 emphasize the pain and anguish of the events in the verse. The B7 chord on "dreams" in measure 32 both provides a sense of determination and love and provides a path back to the key of E♮, which represents a semitone key change from the first chorus.
- **Chorus 2 and tag** (measures 33 through 55): This chorus is dramatically more embellished than the first chorus, with lots of ascending swipes and motion. This represents the sense of hope and urgency, which is further supported by the lead melodic alterations and embellishment of "why don't you know" in measures 41 and 42. The pleas of "don't take my sunshine" in the tag are further supported by harmonic choices, such as the dramatic ♭VI pillar in measure 52.

[40] For more information on public domain laws, please visit here.

Figure 9.1

"You Are My Sunshine," words and music by Jimmie Davis. Arranged by Vicki Uhr.

Stock No. 213943

YOU ARE MY SUNSHINE

as sung by GQ
for SSAA/female voices

Words and Music by
JIMMIE DAVIS

Arrangement by
VICKI J. UHR

Chorus *very freely*

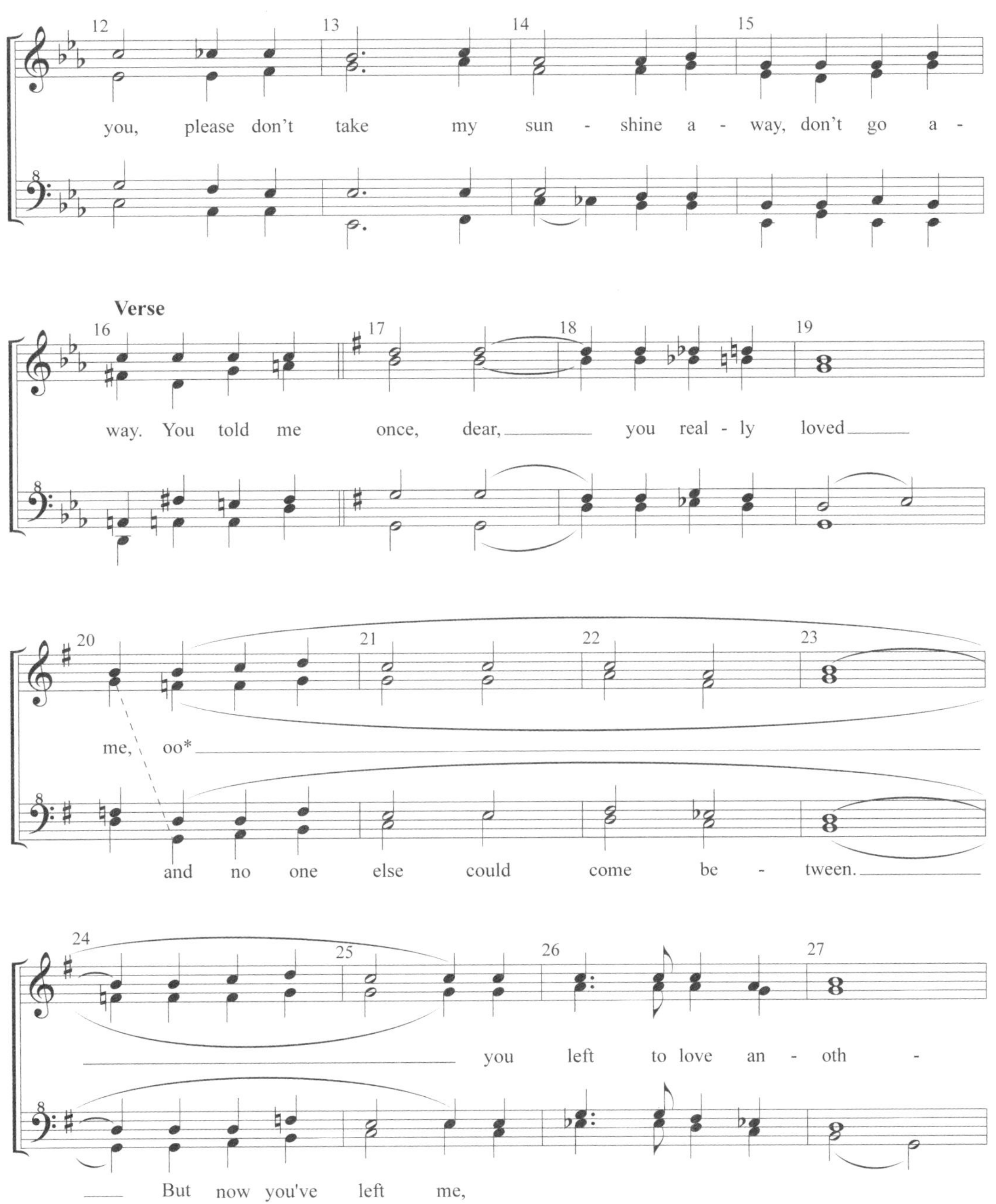

*As an option, you may choose for all parts to sing the lyrics instead of "oo" from mm. 20-25.

You Are My Sunshine 3

28
29
30
31
er, you have shat - tered all my dreams, my

Chorus
32
33
34
35
dreams. You are my sun - shine, my on - ly sun -

36
37
38
39
grey, so
shine, you make me hap - py when skies are grey.
grey, so

40
41
42
43
grey. know,
You'll nev - er know, why don't you know how much I love
grey. know, love, I love
love, how

4
You Are My Sunshine
a - way, don't go a -
you, please don't take my sun - shine a - way.
a - way, don't go a -
Tag
way.
day!
I will love you 'til my dy - ing Don't take the
way.
day,
A - way.
sun, don't take my sun
sun, my sun a - way.
Optional tag
day!
Don't take the sun, don't take my sun a - way.
sun, sun a - way.
day! the sun,

Consider the Inherent Harmonies

One of the most important facets which allows an arrangement to sound like barbershop is characteristic chord progressions featuring secondary dominants and dominant ninths on a variety of roots. Songs that inherently feature these pillar chords and progressions are often easily adapted to the style. Two key considerations:

Harmonic Variety: Are there chords based on a variety of roots in the original? Some very popular songs from the 1950s through the present feature only three chords: I, IV, and V7, which adds the tension to resolve to the tonic. Many blues, country, and early rock songs leverage only these three chords, or perhaps add vi as a fourth featured chord between I and IV. Arrangements of these songs, without careful considerations by the arranger, will feel less satisfying in the style. Adhere too closely to the original harmonizations, and the arrangement will lack the barbershop texture associated with the characteristic chord progressions. Find alternate harmonizations featuring more tritonal energy of the dominant seventh and ninth chords, and the song won't sound like the original version. Neither option will be terribly satisfying as a barbershop contest vehicle, though might work great as a recognizable number in a chorus or quartet's show package.

To feel well-rooted in the barbershop style, the original song should include harmonic pillars based on secondary dominants: an "altered chord (containing at least one tone that is foreign to the key) having a dominant or leading tone relationship to a chord in the key other than the tonic."[41] The most common secondary dominant is the dominant of the dominant, based on the second degree of the scale (II7, or the V7/V). Even better is a song featuring harmonic pillars with dominant seventh chords based on the sixth (VI7, or V7/ii) or third degree (III7, or V7/vi) of the scale, which then progress around the circle of fifths back to the tonic and works well in the style.[42]

Featured Secondary Dominant: For the harmonic variety to generate the sense of musical tension indicative of the characteristic chord progressions of the barbershop style, the dominant seventh chord built on scale tones II, VI or III, must be *featured.* Featured means both by duration—matching the harmonic rhythm of the song, typically at least one full measure, and occurring on a strong beat—and location, e.g., the end of an A section, end of the bridge, or at the title lyrics of the song. Arrangements which feel well-rooted in the style feature secondary dominants built on either the second (II7, or V7/V) or sixth (VI7, or V7/ii) degree of the scale, that then move around the circle of fifths back to the tonic.

When considering a song to arrange, look at the original sheet music and look at the chord symbols above the staff. If the song is in the key of C, is there an A7 (the VI7, or V7/ii) or D7 (the II7, or V7/V) chord symbol in the arrangement? Take the example from *The Muppet Movie* in Figure 9.2, "Rainbow Connection."

---

[41] https://music.utk.edu/theorycomp/courses/murphy/documents/SecondaryDominants.pdf

[42] This doesn't mean that songs lacking secondary dominants in their original harmonizations won't work in the style. Skilled arrangers can adapt harmonizations to feature secondary dominants and circle of fifths movement without changing the original flavor of the song. More information can be found in Vol. 2 in the Advanced Arranging Challenges section.

Figure 9.2

"Rainbow Connection," words and music by Paul Williams and Kenneth Ascher.

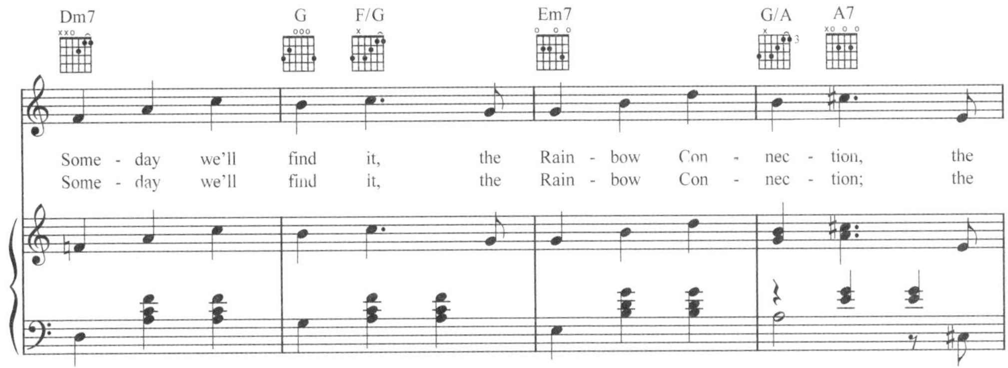

The A7 (VI7) chord then moves to a Dm7 (ii7), further leading to a G7 (V7) and back to the C (I)

Figure 9.3

"Rainbow Connection," by Paul Williams and Kenneth Ascher.

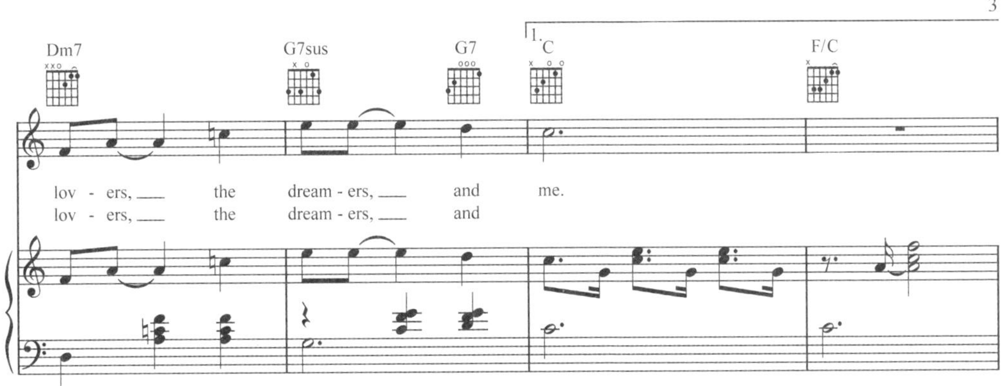

Figure 9.4 shows how these inherent chord progressions could translate to the barbershop style.

Figure 9.4

"Rainbow Connection," arranged by Steve Tramack.

Consider the Lyrics

Barbershop is a lyrical style. Finding a song whose lyrics tell a story helps provides thematic development opportunities within the arrangement and for the performer. One of the things that separates barbershop from other a cappella styles is its primarily *homorhythmic texture*—all four parts singing the same word sounds at the same time. Homorhythmic texture facilitates higher degrees of expansion of sound, which is a hallmark of the style. As is the case with all great music, great barbershop arrangements feature satisfying proportions of unity and contrast. In our case, unity most often involves all four parts singing lyrics.

Summary: Finding the song

Several factors can help contribute to a successful arrangement before you ever write a single chord. Find a song that:

- Inspires you and the intended performer
- Includes harmonic variety
- Features at least one naturally occurring secondary dominant which progresses around the circle of fifths to the tonic
- Has lyrics which tell a story

- Includes a form or construction that fits the style well

If you have these things in the song you've chosen, you're well on your way to creating a successful barbershop arrangement!

Consider the Performer

Whether you're just starting your arranging journey, or you're an experienced arranger, it always helps to have a performer in mind when creating an arrangement. This will help you create an arrangement which is singable by humans. Arrange for your quartet or chorus or for someone you know well. It's much easier to hear them in your head, and it also can help to focus your arranging. How many quartets or choruses, particularly those who don't frequently commission new arrangements, would love to have an arrangement done especially for them? Offer to create an arrangement for a local ensemble who will work with you during the process.

The following is a list of questions which can provide a great deal of input into choices you make in your arrangement.

What Is the Intended Use?

Is this expected to be a contest song? BHS contest rules in 2023 dictate certain arranging choices which map closely to the immutable laws of barbershop.[43] A song intended for a BHS contest, or another barbershop organization's contest, such as Sweet Adelines, will greatly impact chord vocabulary and texture choices. Is this arrangement to be a featured show closer, where the group will spend a great deal of rehearsal time learning and developing the song? This could impact how much development is included in the arrangement. Is this going to be used for a single event or single season as a filler song, and thus not requiring much rehearsal time? You may decide to feature less variety from chorus to chorus, and simplified texture choices, than you would with a song intended to be a featured part of the ensemble's repertoire.

Is there a Reference Performance

Especially when arranging standards from the Great American Songbook of the 20th Century, dozens of performances of a song may be considered iconic. In other cases, where a song was written by or for a specific artist, most people may hear a single iconic performance of that song in their mind's ear. Understanding these aspects to ensure that you capture the desired iconic moments or where you specifically decide to diverge is good to keep in mind during the arranging process.

What is the Performer's Vision for the Song

How does the performer's vision for the song impact your arrangement choices? Many great songs can effectively be interpreted in different ways. In the barbershop style, it's common to hear a true freeform ballad treatment, focusing on a lyrical theme without any underlying sense of meter. Many of those songs could also be effectively delivered in a strict meter sense, or in combination with rubato, allowing more of the rhythmic, melodic and implied harmonic aspects to drive the impact. Arrangements intended to be delivered

---

[43] The rules for BHS contests are updated frequently, and include specific aspects related to the barbershop style. If arranging for contest use, please make sure you check with the Musicality Category of that respective Society to understand the prevailing rules. The current BHS rules are located at https://www.barbershop.org/contests/contests-judging.

in strict meter, compared with one intended for rubato or freeform delivery, are going to look very different—particularly considering embellishments and rhythmic propellants.

Consider the classic Hoagy Carmichael and Stuart Gorrell song, "Georgia On My Mind" in Figure 9.5. This song lends itself to both rubato and strict meter treatments—even within the same arrangement. Note that the homorhythmic texture choices made by the arranger in the verse of the song and the instruction of "freely" clearly imply a freeform, lyrically driven approach.

Figure 9.5

"Georgia On My Mind," words and music by Stuart Gorrell and Hoagy Carmichael. Arrangement by David Harrington.

GEORGIA ON MY MIND

At the chorus of the song, the arranger indicates a delivery change with "start swing" instruction at the end of measure 14. After that, the texture changes substantially, with walking bass downbeats throughout, the bell chord in measure 16, the "blues swing" instruction and syncopation in the lead part in measure 20.

Considering how the arrangement is intended to be performed and providing the ensemble with this kind of notation (both explicitly as part of the expressions, and implicitly via texture choices) are important considerations in the planning process.

In strict meter delivery, intended tempos weigh into choices made by the arranger. For example, decreasing the degree of embellishment and subdivision of the beat as the tempo increases facilitates better execution during performance.

Which Ensemble-specific Information Will Help in Arranging?

Determine:

1. *Ideal ranges for each part.* See chapter 4 the typical vocal ranges for TTBB and SSAA voices. Ranges should serve as a starting point but is not a substitute for discussing specific ranges with the individuals in the ensemble (or sections if a chorus).
   Tessitura is of critical importance. This applies both to the ensemble and the individual. Pay particular attention to the most comfortable part of the singer's range—think of it as the sweet spot for each singer. The sweet spot is the range where the singer can consistently, under pressure, execute at the highest degree of efficiency in the most critical moments of the performance.
2. *Range limits.* What are the absolute limits for each part, and any contingencies, e.g., can the bass sing an E♭ below the scale if they don't stay there for a full measure? This will often determine where a song is pitched, usually based on the bass and lead ranges.
3. *Ensemble and individual strengths.* What are those aspects that the ensemble wants to feature? Can the baritone reliably post an A♭4 for 20 seconds? Is the bass strong rhythmically, singing downbeats against syncopated rhythms? Can all four parts be featured on the melody? These are important factors to consider in both the development of the arrangement, and for the key musical events in the song. Ân example of a commissioned arrangement checklist can be found in Appendix B.
4. *Ensemble and individual weaknesses.* This is perhaps more important than highlighting the ensemble's strengths. Ensembles may be hesitant to provide honest information; you may need to talk with the ensemble's primary coach or close friends. Is the tenor a pure falsetto tenor, and not always capable of balancing chords when on a root of a tightly voiced seventh, or able to effectively sing the melody? Does the bass lose resonance when dipping below an A♭ for more than a note or two? Does the bass sound better in homorhythmic passages than when singing pickups? Does the lead's passaggio create problems for songs in the key of F? Identifying what should be avoided for each member of the ensemble can help to create a less taxing performance.
5. *Is there anything else I should know?* Asking this open-ended question can help to provide unique insight into the group's motivation for choosing a given song, and further inform your arranging process.

Summary: Consider the Performer

Many aspects of the intended performer will impact decisions you make as an arranger. Carefully consider each one so that they and their audiences can have the best singing and performing experience.

Plan the Journey

To make the arrangement process flow as smoothly as possible, it helps to map out as much of the journey as possible—ideally before you ever write a single chord. This can be accomplished by developing a blueprint for the arrangement. The blueprint would include information about the song and the ensemble, as discussed previously in this chapter.

The Blueprint

Different arrangers have different methods of capturing this blueprint, but most would agree that, at a minimum, you need to consider the following:

- *The primary, overarching musical theme: lyrics, melody, rhythm, harmony.* None of these operate in a vacuum, and the themes can change at various places in the arrangement.

- Identifying the basic overall construction can help envision long-line thematic development and identify means of development from section to section of the arrangement.

- *The big idea for this song.* This will highlight the climax, and perhaps provide some insight into key musical events leading up to the climactic moment.
- *The primary key, or keys as the arrangement progresses.* This will dictate voicing choices and highlight if the melody needs to be transferred to the bass (when too low) or tenor (when too high, or up an octave when too low).
- *The intended delivery approach for the arrangement.* Arrangement choices such as embellishments will differ if the planned delivery approach is a freeform ballad, compared to a strict meter interpretation. Decisions such as swing versus straight eighths will also impact notation and development choices.
- *Form and overall construction for the arrangement.* It is important to consider which aspects of the original composition will be leveraged in the arrangement (e.g., verse, chorus, half-chorus reprise, interludes, etc.), and what original material (e.g., introduction, tag, interludes, etc.) would need to be developed. Identifying the basic overall construction can help envision long-line thematic development and identify means of development from section to section of the arrangement.

Blueprint Template

Long before the days of GPS and navigation apps, if we were going somewhere for the very first time, we would map out our journey. Figure 9.6 features an example of an arrangement blueprint template, which allows mapping of the following major elements of the arrangement mapped from beginning to end working from bottom to top:

1. Song and Performance information, including the big idea
2. Construction, broken down by sections of form
3. Keys of the song throughout the musical journey
4. Lyrics associated with each section of form
5. Key textures for a given section of form
6. Melodic highlights worth featuring
7. Harmonic highlights worth featuring
8. Key musical events along the journey

Figure 9.6

Blank arrangement blueprint example. Google Sheet

Key events										
Harmonic highlights										
Melodic highlights										
Texture										
Lyrics										
Key										
Form	Intro	Verse 1	Chorus 1	Verse 2	Chorus 2	A1	A2	B1	Interlude (replaces C)	Chorus

Figure 9.7

Arrangement blueprint example. Google sheet

Harmonic highlights	Establish pillars / progressions. Featured 9th				
Melodic highlights	None - rhythmic chords				
Texture	Match the feel of the piano in the original Kacey Musgraves version. Establish the harmony part textures for the first verse				
Lyrics	Doo doo doo...oh				
Form	Intro	Verse 1	Chorus 1	Verse 2	Chorus 2
			Rainbow		

Summary; Plan the Journey

Whether you choose to map out the elements of an arrangement onto something like this template, or simply consider the individual elements, having an idea about these topics before jumping into the arrangement will aid you in your journey. We'll dive into this more deeply in the Arrangement Planning Use Case, in Chapter 12.

Embark on the Journey

There are varying approaches to laying down the arrangement, several of which are detailed throughout this book. Discovering what works for you through trial and error—perhaps a lot of trial and error—is an exciting part of the arranging journey.

Start With the Melody

In most cases, the place to start is with the melody, mapped into the planned construction and sections of form. For example, if using a software notation program such as Finale or Sibelius, you can start by selecting one of the predefined barbershop templates included with the software. Figure 9.8 shows an arrangement of Cole Porter's "Night and Day," inspired by Frank Sinatra's classic 1962 studio recording.

The song is in common time (4/4), and the basic construction is:

verse | chorus | half chorus | tag

Mapping this to the original sheet music, I plan on 84 measures, with a pickup measure. Sinatra performs the song in the key of C, but this will lie a bit too low for the intended quartet, so we'll start in the key of Eb.

For spacing purposes, I spread the measures out to a standard 4 per system, adjust the spacing in between staffs to accommodate lyrics. I'm now ready to start entering the melody and lyrics.

Figure 9.8

Example of starting an arrangement, this being "Night and Day." YouTube

NIGHT AND DAY

Words and Music by COLE PORTER

Arrangement by STEVE TRAMACK

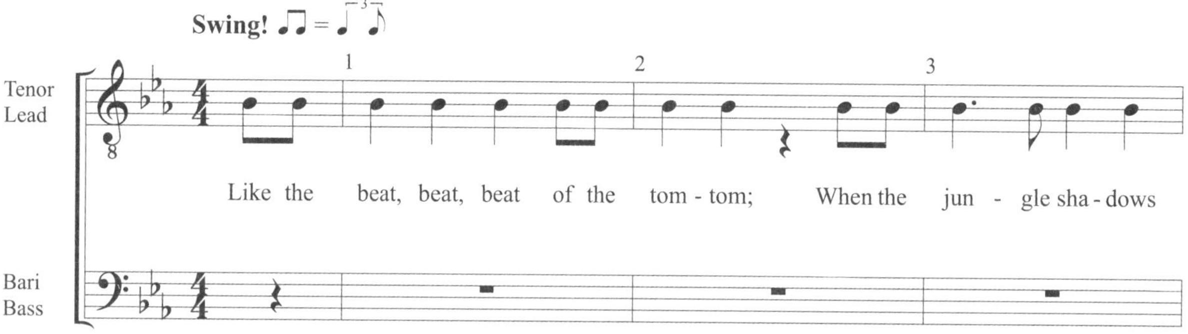

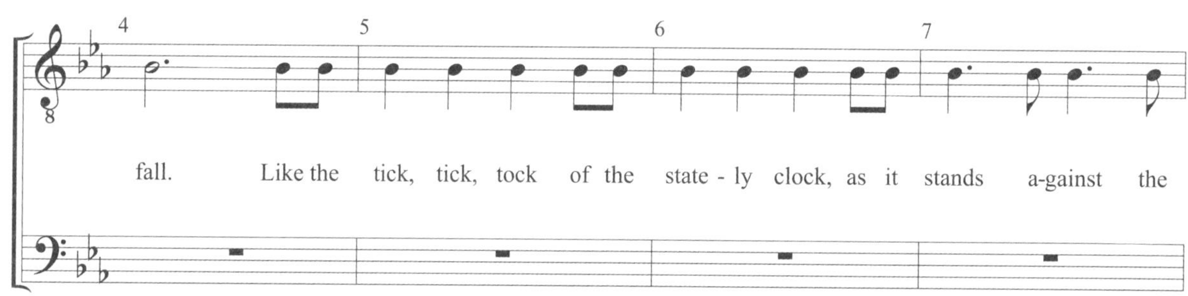

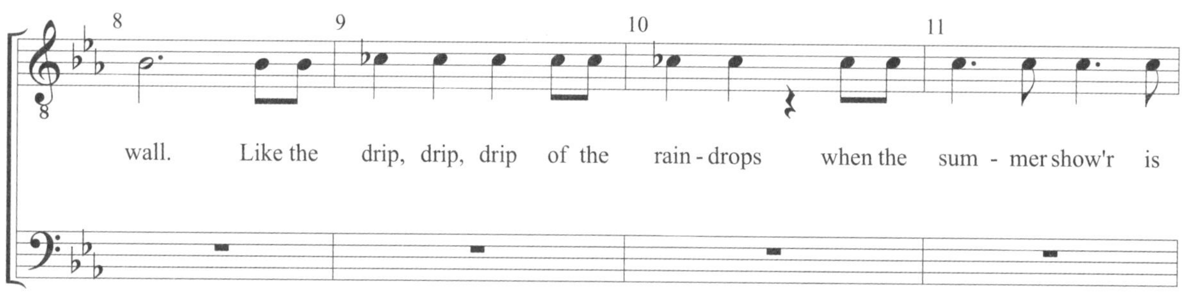

Begin Developing the Arrangement

Once the melody has been entered, the paths through the remainder of the arranging process are as varied as there are songs and arrangers. Several of these paths and processes are covered in detail throughout the remainder of the book. Perhaps the most important aspect is trial and error, determining what works best for you.

Arranging processes tend to change over time as an arranger learns new approaches and gains new perspectives. Master arranger Kevin Keller recommends not obsessing over finding the perfect chord during the first couple of passes through an arrangement. Focus instead on two things: 1) voice leading for all the harmony parts, including the baritone, trusting that you'll find the right chords; and 2) textures for each section of form, e.g., homorhythmic texture for the first A section, more embellished, focusing on lyrics in the second A section, etc.

This can reduce the number of listens to notational software playback functions of the same measures repeatedly. Kevin's advice grants permission to allow your first draft to be imperfect. Later, when polishing your arrangement, focus on the specific chord, inversion, voicing, or voice leading for important word painting opportunities, which make those moments more special.

Summary of Embark on the Journey

One of the most important pieces of advice on getting started is just that: get started. Simply entering the melody into your software or on notation paper can help the creative process begin. It can be easy, then, to move onto the development portion of the arrangement. Hopefully you feel better equipped because of the advice and perspectives of the combined wisdom of barbershop's great arrangers.

Conclusion

Now that we've discussed an overview of the planning process, let's explore some of the different approaches that an arranger might follow in creating an arrangement that meets the performer's vision, fueled by the various sources of inspiration that drive the arranger and honor the original work. We'll explore the spectrum of arrangement types, followed by two case studies.

Part E: Case Studies

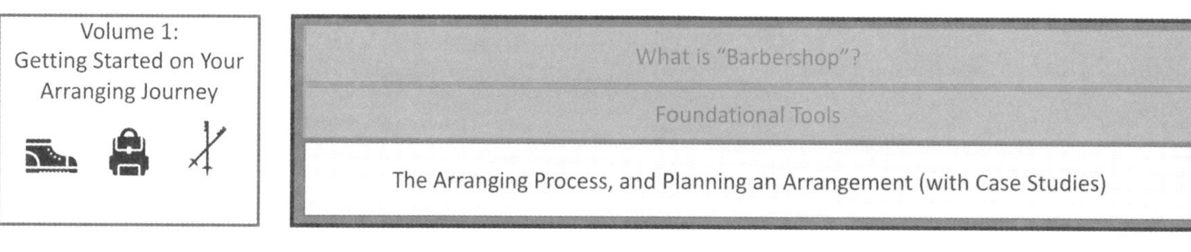

Throughout each volume of *Arranging Barbershop*, we'll explore the topics covered in further depth via case studies. In each, an expert arranger discusses their process and approach and go step-by-step through their own journeys, sharing their experiences and learnings. This part features two such step-by-step case studies.

Chapter 10: Case Study (Planning and Process): The View from 30,000 feet

Kevin Keller explains his process, considerations, and step-by-step approach to developing an arrangement.

Chapter 11: Case Study (Planning and Process): It Had to Be You

Steve Tramack explores the planning process for an arrangement of "It Had to Be You," and how an iconic performance and unique ensemble inspired choices.

Chapter 10. Planning an Arrangement: The View from 30,000 feet

By Kevin Keller

Inspiration

It all starts with the song. Whether the song is commissioned, or you decide to do it on your own, understanding what is inspiring about the song is important. Is it the lyrical message? Is it the rhythms? Is it that you hear barbershop harmonies? Is it a beautiful melody? Is it some combination therein? Knowing why the song inspires will influence your considerations along the way.

If you are inspired by the song, how do you create an arrangement that will inspire the performer? If the performer is inspired by the arrangement, how will the performer and arrangement inspire an audience? One way to create this linkage is to imagine sitting in the audience and hearing the song being performed. How do you want to feel along the way? excited? sad? thrilled? loving? Constantly be aware throughout the arrangement process about inspiration: yours, the performer's, and most importantly the audience's.

Now that you understand the inspiration of the song, it is time to consider how the arrangement takes shape. This is called *construction and form.*

Construction and Form

There are three basic types of song construction we hear in the barbershop style

1. Stanzas
2. Introductory Verse and Story Chorus
3. Story Verse and Refrain

Stanzas

A classic barbershop example of this is "Smilin' Through." Most church anthems are a series of stanzas. Each stanza (or verse) adds more information using the same melody for each stanza.

Decisions:

- Does it need a verse or an intro to get the story going?
- If there are more than three stanzas in the original, which stanzas tell the story you want to tell?
- Are three stanzas too long from a time perspective? More than three minutes of song will be challenging for the audience to stay with the performer hearing the same melody.

From a balance perspective, an odd number of stanzas will feel right to your audience (three or five). A great example of this is the arrangement of "Smilin' Through," as sung by Center Stage, which features three stanzas. *YouTube.* This doesn't mean you can't do an even number but making that choice will require more thought to provide an expected balance.

Introductory Verse & Story Chorus

Most songs from the Great American Songbook (1920–1960) follow this form. The verse is somewhat optional. It provides some introductory material about who we are as a singer and what got us to this point in the story. It tells of an event or events that have led us to the present. The chorus represents how the story unfolds—it tells the story.

Choruses from these songs have their own form. The most popular is AABA, although ABAC and ABCA are other common song forms.

For those not familiar with this notation, the easiest way to determine this is to take the entire chorus and divide the number of measures by 4. The first quarter of the chorus is always labeled A. If the next quarter sounds like the first quarter, it is A. If it has a distinctly different melody, it gets a B. Each time the melody distinctly changes it gets a new letter of the alphabet. If there are just slight alterations to the melody, then musicians will call it A^{I} and A^{II}. For ease, we will just call it A throughout!

Popular performers of the day routinely dropped the verses of these types of songs. Instead, they would have an instrumental intro to get the song started. The strength of the storyline and inspiration of the chorus was sufficient.

Decisions:

- Does the chorus need an intro or a verse to set it up? If so, does the original verse (if one exists) set up the emotion you want in the chorus? Does it support the inspiration?
- Does it need a little setup (4 bars/ intro)
- Does it need a lot of setup (12 or 16 bars / verse)?
- If new lyrics are required, can you write lyrics and melody in the style of the lyricist / composer? If not, can you find source material from other works from the lyricist / composer?
- Is more than one chorus needed?

Ballads and lyric-driven songs may or may not need additional time to render the music. If there are more lyrics beyond the first chorus, it can work. If there is a single chorus, the chorus may be sufficient.

Rhythm songs typically have a relatively short chorus. You will want to consider repeating a portion or all of the chorus. Songs that are AABA form will often be arranged AABABA (a second half chorus).

Story Verse and Refrain

Pre- or early Tin Pan Alley songs (written before 1900), such as "Sweet Adeline" and "Love Me and the World is Mine" have lengthy verses that tell the actual story. The chorus is more of a refrain where the performer shares a central thought or feeling about the story. As the music world entered the Tin Pan Alley era (generally considered from 1885 through the early 1930s), the song forms became mixed. Sometimes the form would be a story verse and refrain, while others were more intro and verse and story chorus. Songs of the rock and roll era (mid-1950s through mid-1960s), songs began taking this older song form. The storyline is found in multiple verses. The refrain becomes something familiar that expresses the performer's thoughts and emotions about the story.

Pre-Tin Pan Alley songs typically do not have many verses that are strong enough lyrically to stand up in today's world. The typical form we find in barbershop is verse/refrain/tag or verse/refrain/half refrain/tag.

The less familiar the verse is, the more the arranger can pick and choose lyrics that will be relevant today and convey the story desired.

Decisions:

- Do you need more than one verse to tell the story?
- Do you need more than a single refrain?

With rock & roll era songs, removal of lyrics could be problematic. Either because it creates gaps in the story, or the song is so familiar to the audience that the absence of lyrics is disappointing. A barbershop arrangement that will be longer than three minutes must require a lot of attention and skill to keep the performer and audience engaged. Ask yourself: if the song is more than three minutes long, what can I do without?

Decisions:

- How long will the song be if you do all verses and refrains?
- Will the song suffer if you remove portions of the song?

Performer

Sometimes an arranger is commissioned to arrange a piece for a particular group. Other times the arranger is simply inspired by a song and the ideas that they have for that song.

When an arranger is commissioned to arrange a piece, there are several things to keep in mind:

- Is this for a quartet or a chorus? The same song could be sung by either, but this decision often will dictate arrangement choices. Some arrangement choices serve quartets better; some serve choruses better. If it is for either, keep that in mind.
- Consider the specific strengths and weaknesses of the individual singers. This was covered in detail in Chapter 6.

Even if the piece is not commissioned, think about the group that would sing it and arrange it with them in mind. Creativity will flow more when thinking about those details.

Audience

Just because the performer is inspired by the song does not necessarily mean the audience will be. But it is true that if the performer is not inspired by it, the audience won't be! Keeping the audience in mind when making arrangement choices will likely yield a successful arrangement.

Most songs can be used in different ways. You can sing a love song through several delivery filters. You could be in love for the first time, when you finally meet the right one, when you propose, when you get married, at an anniversary, or even upon death of that loved one. Each one will sound different, mainly through tempo and dynamics. An arranger can also influence those decisions. Although great songs often can support multiple successful treatments, the best arrangements are often those that influence the performer into a single way of performing the arrangement.

Consider these thoughts:

- What would you like the audience to experience as the song is being performed? More importantly, how should the audience feel at each moment of the song? You can influence this through your choices.
- Why should the audience continue to want to listen? What keeps their attention? Lulls in your arrangement will translate into lulls with the audience. How can you keep the music constantly flowing forward, regardless of tempo or dynamic?
- Just because you think a chord is cool doesn't mean the audience will. As arrangers and barbershoppers, many of us tend to think of music vertically. We listen to the sound of a chord and are enamored with a chord. Audiences think of music horizontally. If the chord is out of context, they might think it is weird. Chords and other choices must serve the horizontal flow of the music. If the choices enhance the emotional journey of the song, then the audience will appreciate it.

Arranging Process Begins

Now we begin. There are some initial steps that are good discipline to do in each arrangement until it becomes second nature:

1. Fill in the title, copyright, and authors.
2. Determine what key the song should be in, at least the first intro, verse, and chorus.
3. Enter the melody of the verse and chorus, noting when the melody is too high or low. Transpose as necessary.
4. Enter the pillar chords as indicated by the sheet music. You are not bound to use the harmonies that the composer used but the pillar chords support the composer's melody, and you can adjust from there.
5. If you are going to repeat anything, then copy and paste the melody.
6. Change the rhythms of any copied melody if the lyrics are different.

First Pass: Basic Chords

This strategy allows one to get most of the arrangement done. Sometimes completing an arrangement is all about momentum. The more that is done, the less daunting it becomes.

1. Arrange the first A section chords, editing the choices until you are satisfied. The pillar chords can be used as guides, but you are not obligated, as long as the harmonization is appropriate and logical. Don't worry about embellishments at this time.
2. Copy the tenor, bari, bass parts into all subsequent A sections. Note: Don't copy full measures with the lead part as lead rhythms and notes may change slightly throughout the song.
3. Fix rhythms in copied sections as the rhythm of the lead might change. If the melody is distinctly different, then fix chords as appropriate.
4. Now work on the B section chords. Copy and paste if repeated.
5. Work on the C section if it exists. Copy and paste if repeated.

At this point you should have a large segment of your chorus done.

Second Pass: Transitions

Now that you have basic chords filled in throughout, now address or fix the transitions from one section to another.

1. Look at transitions between A to A, A to B, etc. Adjust chords to make those transitions work logically, including the use of embellishments.
2. Play the entire piece from the start of the chorus. Does it logically flow with appropriate rises and falls in the music? Don't worry about a lack of climax yet. Do the transitions make sense? Even better, as the masterful arranger Don Gray recommends, "Sing it through." If you can't sing it, it is likely that no one else will be able to do so.

Third Pass: Musical Development

This is where you get to show your creativity. Consider:

Climactic moments: Where do you want the song to have its climax? Are there places to build in additional key musical events and important moments? How do you get the arrangement into (and out of) those moments? Chords and voicings should build towards those moments and then gradually decay unless the climax is the final chord.

Rhythmic feel: You are not tied to the composer's rhythms. Take the time to make the rhythms exactly the way they should be. If you don't, the performer will, and you might not like the outcome. The more they are changing, the less they will be enamored with your work. Take the time to make the rhythms correct. This is a great time to sing through all four parts of the arrangement. Ask yourself, if it feel natural, or if there are places where you feel it could be executed several ways. Which feels most organic and artistic?

Rhythmic changes: Unfortunately, it is a legacy belief that the audience has an incredible memory for details about rhythms; each time the same set of words come along the arranger must change the rhythms of those words to ensure that the audience hears variety. Do not fall victim to this. The audience does not remember and neither does the singer. The singer will ask themselves if it is the first time or the second time for those words. General principle: When the lyrics are the same do not change the rhythms. If lyrics are different, then the singer will memorize whatever rhythms are associated with those lyrics. That is the benefit of copy and paste. You know exactly what rhythms were used the last time. This also applies when the harmonization of repeated material is just different enough to be difficult to memorize for the performer. Avoid making passages slightly different for difference's sake.

Textural changes: The easiest way to create obvious variation is to change the texture of the music. If it is AABA song form, consider the second A section to start with a lead solo with trio backtime for a couple of measures until it makes sense to come in. Maybe a duet? Perhaps someone takes the melody for a couple of bars. An example of this is included in the second verse of David Wright's arrangement of "Hello Mary Lou," shown in Figure 10.1.

Figure 10.1

Example of textural change in verse 2 of "Hello Mary Lou," words and music by C. Mangiaracina and Gene Pitney. Arrangement by David Wright.

Hello Mary Lou

Revoicing: Having copied and pasted your chords from one section to the next, you have the harmonic progressions in place. Now consider where you should revoice the chords to give more drama to the arrangement as the song evolves.

Melodic transfer: Transferring the melody is an easy way to create variation. Transferring to the bass is often used to create additional drama, but sometimes it just helps when the melody goes lower and will be tough for the lead. If the melody is shared by the bass and the bari, make sure the tenor gets involved in the action as well. The audience expects it.

Key Changes: Key changes help in the development of the music. You should have some idea as you started mapping out the song that you want key changes at certain moments of the song. Once the entire chorus is mapped out, play it several times and where the music needs a lift, consider it. Though a half-step key change is unlikely to require new vocal choices, there is a danger that the chords you voiced that were in range may now be out of range, and you'll need to make new choices.

Embellishments, back half of chorus: Embellishments serve two purposes: rhythmic propulsion and lyrical reinforcement (sometimes foreshadowing). By this point the arranger has a good idea of what sort of "gingerbread and fireworks" they can add to the song. If the song has more than one chorus, start after the first chorus. If the song just has a single chorus, start in the middle of the chorus. Keep in mind that echoes are easier to execute than swipes, but echoes can quickly move towards triteness if one isn't careful!

Embellishments, first half of chorus: Once the second half of the song is done, use only as many embellishments as needed in the first half of the song to keep it moving. In 4/4 or cut time, anytime the melody note is a whole note or longer, some embellishment is needed. Note the example in Figure 10.2, from David Wright's arrangement of "Mean to Me."

Figure 10.2

Embellishments of sustained melody notes in "Mean to Me," words and music by Roy Turk and Fred E. Ahlert. Arrangement by David Wright.

In 3/4 a dotted half may not need an embellishment, but if it is more than a measure an embellishment is needed. Regardless of the time signature, keep embellishments to a minimum; nothing can overshadow the back half.

Fourth Pass: Added material

Now that the bulk of the song is developed, consider how the added material amplifies and finishes the song.

Intro or Verse: Now that there is a clear vision of the chorus and the emotional and musical travel it generates, how will the intro and/or verse set up the chorus? If new lyrics are being introduced, are they written in the same language that the composer writes in? In other words, if you replace a Cole Porter verse, you should write in the language of Cole Porter. And the melody and harmonies if changed should sound like the original. A great example of this is David Wright's arrangement of Richard Rogers' *Something Good* from *The Sound of Music.* Note in figure 10.3 how David's verse both evokes the melody motifs and the lyrical subtext and language of Richard Rodgers' original.

Figure 10.3

Original material in "Something Good," words and music by Richard Rodgers. Arrangement by David Wright. YouTube

Tag: How does the tag successfully close the song? The length of the tag should reflect the length of the song. The longer the song the longer the tag should be and vice versa. The tag should also be congruent (harmonically, texturally) with the rest of the arrangement. Introducing new concepts and material in the tag for the first time creates challenges for the performer.

Final Pass: Adjustments

It is quite tempting that once the entire song is completed to consider it done. Take some time to allow new ideas to creep in. Play it for others and get their reactions. What did they like? What confused them? Because you have played it over and over, some weak moments no longer sound weak. If it feels like there are lulls in the arrangement, there are. Every arranger will share that new ideas come to them after the initial arrangement is completed; be open to tweaking it further.

Lyrics: Now that the arrangement is done, it is time to enter lyrics. Sometimes it happens that the perfect embellishment has two musical notes but the perfect echo with the lyrics has three syllables. If a musical compromise can be made to accommodate the syllables, great. Otherwise find new syllables that fit the musical solution. Consider foreshadowing if echoing doesn't work.

Neutral vowels are used quite frequently. They are typically used in two ways:

1. Orchestration: from a volume perspective /a/ (pronounced as the a-sound in "got" in North American English) is the loudest vowel followed by /ɔ/) pronounced as the o-sound in "goat" in North American English), followed by /u/ (pronounced as the oo-sound in "goose" in North American English). For a crescendo use ooh-oh-ah and for a decrescendo use ah-oh-ooh. If there is only room for two vowels, use the two vowels that convey the dynamic level.
2. Emotional:
    a. "Oh" is the word that is said when there are no other words. It is a delay tactic while the speaker is searching for what to say, and then they find the words. "Oh" is the perfect substitute word for pickups if one doesn't exist. *Oh, What a Beautiful Morning* from the Rodgers and Hammerstein musical *Oklahoma* is a good example of this.
    b. "Ah" represents satisfaction, delight, enjoyment.
    c. "Ooh" is interesting, surprising.

Aesthetics: Once the arrangement reaches its final stages, do not underestimate the value of making the arrangement look like a piece of art. Take the time to make it beautiful. Clean everything up. It makes a difference to the performer if you have taken the time to make it look beautiful.

Chapter 11.
Harmonizing a Melody Case Study

By Steve Armstrong

Introduction

Just as it is necessary to have a solid grasp on music theory when one wishes to become an arranger, another fundamental is to be able to write a simple harmonization that is singable and sounds pleasing to the ear. This is really the first step and once this skill has been sufficiently developed, it is possible to explore all the wonderful and creative ways to embellish that harmonization into a true arrangement. This chapter will outline a systematic approach to writing a harmonization that can provide that foundation and be utilized even when an arranger has become quite skilled. This chapter will also walk you through various harmonization scenarios that ends with a case study to help you understand how the process works.

Harmonic Pillars and Harmonic Rhythm

The first step is to identify the *harmonic pillars*. These are the chords that are the main harmony or harmonies for the measure and if you were to sing the song while accompanying yourself on the guitar, these would be the chords you would play. Note that you are not going to play a different chord on each melody note. In fact, most of the time it feels right to change the chord each time you start a new measure. This is partly because rhythmically the first beat of the measure has strength, and you add strength by choosing that moment to also change the chord. This allows the listener to feel a satisfying symmetry as the chords change at consistent intervals of time. This is what we mean by *harmonic rhythm*: the frequency that the main harmony, or harmonic pillars, change. In a fast song the harmonic pillars may last for two full measures. Conversely, with a slower song the pillars may change midway through the measure, e.g, in 4/4 time they might change every 2 beats, meaning they are still changing on strong beats.

The following are examples of inherent harmonic rhythms, moving at different paces:

Figure 11.1

"When I Lost You," by Irving Berlin. Note the pillar chords change every two measures.

Figure 11.2

"Five Foot Two," arrangement by Joe Liles. Note the pillar chords change nearly every measure.

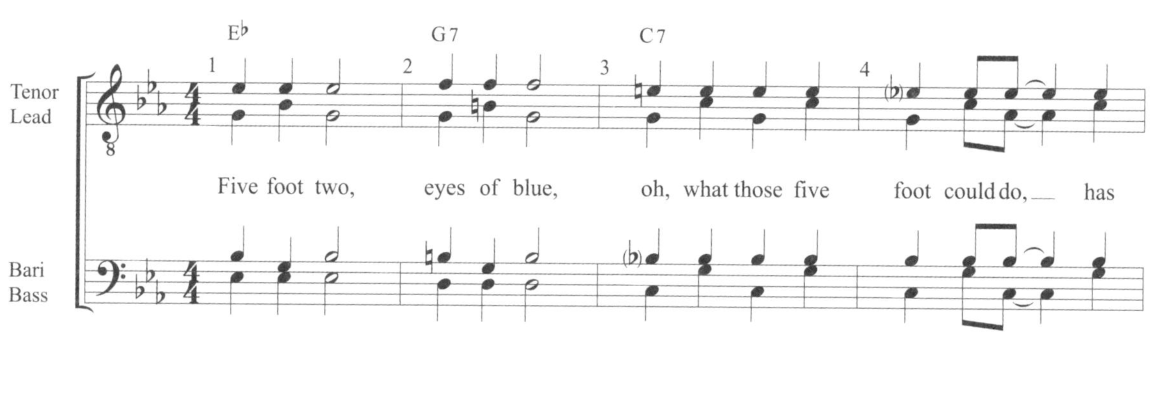

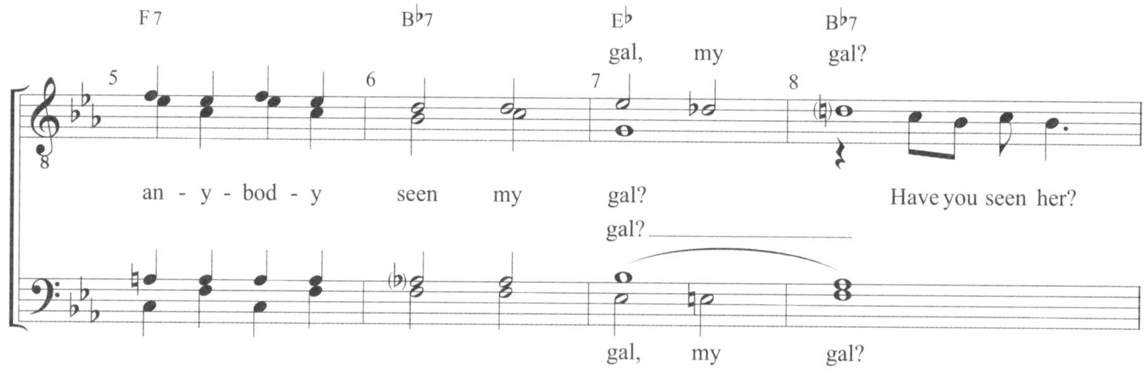

Figure 11.3

"A Nightingale Sang in Berkeley Square," by Manning Sherwin. Note the pillar chords change every 2 beats.

For the remainder of this case study, we'll use "When I Lost You".

Figure 11.4

"When I Lost You," by Irving Berlin.

System Outline

There are seven steps to follow when writing a harmonization: 1) melody and lyrics, 2) identify harmonic pillars, 3) identify non-pillar melody notes, 4) bass harmony, 5) tenor harmony, 6) baritone harmony, and 7) identify potential harmonies for non-pillar notes.

Melody and Lyrics

Enter the melody and lyrics into your notational software. It can be helpful to print page this out for the next steps.

Figure 11.5

Example of the melody and lyrics of the song section.

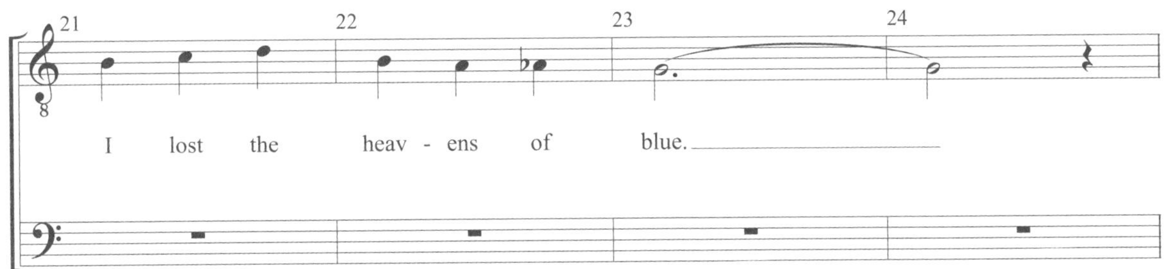

Identify Harmonic Pillars

Write or notate the harmonic pillars above the staff. Sometimes the score you are working from provides this information.

Figure 11.6

Example of harmonic pillar identification.

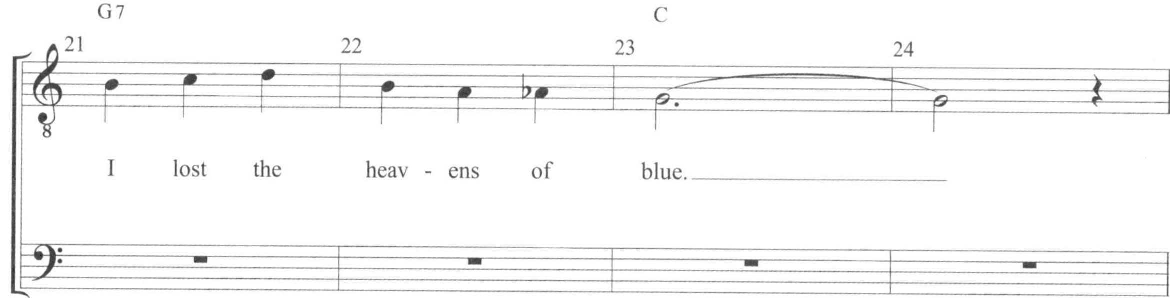

Identify Non-pillar Melody Notes

Go through the melody and circle every note that isn't readily a part of the pillar chord. These will be harmonized later.

Figure 11.7

Example of identifying notes outside the harmonic pillar chord.

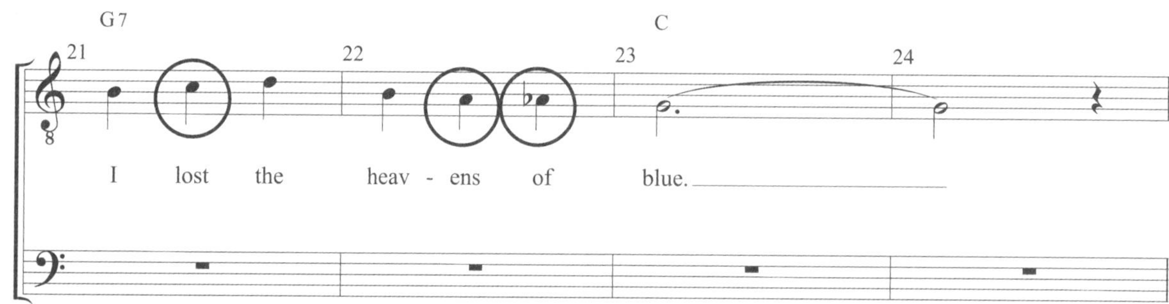

Bass Harmony

Write in the bass note for every melody note inside the pillar chord. Start the bass on the root or fifth for seventh chords and the root for triads. Try to follow the general shape of the melody so that bass notes are higher when the melody is higher and lower when the melody is lower. This will help the voicings to not become too spread. Consider bass voice leading when the harmony implies a seventh chord and the melody is not on the root or fifth.

Figure 11.8

Example of bass part harmonization of the notes within the pillar chord.

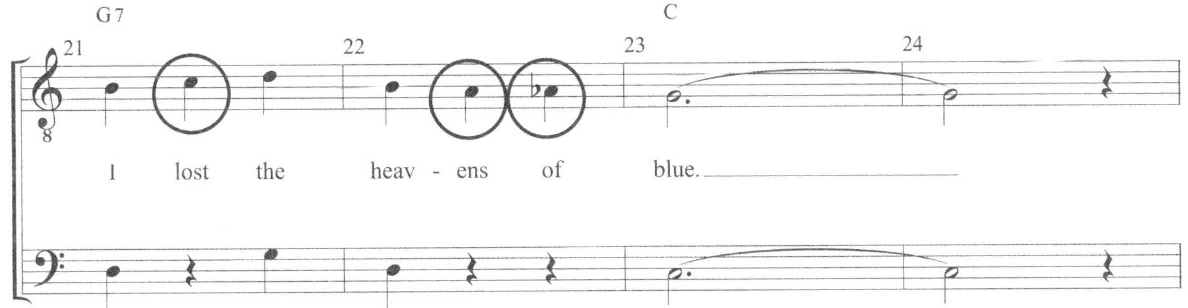

Tenor Harmony

Write in the tenor note for every melody note inside the pillar chord. Use one of the unused notes in the chord or double the root if it is a triad. Consider voice leading and seek for fewer awkward leaps. There may be times when choosing a different bass note would allow a smoother tenor part.

Figure 11.9

Example of tenor and bass part harmonization of the notes within the pillar chord.

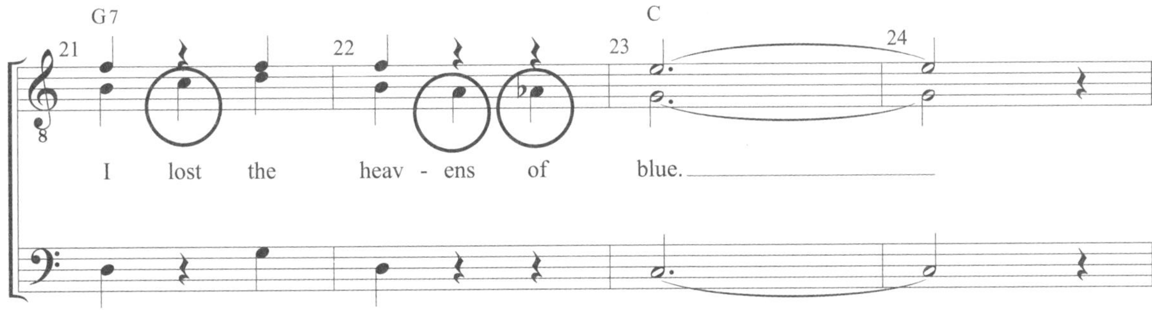

Baritone Harmony

Write in the baritone note for every melody note inside the pillar chord. Completing each chord or double the root if it is a triad. As with the tenor, try to not have the part jump around unnecessarily and consider changing the bass or tenor note if it leads to a smoother baritone part.

Figure 11.10

Example of baritone, tenor, and bass part harmonization of the notes within the pillar chord.

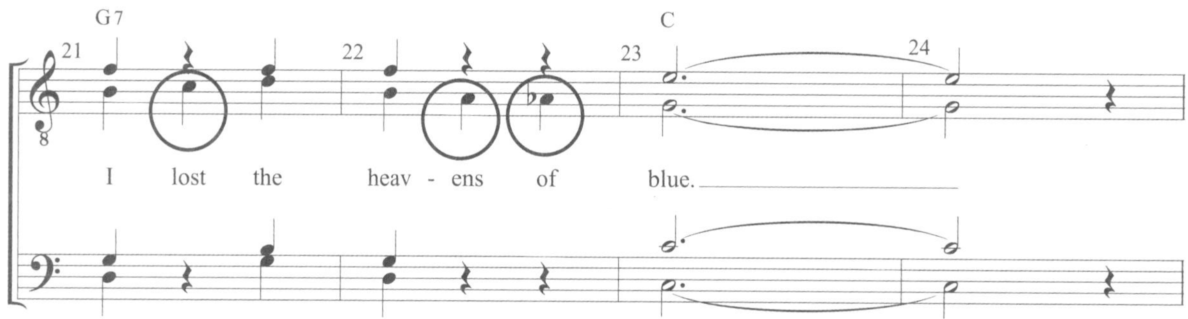

Identify Potential Harmonies For Non-pillar Notes

Examine each circled melody note and determine which of the following options could be used to harmonize it:

Table 11.1

Chord choices for non-pillar chord notes.

Option Number	Chord Type	Distance of Root From Harmonic Pillar
1	Extended chord (add 6th, 7th, or 9th)	On
2	Barbershop 7th	5th above
3	Barbershop 7th	5th below
4	Barbershop 7th	Semitone below
5	Barbershop 7th	Semitone above
6	Barbershop 7th	tritone
7	Diminished 7th	On

These options include every possible pitch. Determine which options include the melody note and try these out. Playing them on a keyboard or using notational software playback are helpful ways to hear the options that sound natural. Choose the one you like the best and write in the bass, tenor and baritone, in that order, following the same guidelines as above.

Figure 11.11

Example of non-pillar chord harmonization options.

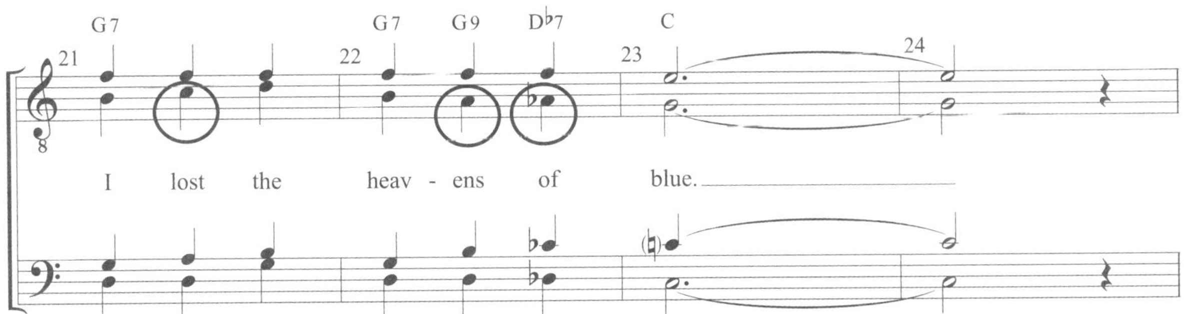

So, in figure 11.11, we used a Dmin7 for the first circled note, a G9 without the root for the second one, and a D♭7 for the third one. Let's examine the options a little further and talk about how we arrived at these, starting in measure 22. The primary harmony is G7 and the first circled melody note is an A.

Table 11.2

Harmonization options for the first non-pillar chord in measure 22. Prevailing harmony: G7. Melody note: A

Option Number	Chord Type	Distance of Root From Harmonic Pillar	Is this an option?
1	Extended chord (add 6th, 7th, or 9th)	On	*Yes*, the A is in G9 chord (missing the root)
2	Barbershop 7th	5th above	*Yes*, the A is the fifth of a D7 chord
3	Barbershop 7th	5th below	*No*, the A is not part of a C7 chord
4	Barbershop 7th	Semitone below	*No*, the A is not part of a F#7 chord
5	Barbershop 7th	Semitone above	*No*, the A is not part of a G#7 chord
6	Barbershop 7th	Tritone	*No*, the A is not part of C#7 chord
7	Diminished 7th	On	*No*, the A is not part of a Gdim7 chord.

From the seven options listed in Table 11.2, we see that we could harmonize this with a G9 chord (option 1), as shown in Figure 11.11. We could also harmonize the second beat of measure 22 as a D7 (option 2), as shown in Figure 11.12.

Figure 11.12

Example of non-pillar chord harmonization options.

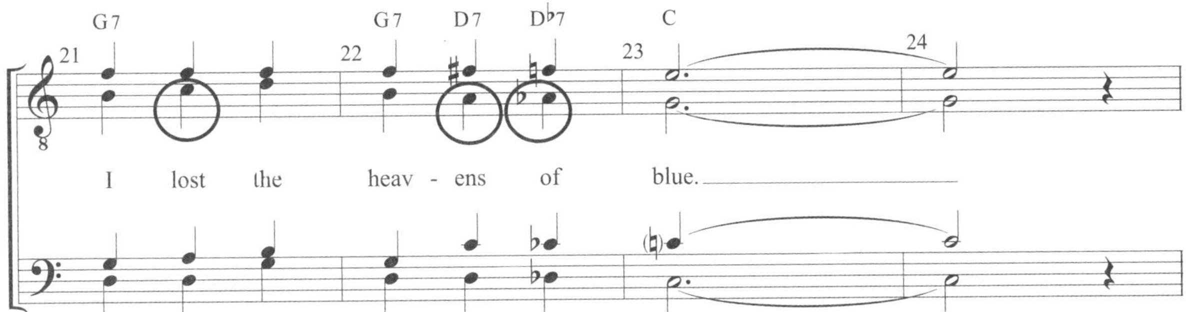

Either one seems like a viable option, but the D7 chord is more strikingly different from the first chord of the measure than the G9 is. There are times when we might prefer that and it often comes down to personal preference, but in this case the stability of maintaining the G7 feel will be our choice and will choose option 1 (G9 chord).

For the second chord in the second measure of figure 11.12, the choices from Table 11.3 are A♭7, Option 5, or D♭7, Option 6. The A♭7 seems a little jarring, particularly because it is the last chord in the measure and in the next measure the primary harmony changes to C.

Table 11.3

Harmonization options for the non-pillar chord, beat 3 in measure 22. Prevailing harmony: G7. Melody note: A♭

Option Number	Chord Type	Distance of Root From Harmonic Pillar	Is this an option?
1	Extended chord (add 6th, 7th, or 9th)	On	*No*, the A♭ cannot be used to extend the G7 chord
2	Barbershop 7th	5th above	*No*, the A♭ is not part of a D7 chord
3	Barbershop 7th	5th below	*No*, the A♭ is not part of a C7 chord
4	Barbershop 7th	Semitone below	*No*, the A♭ is not part of a F#7 chord
5	Barbershop 7th	Semitone above	*Yes*, the A♭ is the root of an A7 (G#7) chord
6	Barbershop 7th	Tritone	*Yes*, the A♭ is the fifth of the D♭7 chord
7	Diminished 7th	On	*No*, the A♭ is not part of a Gdim7 chord.

Figure 11.13

Example of non-pillar chord harmonization option.

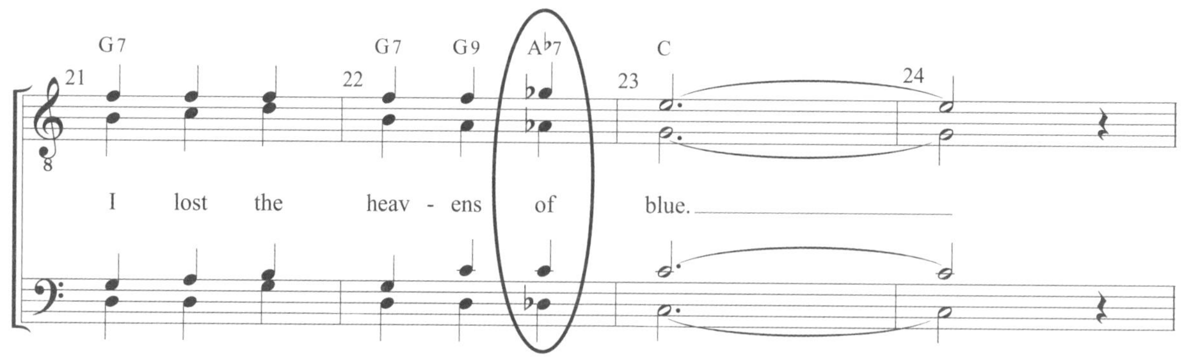

Figure 11.14

Example of non-pillar chord harmonization option.

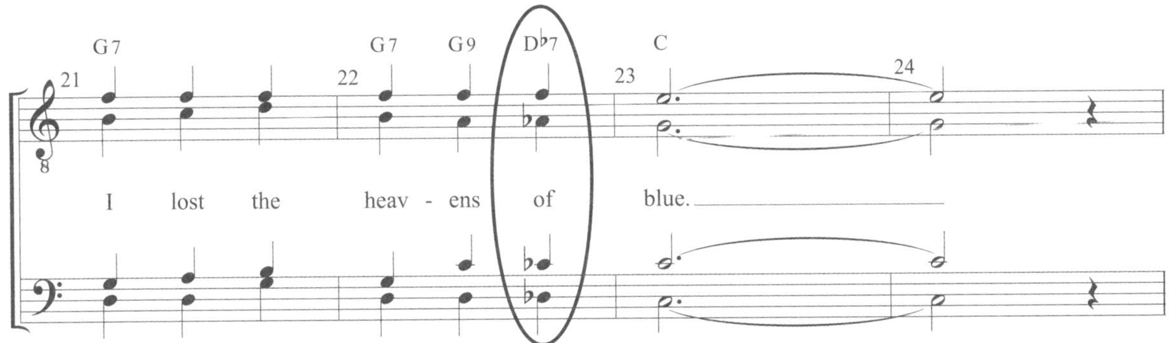

D♭7, as shown in Figure 11.14, works better because it has two notes in common with the G7 chord (the tritone of F and B, or C♭)—so it is closely related to the G7. As a barbershop 7th whose root is a semitone above the harmonic pillar of the next measure, it feels like it fits in measure 22 and it moves smoothly into measure 23.

Returning to the first circled note in measure 21, the C on beat 2, the choices appear to be D7, Option 2 from Table 11.1, C7, Option 3, or A♭7, Option 5. Of all these choices, the A♭7 and especially the C7 sound jarring.

Table 11.4

Harmonization options for the non-pillar chord, beat 2 in measure 21. Prevailing harmony: G7. Melody note: C

Option Number	Chord Type	Distance of Root From Harmonic Pillar	Is this an option?
1	Extended chord (add 6th, 7th, or 9th)	On	*No*, the C cannot be used to extend the G7 chord
2	Barbershop 7th	5th above	*Yes*, the C is the seventh of a D7 chord
3	Barbershop 7th	5th below	*Yes*, the C is the root of a C7 chord
4	Barbershop 7th	Semitone below	*No*, the C is not part of an F#7 chord
5	Barbershop 7th	Semitone above	*Yes*, the C is the third of an A♭7 (G#7) chord
6	Barbershop 7th	Tritone	*No*, the C is not part of D♭7 chord
7	Diminished 7th	On	*No*, the C is not part of a Gdim7 chord.

Figure 11.15

Example of non-pillar chord harmonization, option 3.

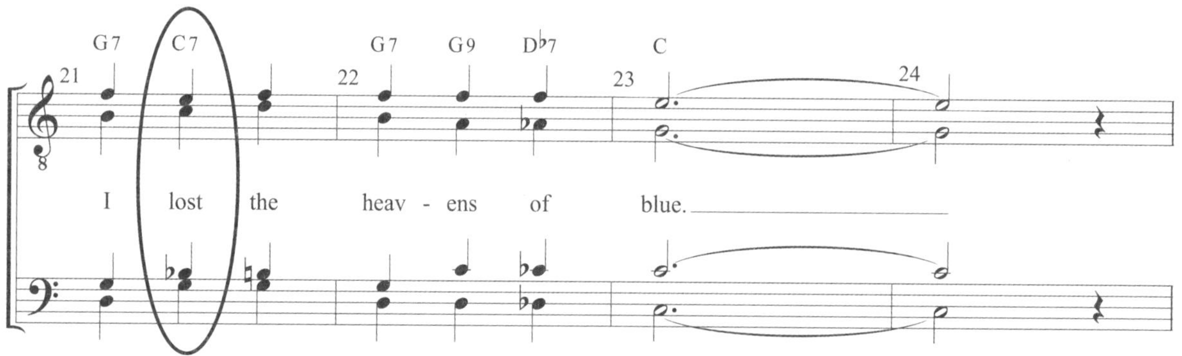

Figure 11.16

Example of non-pillar chord harmonization, option 5.

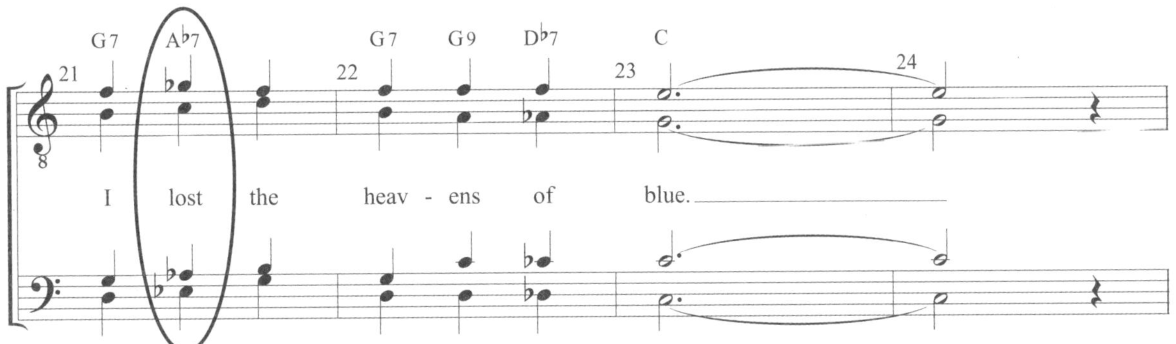

The D7 in the second beat of the first measure in figure 11.17 sounds okay, but the same problem occurs when considering a D7 for the first circled note in the next measure, as shown in Figure 11.12; this chord is strikingly different from the first and last chords of the measure.

Figure 11.17

Example of non-pillar chord harmonization, option 2.

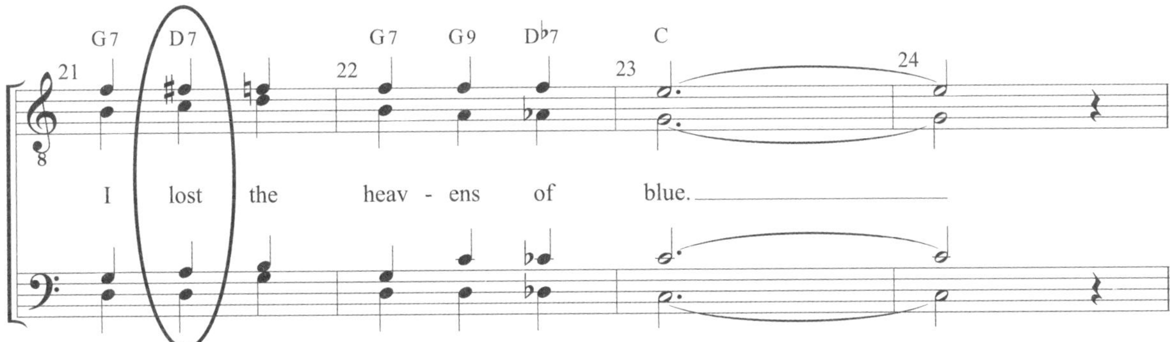

These choices might sound good, but there is another option: extending the harmonic pillar by adding the 11th. This wasn't listed as a choice in Table 11.1 because 11th chords aren't part of the barbershop chord vocabulary. 11th chords also generally consist of five chord tones: root, 5th, 7th, 9th and 11th. However, if the root is omitted, a commonly used barbershop substitution for the 11th chord—sometimes called the sus4 chord—is left. This chord is the *minor 7th* whose root is a 5th above the harmonic pillar, in this case a Dmin7. This choice sounds much smoother, primarily because the tenor note remains straight across on the F rather than move up to the F# on the second chord.

Figure 11.18

Examples of non-pillar chord harmonization, 11th chord extension yielding a minor-minor 7th a fifth above the harmonic pillar.

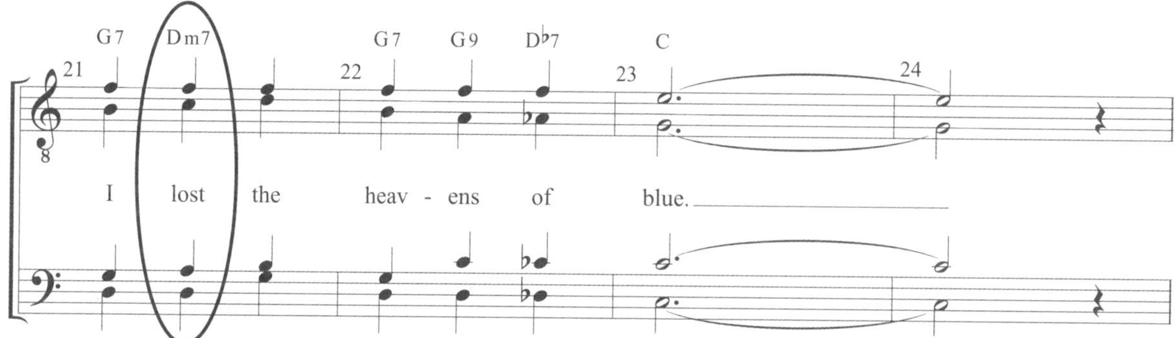

The Dmin7 has two notes in common with the G7 (the Bass D and the Tenor F) chord, making the Dmin7 a commonly used chord as an extension of the G7 harmonic pillar (it sounds very similar to the G9 chord we ended up using on the second circled note.

Following these rules and, using your musical instincts, you'll be able to write a harmonization that is singable and sounds natural. That is a significant achievement, so don't worry about embellishments now. And when considering the various options, take the time to listen to each and decide if it is a pleasing choice in context. Just because one of the options includes the circled melody note doesn't mean it is a good choice. On the other hand, sometimes there will be more than one option that sounds good and then it is up to you to choose based on your personal preference.

The harmonic pillars do not have to be exactly what the published sheet music used. Sometimes there are multiple options that all feel natural, in which case it is personal preference. In other cases, there may be a progression of chords that appear to work in that they accommodate most of the melody notes, but it just doesn't sound like the song, and this makes the listener uncomfortable.

In the Scottish Folk Song, "Annie Laurie", the bridge repeats the same sequence of melody notes, implying the following harmony (I - V7 - I):

Figure 11.19

Excerpt from "Annie Laurie," arrangement by Steve Tramack with traditional chord pillars.

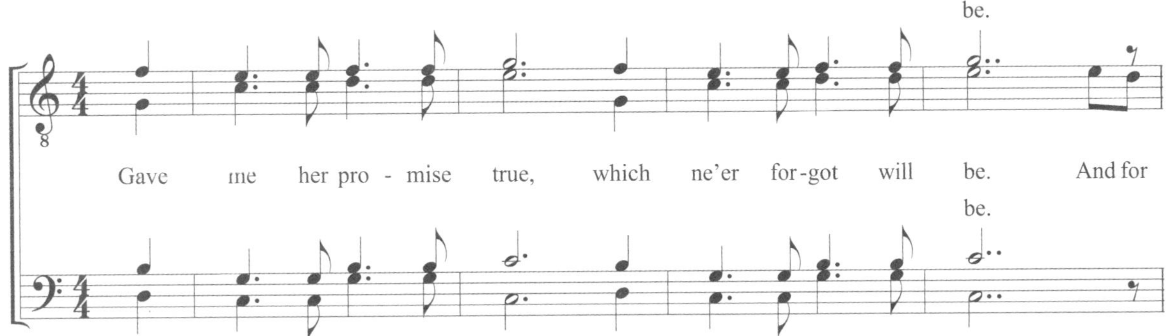

The melody notes would also imply the following harmonization (I—III7—vi), which, when used the second time, leads to the approach in Figure 11.20, providing more variety while still feeling comfortable to the ear.

Figure 11.20

Excerpt from "Annie Laurie," arrangement by Steve Tramack with alternate chord pillars.

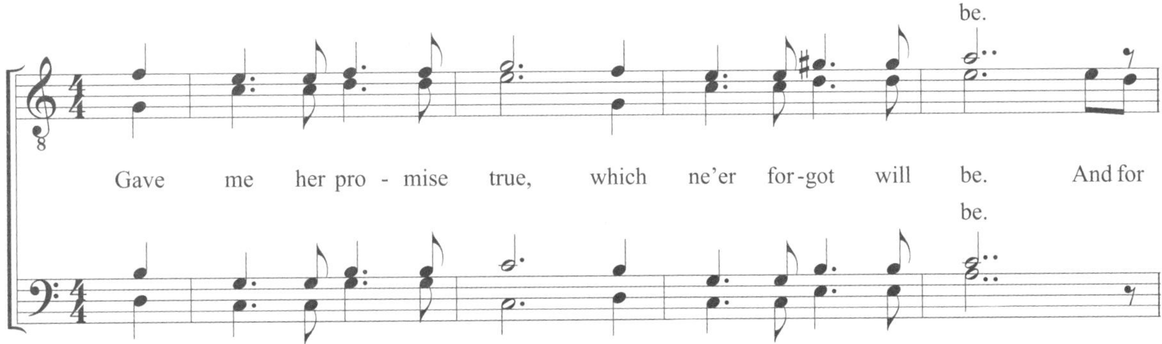

You'll find some additional examples in chapter 16 of *Arranging Barbershop,* Vol. 2, Harmonic Rhythm.

Case Study

The following case study looks at the development of the barbershop arrangement, fleshing out the steps outlined above. Once you have identified the harmonic pillars, write out the melody in the lead part and add in the names of the chords at the points where the pillars change.

Figure 11.21

Melody of "When I Lost You," by Irving Berlin with identified harmonic pillars.

2
When I Lost You
E G7 C B7
you. I lost the sun - shine and ros -
G7 C
es, I lost the heav - ens of blue.
A7 Dmin D7
I lost the beau - ti - ful rain - bow, I lost the
G7 C
morn - ing dew. I lost the an - gel who

Next, identify non-chord tones. For now, if the melody note is part of the chord you have identified as the harmonic pillar, you will use that chord. When you advance beyond writing harmonizations to full-blown arrangements with use of embellishments to create interest and development in the musical performance, you may well choose an alternate chord, but that will come later.

Figure 11.22

"When I Lost You," by Irving Berlin. Melody with harmonic pillars and identified non-chord tones.

WHEN I LOST YOU

Words and Music by
IRVING BERLIN

Arrangement by
STEVEN ARMSTRONG

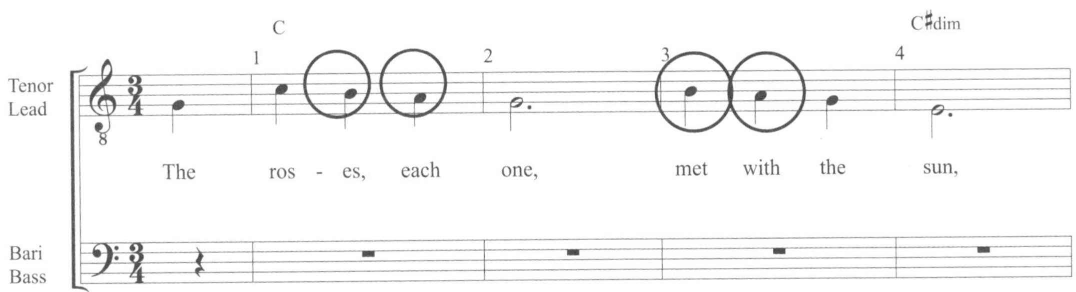

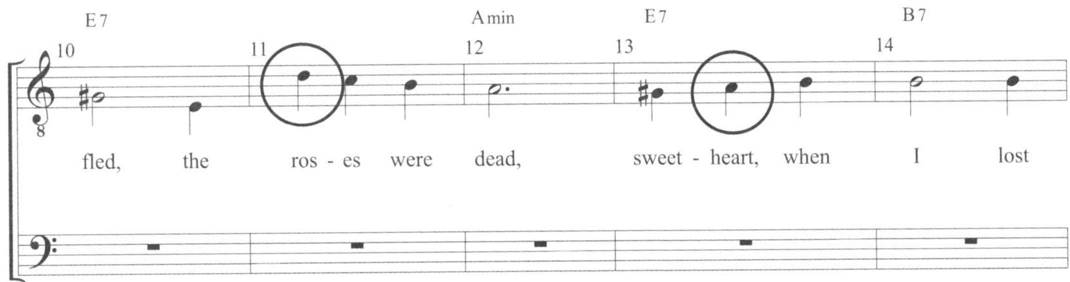

2

E
G7
C
B7
15
16
17
18
19
you.
I lost the sun - shine and ros -

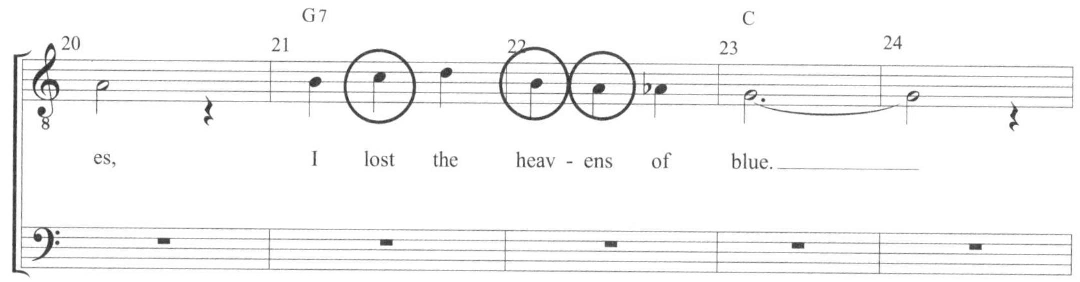
G7
C
20
21
22
23
24
es,
I lost the heav - ens of blue.

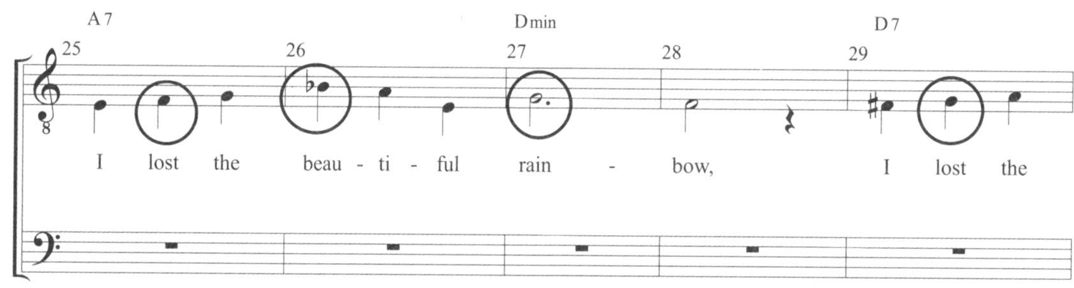
A7
Dmin
D7
25
26
27
28
29
I lost the beau - ti - ful rain - bow,
I lost the

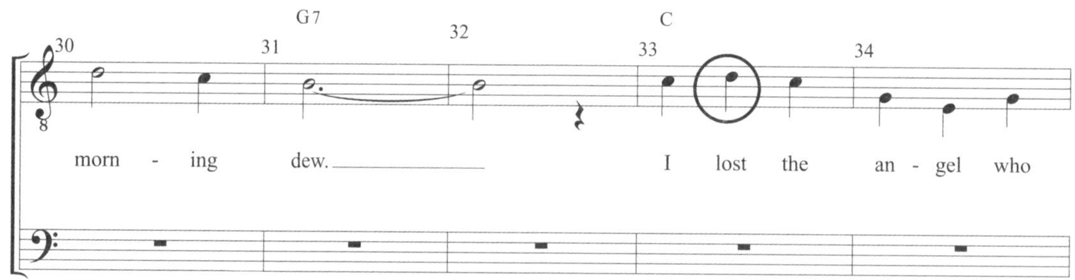
G7
C
30
31
32
33
34
morn - ing dew.
I lost the an - gel who

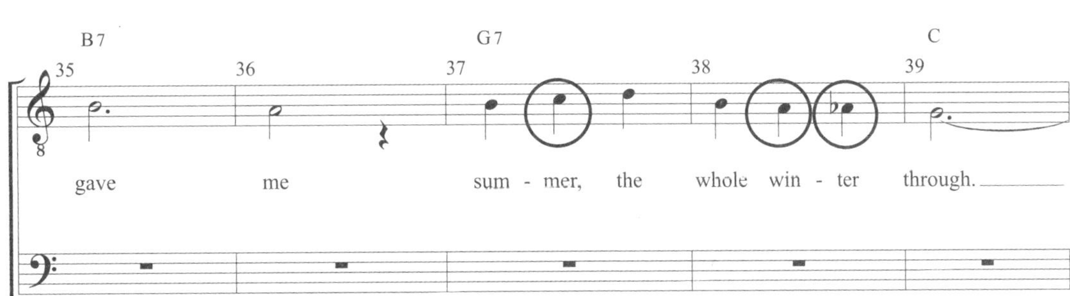
3
B7
G7
C
35
36
37
38
39
gave me sum - mer, the whole win - ter through.

A7
D7
40
41
42
43
44
I lost the glad - ness that turned in - to sad - ness when

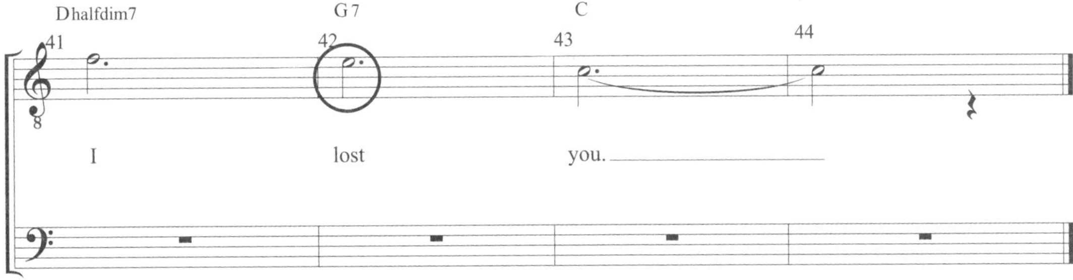
Dhalfdim7
G7
C
41
42
43
44
I lost you.

Harmonize the Bass Line

Next, write in the bass notes for any melody notes that are part of the harmonic pillar.

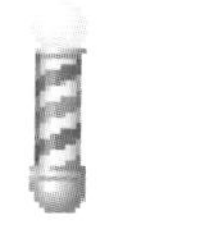	Keep in mind that for triads, the bass is usually on the root. With seventh chords, the bass is either on the root or fifth. The bass note on the root or fifth is considered a strong voicing and is easier for barbershoppers to tune.

Strive for a smooth, easy-to-sing line. If a choice exists of changing the note when the measure changes or within the measure, it is usually best to have the note change at the beginning. This adds strength to the listener's perception of the harmonic rhythm.

Figure 11.23

"When I Lost You," by Irving Berlin with lead and bass harmonization of melody notes within the harmonic pillars.

WHEN I LOST YOU

Words and Music by
IRVING BERLIN

Arrangement by
STEVEN ARMSTRONG

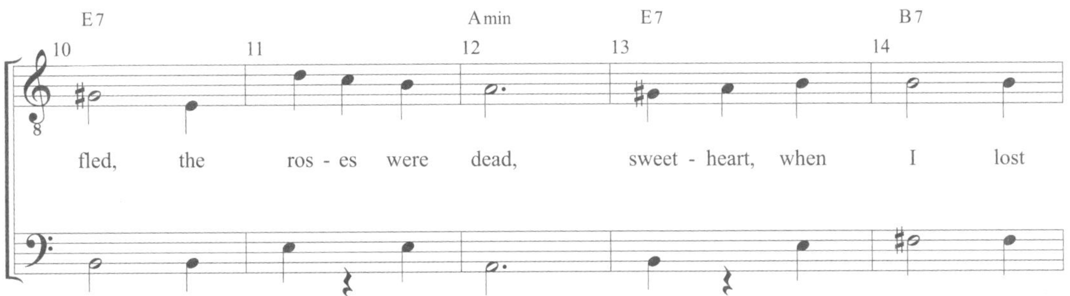

2

When I Lost You

E G7 C B7

15 16 17 18 19

you. I lost the sun - shine and ros -

G7 C

20 21 22 23 24

es, I lost the heav - ens of blue.

A7 Dmin D7

25 26 27 28 29

I lost the beau - ti - ful rain - bow, I lost the

G7 C

30 31 32 33 34

morn - ing dew. I lost the an - gel who

Harmonize the Tenor Line

Next, write in the tenor part, filling in one of the remaining parts of the chord. Again, being sure to write smooth, easy-to-sing lines.

Figure 11.24

"When I Lost You," by Irving Berlin. Lead, bass, and tenor harmonizations of melody notes within the harmonic pillars.

Note that most of the contiguous tenor notes are either a repeated note, or intervals of a third or less. Things were going well until measure 11, as shown in Figure 11.25. At this point, the only two available tenor notes are a G#, which would make an awkward jump of a tritone, or B, which would mean taking the tenor below the lead.

Figure 11.25

"When I Lost You," by Irving Berlin. Tenor harmonization challenge.

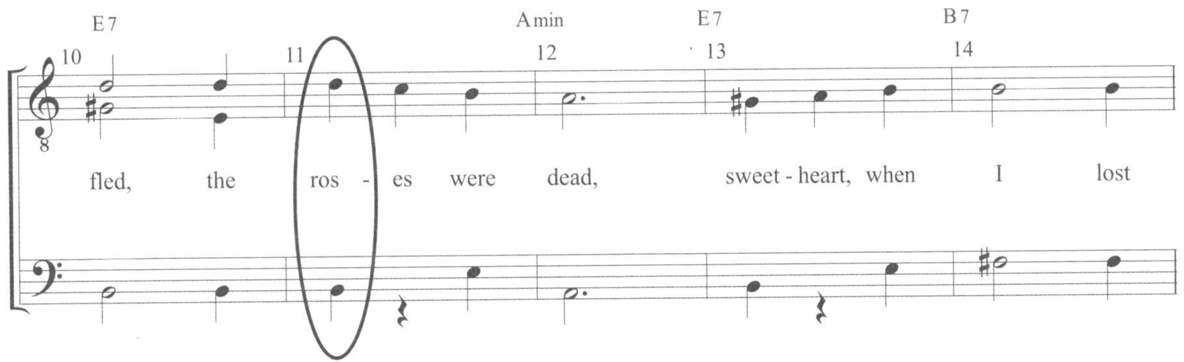

The problem can be solved if we adjust what we had written in the bass line and put the bass on the B (the fifth) instead of E. That will allow us to put the tenor on an E, making a nice smooth line.

Figure 11.26

"When I Lost You," by Irving Berlin. Lead, bass, and tenor harmonizations of melody notes within the harmonic pillars.

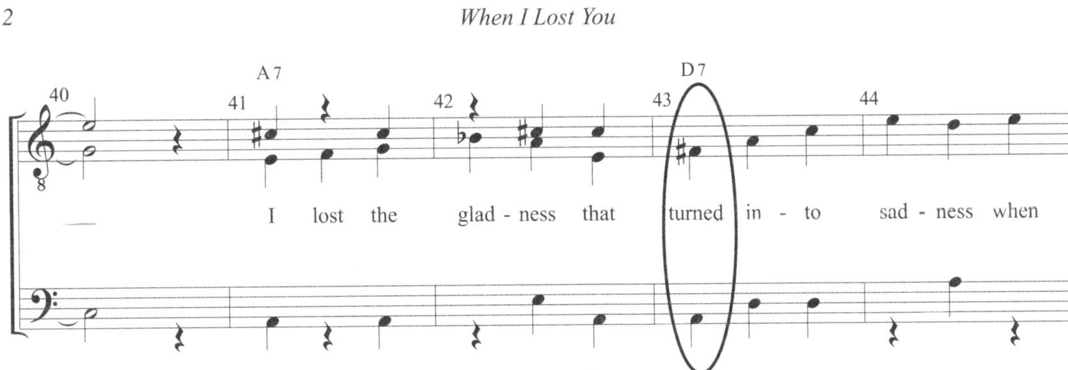

We run into the same sort of problem in measure 42, as shown in Figure 11.27. We could put the tenor on a C for the first two quarter notes, but then it would require a tritone jump up to an F# on beat three or taking the tenor below the lead on that chord. If we change the bass note on beat one to be an A, we can again make for a smoother tenor line.

Figure 11.27

"When I Lost You," by Irving Berlin. Lead, bass, and tenor harmonizations of melody notes within the harmonic pillars.

Harmonize the Baritone Line

Now it is time to complete the chord by adding the baritone part. Be careful that you don't inadvertently double notes of a 4-part chord (which means leaving one of the notes out). The barbershop baritone is used to having lines that jump around a little, but we still want to avoid difficult-to-sing lines.

Figure 11.28

"When I Lost You," by Irving Berlin with four-part harmonizations of melody notes within the harmonic pillars.

WHEN I LOST YOU

2
When I Lost You
E G7 C B7
15 16 17 18 19
you. I lost the sun - shine and ros -
G7 C
20 21 22 23 24
es, I lost the heav - ens of blue.
A7 Dmin D7
25 26 27 28 29
I lost the beau - ti - ful rain - bow, I lost the
G7 C
30 31 32 33 34
morn - ing dew. I lost the an - gel who

We made it almost all the way through without running into any problems but when we come to measure 43, as shown in Figure 11.28, the only remaining note is a C. The low C would sound too muddy, and the higher C makes for an interval of a 6th. This could be sung by a baritone, but it is worth looking to see if there is an option that leads to a smoother line. Since this is leading into a higher melody line and, in fact, the climax of the melody, we might want to consider higher voicings here.

A natural spot to do this would be at measure 41, as shown in Figure 11.29, so instead of the tenor and baritone coming down from their previous notes they may go up a little. If we do that, we end up with this, which is a nice smooth line for everybody.

Figure 11.29

"When I Lost You," by Irving Berlin with modified harmonizations of melody notes within the harmonic pillars.

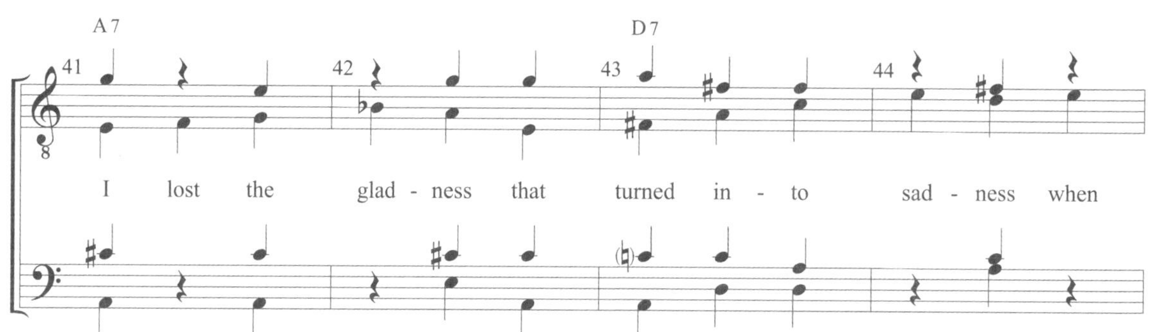

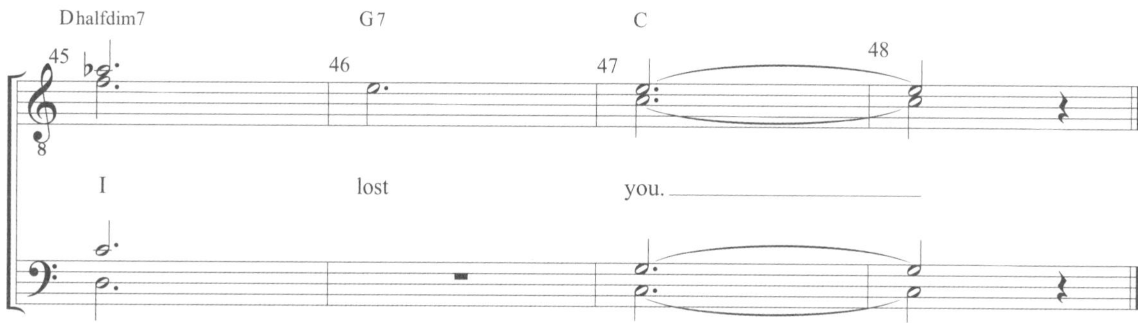

Harmonize Non-Chord Tones

The next step is to determine how to harmonize these non-pillar chord notes. For each note, consider the following options. It is best to play each one on a keyboard or plug them into your music notation software and play it back so you can hear what it sounds like. As a reminder, the options are shown in Table 11.5.

Table 11.5

Chord choices for non-pillar chord notes.

Option Number	Chord Type	Distance of Root From Harmonic Pillar
1	Extended chord (add 6th, 7th, or 9th)	On
2	Barbershop 7th	5th above
3	Barbershop 7th	5th below
4	Barbershop 7th	Semitone below
5	Barbershop 7th	Semitone above
6	Barbershop 7th	Tritone
7	Diminished 7th	On

Let's look at some of the non-pillar notes in our example and consider the options. Since bars 1 and 3 each have two non-pillar notes, let's start by looking at measure 5 (we'll come back to bars 1 and 3) and consider each of the seven options above. The harmonic pillar is a G7, and the melody note is an A.

- Can we add this note into the harmonic pillar? ***Yes*, we could use a G9.**
- Can we use the barbershop 7th chord whose root is a 5th above the root of the harmonic pillar? ***Yes*, we could use a D7.**
- Can we use the barbershop 7th chord whose root is a 5th below the root of the harmonic pillar? *No*, the melody note A is not in a C7 chord.
- Can we use the barbershop 7th chord whose root is a semitone below the root of the harmonic pillar? *No*, the melody note A is not in an F#7 chord.
- Can we use the barbershop 7th chord whose root is a semitone above the root of the harmonic pillar? *No*, the melody note A is not in an A♭7 chord.
- Can we use the barbershop 7th chord whose root is a tritone away from the root of the harmonic pillar? *No*, the melody note A is not in a C#7 chord.
- Can we use the diminished 7th chord that shares the same root as the harmonic pillar? *No*, the melody note A is not in a G dim 7 chord.

So, we have two options to consider:

Figure 11.30

"When I Lost You," by Irving Berlin with option 1 for harmonizing the non-chord tone.

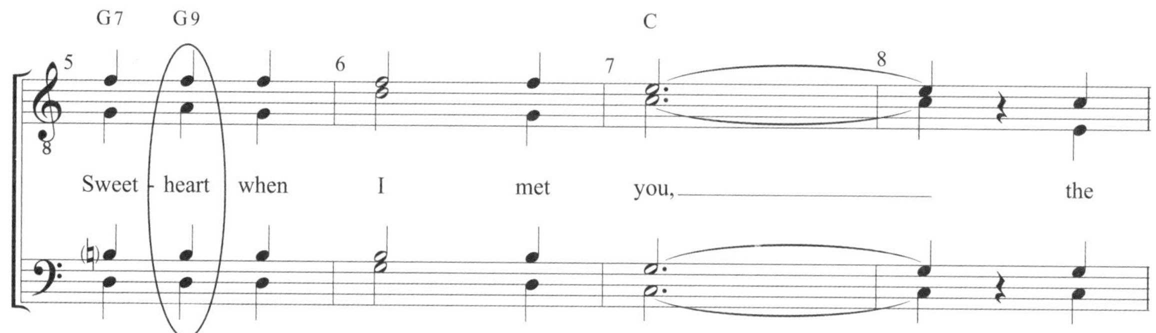

Figure 11.31

"When I Lost You," by Irving Berlin with option 2 for harmonizing the non-chord tone.

Either could work, but the first option, shown in Figure 11.30, just feels a little smoother. Let's go with that.

Next let's look at measure 9 and again consider each of the 7 options. The harmonic pillar is an A min, and the melody note is a B.

- Can this note be added into the harmonic pillar? *No*, B can't be added to A min and make a chord in the barbershop chord vocabulary.
- Can we use the barbershop 7th chord whose root is a 5th above the root of the harmonic pillar? ***Yes*, we could use an E7**
- Can we use the barbershop 7th chord whose root is a 5th below the root of the harmonic pillar? *No*, the melody note B is not in a D7 chord.
- Can we use the barbershop 7th chord whose root is a semitone below the root of the harmonic pillar? *No*, the melody note B is not in a G#7 chord.

- Can we use the barbershop 7th chord whose root is a semitone above the root of the harmonic pillar? *No*, the melody note B is not in a B♭7 chord.
- Can we use the barbershop 7th chord whose root is a tritone away from the root of the harmonic pillar? *No*, the melody note B is not in an E♭7 chord.
- Can we use the diminished 7th chord that shares the same root as the harmonic pillar? *No*, the melody note B is not in an A dim 7 chord.

We only have one choice, but thankfully this one sounds really good and works well.

Figure 11.32

"When I Lost You," by Irving Berlin with option 2 for harmonizing the non-chord tone.

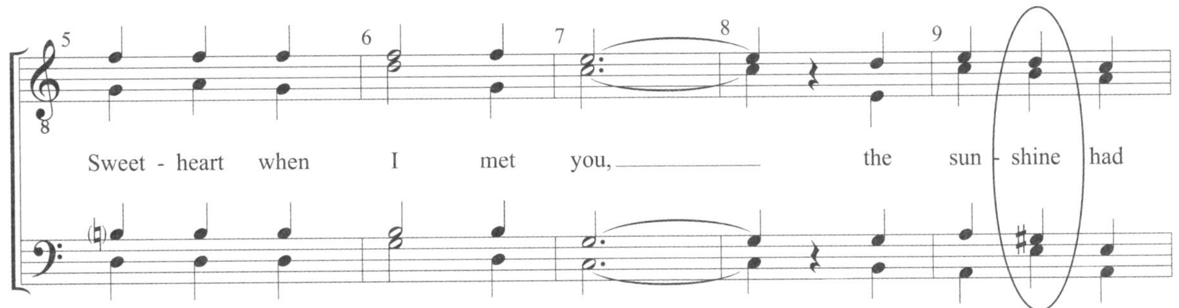

Let's look at another example, in Figure 11.33, measure 13:

Figure 11.33

"When I Lost You," by Irving Berlin with identified harmonic pillars.

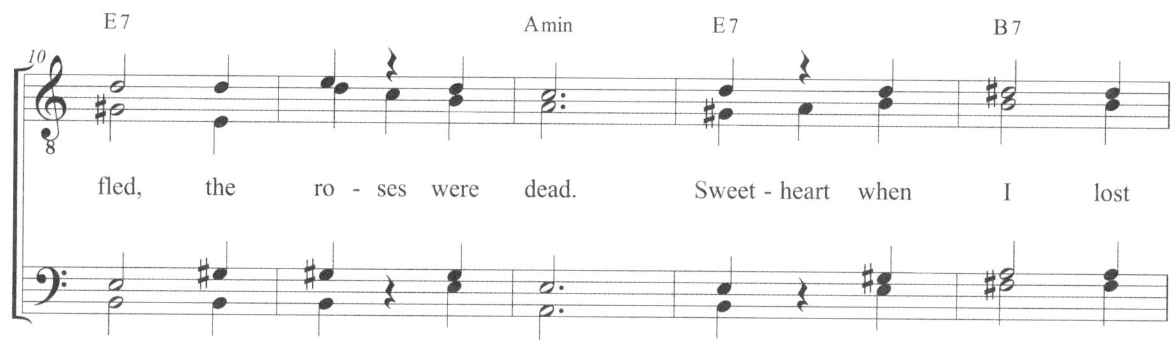

The harmonic pillar is an E7 chord, and the melody note (on "sweet*heart*" in the second beat of measure 13) is an A. Let's look at the seven options, and what the chord would look (and sound, if this is the online version) like:

- Can this note be added into the harmonic pillar? *No*, A can't be added to E7 and make a chord in the barbershop chord vocabulary.
- Can we use the barbershop 7th chord whose root is a 5th above the root of the harmonic pillar? ***Yes*, we could use a B7**.

This feels natural as well:

Figure 11.34

"When I Lost You," by Irving Berlin with option 2 for harmonizing the non-chord tone.

A variation on this theme, which also would work well, would be to use the minor 7th chord (min/min7) whose root is a 5th above the root of the harmonic pillar. In this option, the tenor stays on the D for all three notes in the measure, and the minor seventh seems more appropriate to the lyrical subtext of "sweetheart when I lost you".

Figure 11.35

"When I Lost You," by Irving Berlin with a modified option 2 for harmonizing the non-chord tone.

- Can we use the barbershop 7th chord whose root is a 5th below the root of the harmonic pillar? ***Yes*, the melody note A is the root of the A7 chord.**

This sounds a bit awkward, though the progression works:

Figure 11.36

"When I Lost You," by Irving Berlin with option 3 for harmonizing the non-chord tone.

Sweet - heart when

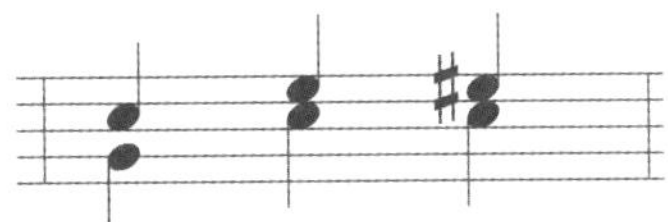

- Can we use the barbershop 7th chord whose root is a semitone below the root of the harmonic pillar? *No*, the melody note A is not in an E♭7 chord.
- Can we use the barbershop 7th chord whose root is a semitone above the root of the harmonic pillar? ***Yes*, the melody note A is in an F7 chord**.

This is an interesting option, though the voice leading for the bass and baritone may be tricky:

Figure 11.37

"When I Lost You," by Irving Berlin with option 5 for harmonizing the non-chord tone.

Sweet - heart when

- Can we use the barbershop 7th chord whose root is a tritone away from the root of the harmonic pillar? *No*, the melody note A is not in an A#7 chord.
- Can we use the diminished 7th chord that shares the same root as the harmonic pillar? *No*, the melody note A is not in an E dim 7 chord.

Which option should you choose? Several factors are at play. Which option best conveys the subtext of the musical line? Which tug at the listener's ear less or more than others, which should weigh into your decision. Which is easiest to sing, particularly considering this is on a weak beat in the measure, in the middle of a phrase? All these factors play a role in determining what's right for this chart.

Time to try some for yourself! What options would be available in measures 8, 24, 27, 30 and 31? From the available options, what do you choose?

Figure 11.38

"When I Lost You," by Irving Berlin. Worksheet for practicing harmonization.

WHEN I LOST YOU

Words and Music by
IRVING BERLIN

Arrangement by
STEVEN ARMSTRONG

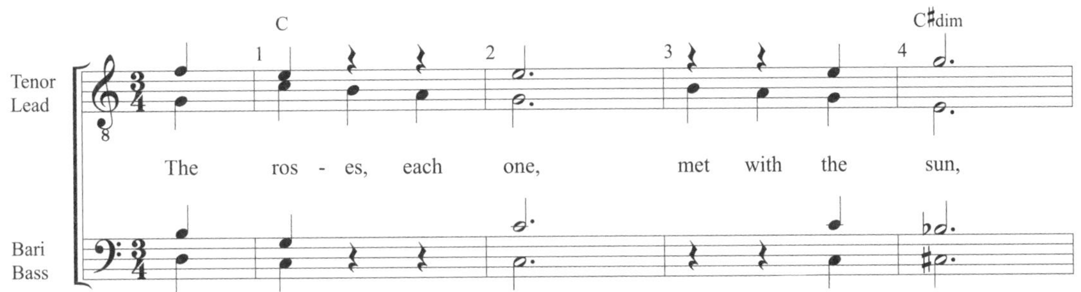

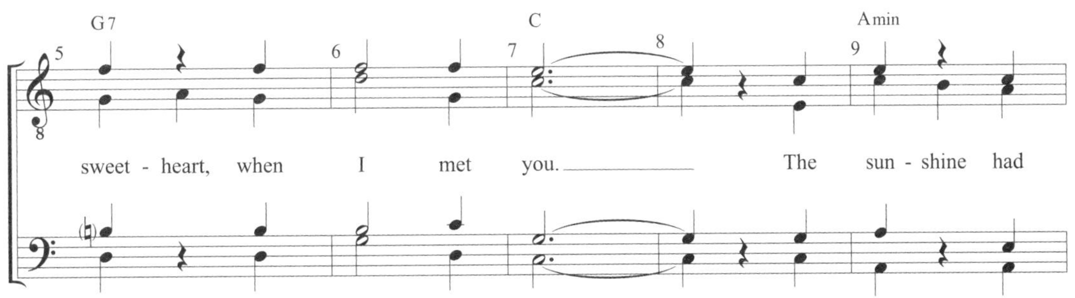

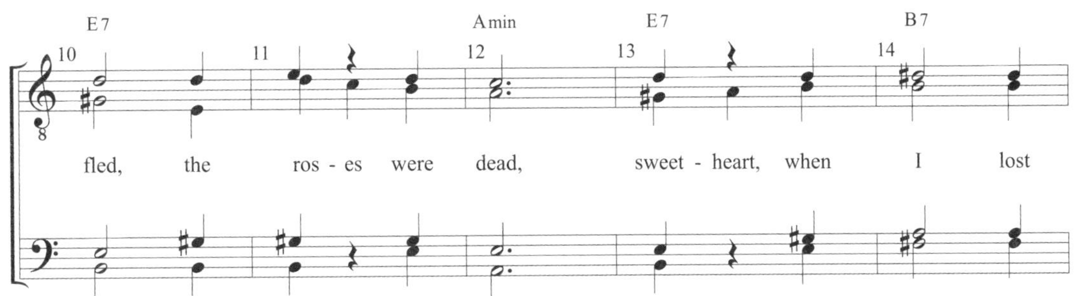

2
When I Lost You
E G7 C B7
15 16 17 18 19
you. I lost the sun - shine and ros -
G7 C
20 21 22 23 24
es, I lost the heav - ens of blue.
A7 Dmin D7
25 26 27 28 29
I lost the beau - ti - ful rain - bow, I lost the
G7 C
30 31 32 33 34
morn - ing dew. I lost the an - gel who

Let's now look at a completed version of the chart.

Figure 11.39

"When I Lost You," by Irving Berlin. Completed arrangement from the Harmony University Beginning Arranging Class, 2019.

WHEN I LOST YOU

Words and Music by
IRVING BERLIN

Arrangement by
STEVEN ARMSTRONG

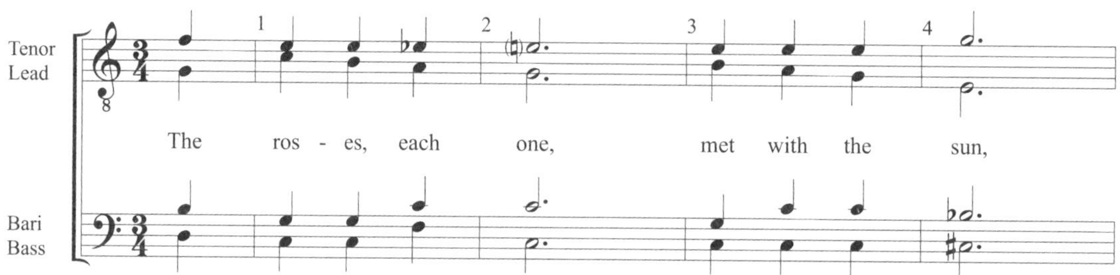

2
When I Lost You

15
16
17
18
19
you.
I lost the sun - shine and ros -

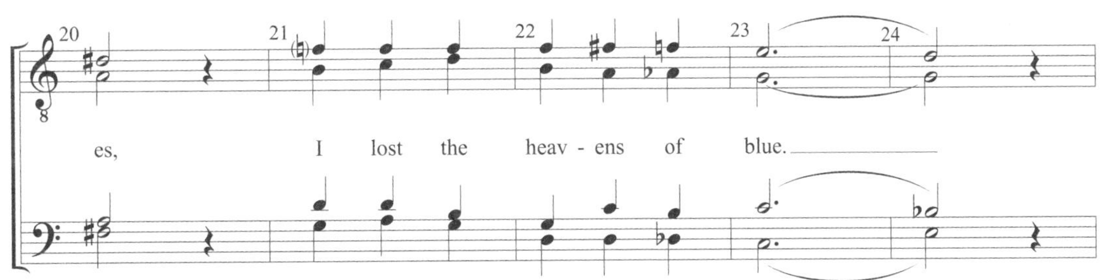
20
21
22
23
24
es,
I lost the heav - ens of blue.

25
26
27
28
29
I lost the beau - ti - ful rain - bow,
I lost the

30
31
32
33
34
morn - ing dew.
I lost the an - gel who

Conclusion

Harmonizing a melody in the barbershop style is both an art and a science. There are seven steps to follow when writing a harmonization: 1) melody and lyrics, 2) identify harmonic pillars, 3) identify non-pillar melody notes, 4) bass harmony, 5) tenor harmony, 6) baritone harmony, and 7) identify potential harmonies for non-pillar notes.

Considering the harmonic rhythm—the rate of change of the harmony—and the harmonic pillars—the prevailing harmony which designates the mileposts for the harmonic rhythm—is an important first step. These harmonic pillars are often found above the staff in printed sheet music and can be further validated by the melody notes within that measure.

Once identifying the harmonic pillars, the next step is identifying which melody notes fall outside that pillar. The harmonization process involves identifying and considering choices for harmonizing those non-chord tones while maintaining good voice leading and pleasing harmonic flow. This chapter reviewed these rules starting with Table 11.1.

Starting with the bass harmony and establishing strong voicing—root position and second inversion chords wherever possible—creates a solid foundation for the barbershop style. Baritone and tenor harmonies are often dictated by a combination of identifying the remaining notes in complete chords and voicing leading considerations.

Chapter 12 applies all the concepts from Vol 1 of *Arranging Barbershop* to look at an arrangement from concept to the stage. It introduces several concepts which will be detailed in Vol. 2 of *Arranging Barbershop*, The Arranging Journey.

Chapter 12. The Arranging Process, Applied: Case Study of "It Had to Be You"

By Steve Tramack

Introduction

In this chapter, we'll focus on the arranging process starting with the creation of a blueprint of the chart prior to writing a single chord. We'll then follow the progress of applying this blueprint to an arrangement of "It Had to Be You," arranged for a mixed quartet (Alto-Alto-Tenor-Bass, or AATB). This arrangement was inspired by a duet performance by Michael Bublé and Barbra Streisand. *YouTube*.

The song was written in 1924 by Gus Kahn and Isham Jones and has been featured in movies such as *When Harry Met Sally, A League of Their Own*, and *Annie Hall.* Aside from the Streisand/Bublé duet, performers ranging from Frank Sinatra, Louis Armstrong, Carrie Underwood, Rod Stewart, and Harry Connick Jr. have put their stamp on this song. The song is versatile, supporting several delivery styles from freeform or rubato ballad, to slow swing, to up-tempo shuffle. This provides great latitude to the arranger in developing a chart specifically to match the intended group's strengths.

As a recap, the high-level arranging process is:

1. Find a song to arrange
2. Consider the performer for whom you're arranging
3. Plan the journey by building a blueprint
4. Embark on the journey by laying down the melody and begin developing the arrangement

We're going to focus just on the first three steps, summarize the fourth, and then deep dive into the final version of the chart in this case study.

Find a Song

As an arranger, sometimes you find a song, and sometimes the song finds you. Even when presented with a song to arrange by an ensemble, determining the approach, as outlined in Chapter 7, and sources of inspiration all contribute to the arranging finding the song.

For this case study, we'll review an arrangement specifically developed for Sweet & Sour Quartet. This quartet consisted, at the time, of three siblings and a fiancé: two sisters on lead and tenor, their brother on bass, and the lead's fiancé (now her spouse) on baritone. It was arranged by their father (me) to be sung at the wedding.

There are multiple versions of the song which were considered as part of the arranging process. These include:

- Harry Connick Jr.'s version from the "When Harry Met Sally" soundtrack, found here. This version is upbeat, with an orchestral introduction which feels separate thematically from the rest of the song.

It does create a sense of grandeur and anticipation, leading into a rather simplified first chorus (singer + piano + small combo), which continues to grow and build to the full orchestra in chorus two.

- Frank Sinatra's classic version, found here. Frank's version features the verse, sung with a slower rubato delivery and a sense of all the pain and tribulations Frank endured in various relationships through the years. During a review of this chapter, the brilliant arranger Anthony Bartholomew observed how the underlying melancholy in the romantic jazz adds an additional emotional layer to the performance. The difference in texture and tone of the song as we emerge from the verse into the first "It Had to Be You" parallels Sinatra emerging from the pain and tribulations in his life. The "wonderful you" clearly honors the person that helped him to do so.
- Tony Bennett's incredible version from the MTV Unplugged series, found here. Tony's version, almost freeform in nature, focuses largely on the lyrics. Anthony Bartholomew, in his review of this chapter, observed how this short and sweet performance focuses more on the crooning and lyrics delivered in a rubato fashion, rather than the emotional content. To the point, this reinforces the timeless cool, hip nature of Tony Bennett, more so than telling a story. This kind of approach can also inform choices (including structure, rhythmic treatment, chord vocabulary, etc.) made by the arranger.
- Michael Bublé and Barbra Streisand's version, which ultimately served as the primary inspiration for the arrangement, is located here. In addition to the melody-passing duet, this version blended some of the rhythmic energy from the Connick Jr. version, Sinatra's emotional journey from past to present (and future), and cool factor from Tony Bennett. Several of the arrangement's elements, including the interlude and tag orchestration feel, the rhythmic figures and the key changes, were directly adapted from the Bublé/Streisand version.

Barbershop Style

As a quick summary, there are a handful of shared elements of the barbershop style. Arrangements featuring these elements, the previously referred immutable laws of barbershop, are easily recognizable by fans of the style, even if they are unfamiliar with the music theory aspects.

> *Always*: 1) Four-part a cappella texture; 2) Characteristic chord progressions, with featured secondary dominants.
>
> *Most of the time*: 1) Melody in an inside voice, meaning harmony above and below the melody; 2) Lyrics sung by all four parts as opposed to solo plus neutral syllables.
>
> *Other arrangement choices*: 1) Expanded sound enabled by choice of voicing, inversions, chord vocabulary, and homorhythmic textures; 2) Balanced form; 3) Embellishments; 4) Construction, e.g., tags.

There have been several arrangements of "It Had to Be You" done in the barbershop style, so, in this case, there were no real concerns about whether it would work. It can easily be harmonized with an inside voice melody, features harmonic variety, and several examples of featured secondary dominants which move toward the tonic around the circle of fifths. The lyrics fit well in the style and can be adapted to several different types of delivery approaches.

In this case, I knew the answer before even embarking on the arrangement journey; the only question was how much of the Bublé/Streisand version's inspiration could be captured in this arrangement for Sweet & Sour.

Get the Sheet Music

The sections of form in the chorus of "It Had to Be You" are divided into 8 measure segments. The form is ABAC. Figures 12.1–12.4 displays the form.

Figure 12.1

Excerpt of "It Had to Be You" A section, pickup + 8 measures.

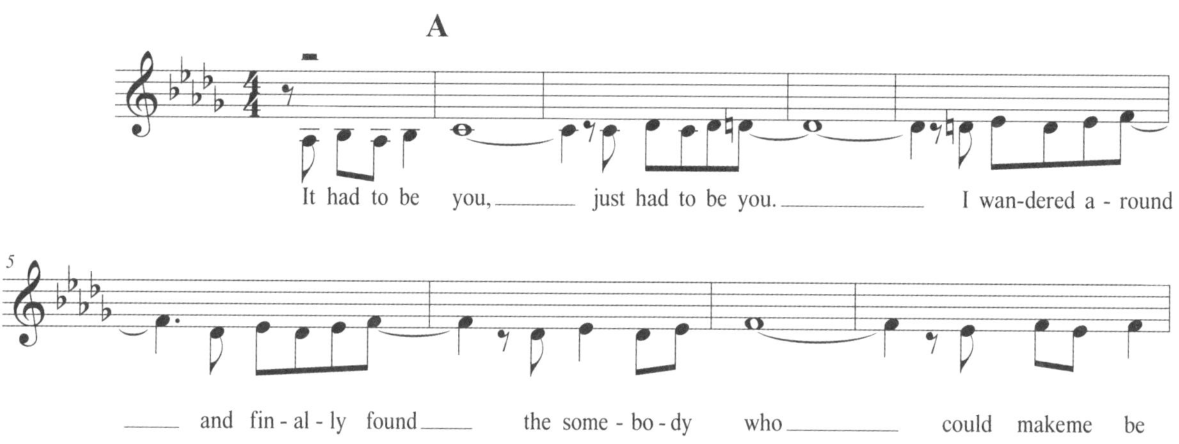

Figure 12.2

Excerpt of "It Had to Be You" B section, 8 measures.

Figure 12.3

Excerpt of "It Had to Be You" return of A section, 8 measures.

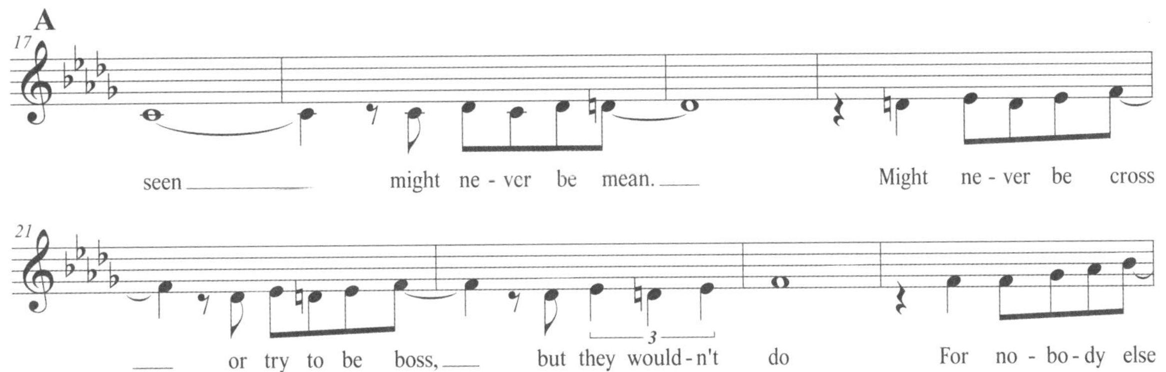

Figure 12.4

Excerpt of "It Had to Be You" C section, 8 measures.

This form provides enough interest to create a complete musical journey without any added material. This journey could include a repeated half chorus, starting with the second A section. The overall form in this case would be ABACAC:

Figure 12.5

Chorus / reprise structure of "It Had to Be You."

Section of form	Lyrics
A	It had to be you, it had to be you. I wandered around and finally found the somebody who, could make me be
B	True, could make me be blue. Or even be glad, just to be sad, thinking of you. Some others I've
A	Seen, might never be mean. Might never be cross, or try to be boss, but they wouldn't do. For nobody
C	Else gave me a thrill. With all your faults, I love you still. It had to be you, marvelous you, it had to be you. It had to be
A	You, it had to be you. I wandered around and finally found the somebody who. For nobody
C	Else gave me a thrill. With all your faults, I love you still. It had to be you, marvelous you, it had to be you.

The original song also features a verse that could easily precede the chorus in an arrangement: verse, chorus (ABAC).

Figure 12.6

Verse / Chorus structure of "It Had to be You."

Section of form	Lyrics
Verse	Why do I do just as you say? Why must I just give you your way? Why do I sigh? Why don't I try to forget? It must have been that something lovers call fate, kept me saying, "I had to wait." I saw them all, just couldn't fall 'til we met.
A	It had to be you, it had to be you. I wandered around and finally found the somebody who, could make me be
B	True, could make me be blue. Or even be glad, just to be sad, thinking of you. Some others I've
A	Seen, might never be mean. Might never be cross, or try to be boss, but they wouldn't do. For nobody
C	Else gave me a thrill. With all your faults, I love you still. It had to be you, marvelous you, it had to be you. Some others I've

There are other considerations for structuring the verse mid-arrangement. These include leveraging two full choruses with the verse sandwiched in between. Possible structures include chorus 1 (ABAC) | verse | chorus 2 (ABAC) or using a half chorus (AC) instead of the second chorus.

Consider the Inherent Harmonies

One of the most important of the immutable laws of barbershop that allows an arrangement to sound like barbershop is related to characteristic chord progressions with featured secondary dominants on a variety of roots. In figure 11.7, "It Had to Be You" is written in the key of C. Note the featured occurrences of the VI7 chord, A7, in the third and fourth measures of the A section.[44]

Figure 12.7

Excerpt of "It Had to Be You" with a secondary dominant (A7) in the displayed measures.

This leads to a D9 chord in the 5th measure of the A section, which could easily support a dominant ninth (D9) pillar.[45]

[44] A featured occurrence of the prevailing harmony is one which matches the harmonic rhythm, or rate of harmonic change, of the song. The harmonic rhythm typically dictates changes every 1–2 measures, though slower songs may dictate a change on the half-measure, or even on a beat itself.

[45] A dominant ninth chord is a combination of the dominant seventh chord (including the minor seventh) and a major ninth. This chord omits the root when used in barbershop arranging. The dominant ninth is different from the Added 9th (or add9) chord, which adds the ninth to a major triad.

Figure 12.8

Excerpt of "It Had to Be You" with a dominant ninth (D9) in the displayed measures.

The inherent progression then moves to V, a G major triad, which logically could also be V7, at the beginning of the B section of the form. From there, rather than progressing back to the tonic, the song moves to the III7, E7, on the words "could make me," and then continues with a circle of fifths progression, noted in Figure 12.9.

Figure 12.9

Excerpt of "It Had to Be You" with secondary dominants in the displayed measures resolving around the circle of fifths.

At the end of the B section (featured by location), the song features a G7 (V7) *pillar*, resolving at the beginning of the next A section to the CMaj7 (IMaj7).

	The harmonic *pillar* refers to the prevailing harmony associated with the melody notes and implied by the chord progression. These pillars most often fall on strong beats (first or third beat of the measure), and define the harmonic rhythm of the song.

Figure 12.10

Excerpt of "It Had to Be You" with secondary dominants in the displayed measures.

The harmonic variety of the song as originally composed —featuring dominant seventh chords on II, III, V and VI—provides both the sense of travel and inherent t*ritonal energy* that we associate with the barbershop style.

Tritones (e.g., the interval between the major third and the flat seventh) are discussed in detail in Chapter 2. The tension between the notes demands onward movement around the circle of fifths, and the practice of leveraging circle of fifths movement which progresses from secondary dominant to secondary dominant was described by prominent arranger Kevin Keller as *tritonal energy*. This harmonic energy, as part of a chord featuring, when in root position or second inversion, both high levels of consonance and tension to move are a characteristic feature of the barbershop style.

Featured Secondary Dominant

You'll notice a featured secondary dominant, a VI7, as the first harmonic pillar change, in the third measure of the first A section, as shown in Figure 11.10. This progression from CMaj7, a IMaj7 pillar, provides tritonal energy to move to an A7, or VI7. Note the raised tonic, a C♯ in the melody, which serves as the major third in the chord, creates a tritone interval with the G (the minor seventh in the A7 chord), as shown in Figure 11.11— from CMaj7 (IMaj7), implies a move to A7, or VI7, shown in Figure 11.11.

Figure 12.11

Excerpt of "It Had to Be You" showing the tritone using a C♯, providing harmonic energy and movement to A7 (VI7).

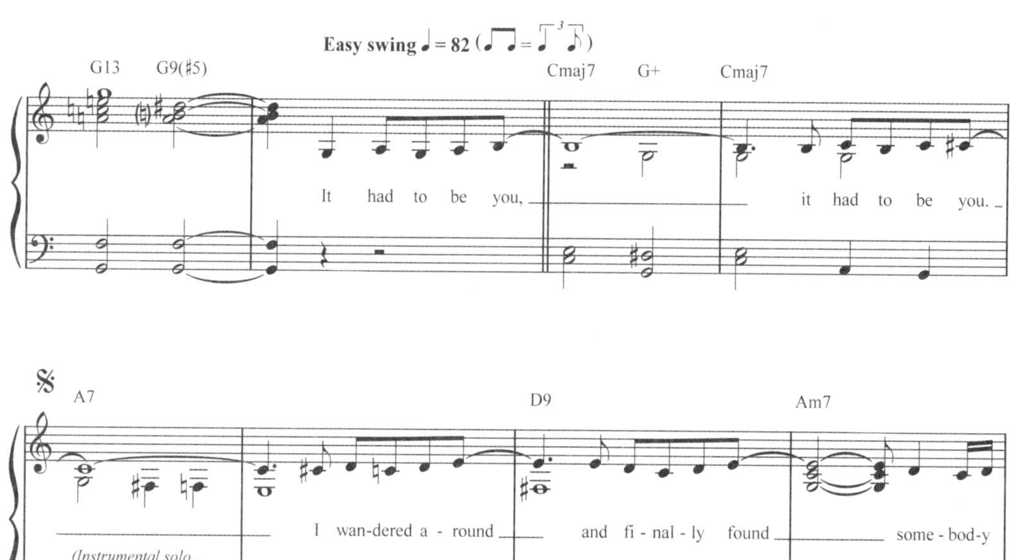

Note the secondary dominant, the E7 (III7), in the bridge, as shown in Figure 12.12. We see a progression from E7 (III7), to Amin (vi).

Figure 12.12

Excerpt of "It Had to Be You" showing the movement from E7 (III7) to Am (vi).

Barbershop features a variety of chords in the style's vocabulary. The Am and proceeding Am7 provide contrast and harmonic variety and match the lyrical subtext of "make me be blue." However, songs that don't feature naturally occurring secondary dominants won't feel as solidly rooted in the style. It's not enough to simply replace a minor seventh with a dominant seventh chord pillar. Imagine doing so in this section of "It Had to Be You;" doing so would change the entire feel of that phrase, and perhaps the entire song. "It Had to Be You" features plenty of secondary dominants (sevenths and ninths), as we've seen thus far, so there's no need to do so in this case. Still, given the inherent variety of secondary dominants, coupled with the fact that the bridge then progresses to II (which could also support a II7 chord without changing the melody), the presence of the minor seventh simply adds more variety to the overall journey of the song.

Is there a D7 chord symbol—note: not Dm7—which then progresses to G7, and then back to C? If so, you have the makings of a solid barbershop arrangement in your hands. In this case, the original sheet music shows D, which could support a D7, progressing through Dm7 to G7. Because the melody spends time on E in these two measures, a D9 (dominant seventh chord with the added ninth, missing the root) is also a feasible choice. The Dm7 harmonic pillar could remain as a D7 and D9, which may feel more rooted in the barbershop style. See Figure 12.13.

Figure 12.13

Example of a II chord (D), progressing to a Dm7, to a G7.

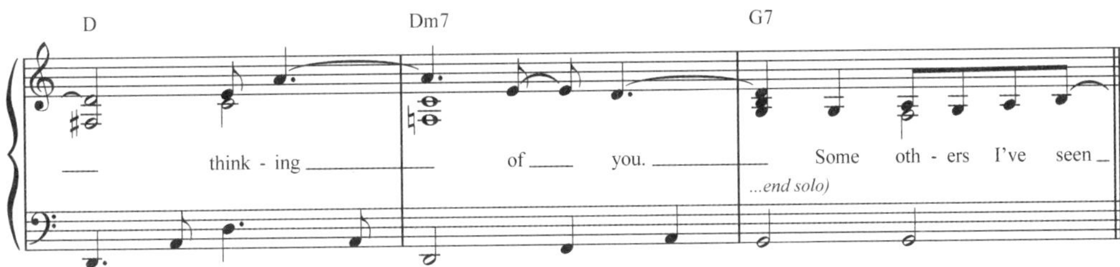

Lyrics

In the case of "It Had to Be You," the lyrics succeed in telling a story of a real relationship: one that includes a range of emotions, complete with conflicts and a realization of what goes into the kind of relationship that can withstand challenges. It speaks about the fact that false, superficial harmony isn't the foundation for a lasting relationship. The internal rhyme scheme provides both interest and contrast, implying dynamics (based on the openness and closedness of the sustained vowels).

> It had to be you, it had to be you
> I wandered around, and finally found the somebody who
> Could make me feel blue, could make me be true
> And even be glad, just to be sad, thinking of you.
>
> Some others I've seen might never be mean
> Might never be cross or try to be boss, but they wouldn't do
> For nobody else gave me a thrill. With all your faults, I love you still
> It had to be you, wonderful you, it had to be you.

Consider Who You're Arranging For

Here is the list of questions that I use in considering choices in a commissioned arrangement:

1. *What is the intended use?* Is this expected to be a contest arrangement? BHS contest rules dictate certain arranging choices which map closely to the immutable laws of barbershop.[46] An arrangement intended for a BHS contest, or another barbershop organization's contest, such as Sweet Adelines International (SAI), will greatly impact chord vocabulary and texture choices.

   Is this arrangement intended to be a featured show closer, where the group will spend a great deal of rehearsal time learning and developing the song? This could impact how much development is included in the arrangement.

   Is this going to be used for a single event or single season as a filler song, and thus won't get much rehearsal time? You may decide to feature less variety from chorus to chorus and simplified texture choices than you would with a song intended to be a featured part of the ensemble's repertoire.

   In the case of *It Had to Be You,* the quartet intended to use it during the wedding ceremony, as a contest song, and as material for a recording. Thus, the chart needed to comply with current—as of 2022—BHS contest rules and needed to provide the kind of development opportunities indicative of a featured performance.

2. *Is there a reference performance of the song that you'd like to capture?* Especially when arranging standards from the Great American Songbook of the 20th Century, dozens of performances of a song may be considered iconic. In other cases, where a song was written by or for a specific artist, most people may hear a single iconic performance of that song in their mind's ear. Understanding these aspects to ensure that you capture the desired iconic moments, or specifically deciding to diverge, is key to the arranging process.

   There were several elements of the Michael Bublé and Barbra Streisand performance that the quartet and I wanted to capture, including:

   - The modified lyrics in the verse.
   - Passing the melody, with the lead singing the Streisand melodies and baritone singing the Bublé parts. This also implied key changes like the original performance.
   - The duet (call and response) section in the second chorus.
   - The orchestration motif, which served as the interlude between the verse and chorus and reappeared in the tag.
   - A similar tempo and rhythmic subtext.

   All these factors are prominently featured in the final arrangement.

3. *What is the performer's vision for the song, and how does that impact your arrangement choices?* Many great songs can effectively be interpreted in different ways. In the barbershop style, it's common to hear a true freeform ballad treatment, focusing on a lyrical theme (without any underlying sense of meter). Many of those songs could also be effectively delivered in a strict tempo sense, or in combination with rubato, allowing more of the melodic and implied harmonic aspects to drive the impact. Arrangements intended to be delivered in strict meter, compared with one intended for rubato or freeform delivery, are going to look very different (particularly considering embellishments and rhythmic propellants).

---

[46] The rules for BHS contests are updated frequently, and include specific aspects related to the barbershop style. If arranging for contest use, please make sure you check with the Musicality Category of that respective Society to understand the prevailing rules. The current BHS rules are located at https://www.barbershop.org/contests/contests-judging.

The quartet was most enamored with choices from the Bublé/Streisand version of the song. This served as the form and construction blueprint and provided insight into textural development and featured aspects of the arrangement, e.g., key changes and melody passing.

4. *What are the unique qualities of the ensemble?* Because the quartet is composed of my children (3 by birth, 1 by marriage to my daughter), I happened to know these voices well. Consequently, the following guidelines would lead to the best outcome:

   - The lead and tenor are sisters and have similar ranges. The tenor has a great full/mixed voice post in the A♭ range and can post for 20+ seconds on an open vowel. The lead's alto range is best when sitting a bit lower, closer to a tenor 2 range, and she has a great head voice above a B4.
   - The baritone has a great range and can sing all four parts in a TTBB quartet. His strongest range is F3 to F4.
   - The bass—the brother to the two sisters—is a natural baritone and has a great rhythmic sense as well as upper range. Ideally, he should stay within the staff and avoid anything below an A♭ 3 or staying down there for too long.
   - The quartet handles jazzy rhythms and textures exceedingly well.
   - The lead is outstanding at interpreting a lyric line; solo + three textures highlight their strengths.
   - The quartet rings an E♭ major triad (1-5-1-3) best on any variety of open vowels.

Plan the Journey

One valuable piece of advice that I received as a new arranger was to start simple. If you're just trying to get started, don't try to write a gold medal arrangement with your initial efforts. Write something that you could hand to a lead singer with three good *woodshedders*, with the goal of having them sing at least 80% of what you wrote. How does that happen?

In barbershop, *woodshedding* refers to the art of harmonizing by ear (or without notated music). Singers create their own harmonies around a melody, determining the chord progression implied by the melody. This practice goes back to the early days of barbershop music, when most arrangements were improvised by ear, without notated music.[47]

Stick to the harmonic rhythm, or the rate of change of the chords, of the original version. Unless there's a good reason not to do so, stick with the original harmonizations, particularly the first time through the song. Also, don't modify the melody to support chord progressions which are not implied.

To make the process flow as smoothly as possible, it helps to know how you want the finished arrangement to sound, ideally before you ever write a note on physical or virtual paper. Building a roadmap for the song helps to flesh this out. Long before the days of GPS and Google Maps, if we were going somewhere for the very first time, through uncharted territory, we'd map out our journey. Here's an example of an arrangement blueprint template, using a spreadsheet or timeline approach:

---

[47] Cole, Richard; Schwartz, Ed. "Dictionary On Music". *dictionary.onmusic.org*. Connect For Education Inc. Retrieved March 9, 2019.

Figure 12.14

Example of an arrangement roadmap.

Key events												
Harmonic highlights												
Melodic highlights												
Texture												
Lyrics												
Key												
Form	Intro	Verse 1	Chorus 1	Verse 2	Chorus 2	A1	A2	B1	Interlude (replaces C)	Chorus	Extension	Tag
Tell 'em what you'll tell 'em		Tell 'em										Tell 'em what you told 'em

Song: ____________ Key approach / theme(s) ____________

Group: ____________ Notes ____________

Whether you choose to map out the elements of an arrangement onto something like this template or simply consider the individual elements, having an idea about these topics before jumping into the arrangement will aid in your journey. Let's dive in deeper, working from the bottom up.

Song Info

Capture the essential, overarching elements in this section:

- Who are you arranging for?
- What is the "big idea" for the arrangement?
- What's the key musical theme: lyric, melody, rhythm, harmony, or other? Does it change at different times in the song? For example, many up-tunes start with a harmonically themed, freeform delivery intro, which can feel like a tag, then kick into tempo at the chorus, becoming rhythmically themed. A reprise might have a section where the lyric becomes the feature in the bridge, and back to rhythmic theme before a harmonic themed tag acts as the perfect bookend to the musical journey.

Figure 12.15

Excerpt of an arrangement roadmap detailing overarching aspects to the song.

Song: ____________ Key approach / theme(s) ______________________________

Notes ______________________________

Group: ____________ ______________________________

Form/Construction

Lou Perry, arranger for groups such as The Boston Common and The Four Rascals, once said that music follows the Dale Carnegie philosophy of "Tell 'em what you're going to tell 'em, tell 'em, and tell 'em what you told 'em." In terms of the construction of an arrangement, this often results in:

- *Tell 'em what you're going to tell 'em:* intro and/or verse.
- *Tell 'em:* chorus.
- *Tell 'em what you told 'em*: optional reprise and tag.

Figure 12.16

Excerpt of an arrangement roadmap detailing the form of the song.

Key												
Form	Intro	Verse 1	Chorus 1	Verse 2	Chorus 2	A1	A2	B1	Interlude (replaces C)	Chorus	Extension	Tag
Tell 'em what you'll tell 'em		Tell 'em										Tell 'em what you told 'em

Identifying the construction of the chart is essential to the arranging process and should be the bare minimum for what an arranger determines prior to getting too far into the arranging process.

Key Signatures

Without knowing where you're headed, how will you know how to get there? This concept is important in the arranging process. Mapping out the key signatures corresponding to the form can provide a sense of the long line journey of the arrangement. Some important points to consider:

Form and Development

- If the key remains constant throughout the chart, development and building anticipation will depend more on other factors.
- If you intend to pass the melody, what key works best in that section for the intended voice part, and how can you best arrive there?

Voice Part Ranges

- Based on the melody and the range of the lead singer or section, what key keeps the melody in the sweet spot of their range?
- Look at the overall range of the melody. Melodies typically fall into two camps: *do–do* or *sol–sol*. This will drive consideration of the key, tying into considerations about the lead's *passaggio*, and will also highlight places where the melody may need to pass to the bass or tenor.

Do–do and *sol–sol* are shorthand terms for how the melody is composed, either generally staying within the range from the first note of the scale degree, *do*, and the highest note, sometimes called *high do*, or following the same pattern between the fifth scale degrees, *sol* and *high sol.*

The *passaggio* is a transition area between vocal registers.

- Considering the range of the bass, what's the lowest key in which the song will work?
- Considering both the melody and the bass part, assuming the bass will often sing the root of the chord, how does the overall tessitura of the key feel?

Musical Events

- Are there key musical events where a key change would add impact or drama?
- If the tag is intended to be climactic, e.g., ending on a high, powerful note, what is the ideal note for the intended voice part to sustain (called *posting* in barbershop)? How does that compare with what precedes it, and, if a key change is necessary, where's the ideal place?

A *post* is a sustained note, typically by one voice part on the tonic, while the other voice parts sing additional words and/or notes on the same word sound. Posts are often found in tags, such as the one by the lead part in Figure 12.17.

Figure 12.17
Tenor post from "Liar Medley Tag," arranged by Renee Craig.

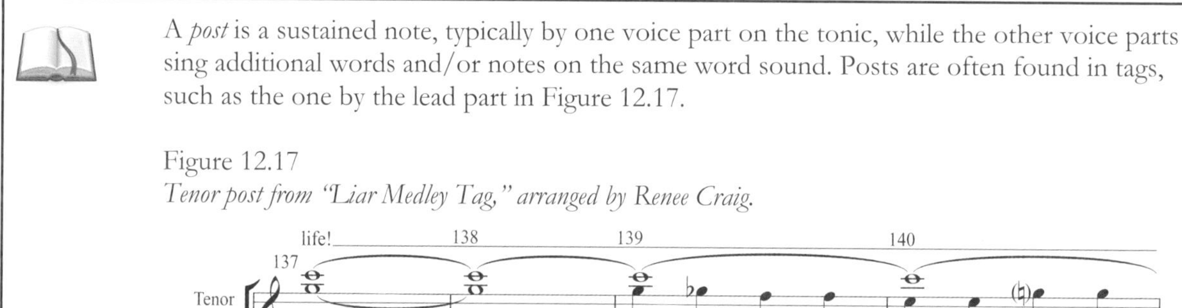

Lyrics

Once you've identified the form and construction of the arrangement, it's time to start mapping the lyrics. Lyrics, like melody, help to underscore form. They emphasize articulation, meter, and symmetry, which can also be taken into consideration when developing the arrangement. Looking at the lyrics separately, particularly for lyrically themed songs, can also help to highlight key moments in the arrangement.

Other lyrical aspects to consider as part of the arranging process:

- Text versus subtext. The text is the main body of printed or written matter on the page. But the musicality and impact often lie in the subtext: the implicit or metaphorical meaning of the material. The arranger should consider the subtext intended by the lyricist supported by the composer and have an opinion on a given subtext as well. This will drive choices of voicing, inversions, embellishments, progressions, and chord choices.
- Lyrics can serve three purposes
    - Tell the story: what's happening?
    - Convey emotion: how do I feel about what's happening?
    - Evoke imagery: what does it look like?

Understanding the function of a given phrase or line of lyrics can help to influence choices made by the arranger.

Textures

Textures, mapped to sections of form, are an often-overlooked aspect of developing an arrangement. Determining the texture of a given section of form before starting the arrangement can help to create interest, variety, and an overall sense of development and balance in the long line of the arrangement. Examples to consider include:

- Homorhythmic (everyone singing the same words or word parts at the same time)
- Solo against trio (neutral syllables or back time)
- Embellished, using primarily
    - Swipes, which are movements from chord to chord on the same word
    - Echoes, where one or more parts sing lyrics, often repeating was what just sung, while the other part(s) sustain a note
    - Solos, duets, or trios
    - Other embellishments[48]
- Voicing (higher or lower tessitura, or the same as previous sections of form)

Note: these textural devices need not be employed for entire sections to be effective. Any moment of a song that jumps out as a clear candidate for a given effect can be a useful part of an outline. An arranger need not restrict themselves to one texture for an entire section.

Melodic Highlights

Recognizing the journey of the original melody, as mapped out by the composer, is important information for the arranger.

---

[48] Embellishments are covered in more detail in *Arranging Barbershop*: Vol. 2

The *Harvard Concise Dictionary of Music and Musicians* defines *melody* as "a coherent succession of pitches...accepted as belonging together."[49] Further,

> It is obviously impossible to separate rhythm completely from melody, since every pitch must have a duration, and duration is part of rhythm. In Western tonal music, melody is fundamentally inseparable from harmony, since melodies… clearly imply (harmonies). [50]

Aspects of melody to consider include:

- Movement and shape
- Patterns or motifs
- The creation and resolution of musical tension
- Narrative content and/or emotional character

Identifying key melodic aspects and highlights can help to drive arrangement choices at key musical events. Key melodic events include:

- Intervals
- Contour
- Tension and release
- Climax
- Surprise

A great example of all these aspects is the C section of "You Make Me Feel So Young," arrangement by Mark Hale. Note:

- An extended section of form (12 measures) as opposed to the 8-measure A and B sections. YouTube
- Features smooth (conjunct) movement (measures 41–43, 49–51), in addition to disjunct leaps (measures 44 and 47).
- Ascending (measures 41–43) and descending (measures 49–51) contour.
- The surprise of an octave leap (measure 43–44). YouTube
- Tension built from repeated melodic notes (measures 44–46) before a melodic leap (measure 47). YouTube
- A sense of completion via descending melody back to the tonic (measures 49–51). YouTube

---

[49] Randall, Don Michael (1999). *The Harvard Concise Dictionary of Music and Musicians.* The Belknap Press of Harvard University Press, 401

[50] *ibidem.*

Figure 12.18

"You Make Me Feel So Young," arrangement by Mark Hale, with excellent examples of highlighting melody. YouTube

Harmonic Highlights

Oftentimes, the harmonic highlights will emerge later during the arranging process. However, key harmonic events—critical chords at key moments, key changes from an iconic performance, etc.—will be obvious during the planning process for the arrangement. If you have a strong feeling about a given chord or progression, it's good to capture this as part of the planning process, as that moment can influence other choices in the arrangement.

For example, when arranging Irving Berlin's "When I Lost You," I spent time investigating the background of the original song, which Berlin wrote as a catharsis to help deal with the loss of his wife. It is said that after a long period of not being able to write anything after his loss, this song provided a vessel for his emotions, allowing him to unlock more music and, in some ways, move on in his life.

To "tell 'em what we told 'em" in the tag, I leveraged lyrics from the original second verse. The actual moment of catharsis, the song's climax, was the chord on "wrong" in measure 68, as seen in figure 11.19. The specific chord that conveyed that emotion was a high tessitura, tightly voiced II halfdim7. This chord had the energy from the preceding harmonic progression, and then dissolved away to the final chord. The baritone is the agent of change, as the root of the climactic chord, and serves to unlock the emotions and melt away the pain through its motion on the subsequent chords.

Figure 12.19

"When I Lost You," words and music by Irving Berlin. Arranged by Steve Tramack, this figure highlights the harmonic climax in measure 68.

Other harmonic considerations include:

- Minor to major mode changes
- Alternate harmonizations in later sections of form, especially during the development of a chart
- The power of occasional, brief, and appropriate unison or octaves

Other Key Events

As you're planning the course of your musical journey, consider the *long line* of the arrangement.

Long line refers to the arc of emotive and musical variations leading the listener/observer/audience through to a clear, emotionally fulfilling culmination and experience. The long line of the song considers the macro view of development, focusing on how each successive section of form and construction builds on the preceding.

What are those key musical events that serve as points of arrival? Consider mapping those during the planning process to serve the high-level roadmap for the arrangement. These may include:

- The introduction. What is the inspiration?
- Key changes
- Climaxes
- Places where the melody moves to another voice part
- Original or added material
- Reprise
- The golden ratio moment, roughly ⅔ of the way through the chart
- The tag. What's the inspiration? Is there a sense of symmetry with the introduction?

Fans of the Dan Brown book *The DaVinci Code* are likely familiar with the Fibonacci Sequence. Also nicknamed nature's code, the Fibonacci Sequence is a series of numbers: 0, 1, 1, 2, 3, 5, 8, 13, 21, 34, 55, 89, 144, 233, 377, 610…The next number in the sequence is determined by adding the two numbers before it. The ratio for this sequence is approximately 1.618, which is called *the golden ratio.*

In addition to examples from mathematics, architecture, geometry, nature and art, the golden ratio can be found within music as well. For example, the notes of a major triad (1, 3, 5 and 8) are all within the Fibonacci Sequence. The ratio between the dominant scale tone (the fifth, which is the 8th note in a 13-note chromatic scale) and the 13th note (octave) is .615, or very close to the golden mean ratio. Composers, arrangers and performers leverage this ratio for high impact moments, such as placement of key changes. Note the following example from David Wright's arrangement of "California, Here I Come," with the dramatic, half-time melody in the second chorus at measure 91, which (of 158 measures) is roughly the golden mean moment in the arrangement.

Figure 12.20
"California, Here I Come," arranged by David Wright, YouTube.

while the ver - y thought of home will
Tenor
Lead
and then the thought of home will make you smile.
while the ver - y thought of home will
Bari
Bass
6
That's why I must fly out yon - der, where a frown is might - y hard to
find.
Chorus 2
Oh, my Cal - i - forn - ia,
12
find. That place is on my mind. Ca - li -
find Can't ya hear me cal - lin' Oh, my Cal - i - forn - ia,
find.
how I've been long - in' for ya,
18
for - nia, Ca - li - for - nia, here I come.
how I've been long - in' for ya,
come. I'm head - in'
24
I've wan - dered here and there but this time I'll be stay - in' where I start,
right back where I, right back

Example Completed Roadmap

Following these concepts and using the blueprint template, Figure 12.21 shows an example of the completed roadmap for the arrangement of "It Had to be You."

Figure 12.21

Completed roadmap of "It Had to Be You," arranged by Steve Tramack.

Key events	Set up two features: lead first, with key change...	... passing the melody to the baritone	Key change from bari melody; introduce rhythmic themed element	Title; start journey	Emotional words - highlight	Feature lead	First climax; ramp down, and then ramp up into the real heart of the song	**Key moment:** Feature bari melody and lead resposne	Climax - nobody ELSE. Most touching moment: **I love you still (always will)**	**Call/response vamping feel.** Enjoy the lead/bari relationship. Fading to black...	Final line features lead as top voice, walking up to the high root
Harmonic highlights	**Use major seventh (melodic feature in chorus) and voicings to create a sense of melancholy past**	**Key change with melodic pass to baritone; create excitement into chorus (past to present)**	"Power V7" chords in middle - create impact to match present joyous feelings	Major seventh, aug "crunch" at title - implies intimacy and love despite faults. Dom 9ths provide excitement	Use **colorful chords** to emphasize difference between "true" and "blue". Glad - use triad, not seventh. Climactic V7 at end	**Lead solo at improvised melody.** Tighter chords at responses to start building sooner toward first climax	Higher tessitura at **first climax**; use tessitura and voicings to create symmetry with first A; ramp with key change into reprise	iv6 power chords transition to C	**Highest voice chord at climax.** Use spread harmony at "always will" echo.	Use the orchestration to land the 2nd inversion V7 (tenor root); with a feeling of ebb and flow	Use the major seventh one more time (deceptive cadence-type feel)
Melodic highlights	Opening line sets up repeated motif	Improvised melody at the end of the verse to create excitement into the chorus.	Motif from Buble/Streisand version; revisit in tag	**Major seventh! Ascending conjunct motion, building anticipation**	More **leaps** (ascending, descending). Hits highest note at end	Improved melody at first line (a la Streisand) to major seventh - **feature this**	Melodic climax at "nobody else" - sets up final climax in reprise. Repeated motif from beginning of chorus	Bari melody with lead (often times in tenor line) responses. Don't lose melody!	**Melodic climax - nobody ELSE.** Improvised melody after climax leading to intimate moment	None	**Improvised melodic riffs (from original); Walk up to high root**
Texture	**Homorhythmic to feature lyrics,** and start to set up the lead/bari feature with a duet (could be, should be). Embellish in transitions.		**Instrumental feel, matching original**	Introduce easy swing features to support lyric and melodic highlights	More embellished, **more rhythm** - feeling of the band building toward a first climactic event at the end of B	Start to build in **call/response** feel (melody with harmony part echoes). Use bass downbeats to create feeling of deep brass pulses	**Homorhythmic - focus on lyrics** (first time through C section). These lyrics are the point of the song.	**Call / response (from original). Bari melody, lead responses.** Bass/tenor reinforce bari/lead	Homorythmic. Use bari echo for intimate moment. Reinforce duet one more time at the title	Bring back into the **interlude orchestration feel** with call and response extension	Embellished, winding down feeling (similar to original)
Lyrics	*Seems like dreams that I always had, could be, should be making me glad. Why am I blue? It's up to you to explain.*	*I'm thinking maybe, baby, you'll go away. Someday, some way, you'll come and say: "it's you I need", and you'll be pleading in vain.*	*Big band Scat*	*It had to be you, just had to be you. I wandered around and finally found the somebody who*	*Could make me be true, could make me be blue. Or even be glad, just to be sad thinking of you.*	*Some others I've seen might never be mean. Might never be cross, or try to be boss, but they wouldn't do.*	*For nobody else gave me a thrill. With all your faults, I love you still. It had to be you, marvelous you, It had to be you.*	*It had to be you, just had to be you. I wandered around and finally found the somebody who*	*For nobody else gave me a thrill. With all your faults, I love you still* ***(always will)****. Had to be you, wonderful you, no one but you.*	*Repeated call / response*	*Repeated lyrics*
Form	1st half (Verse)	2nd half (Verse)	Interlude	A (Chorus 1)	B (Chorus 1)	A (Chorus 1)	C (Chorus 1)	A (Reprise)	C (Reprise)	C ext (Tag)	Final riff (Tag)
Key	Db	E	Db	Db				D		D	
	Tell 'em what you'll tell 'em		**Tell 'em**							**Tell 'em what you told 'em**	

Song: It Had to Be You

Group: Sweet and Sour

Key approach / theme(s): Duet between lead and baritone; lyric theme with strong melodic and rhythmic themed support.

Notes: Inspired by the Michael Buble / Barbra Streisand version. Feature lead/bari melody passing. Contestable

Keep the bass part in the staff (lowest note = Ab) and leverage lead voice for features (above and below teno

While this may seem daunting, many of these details were effectively predetermined by choosing to follow the overall approach of the reference performance. By tracking the form and iconic aspects of the source performance, the following aspects were easily adopted:

Figure 12.22

Shorthand to the arrangement roadmap of "It Had to Be You," arranged by Steve Tramack.

Form: Verse | Interlude | Chorus | Reprise | Tag	1
Key changes	2
Lyric changes from original, verse and chorus	3
Key melodic passing moments in the verse and reprise	4
Melodic improvisation moments	5
Call and response in the reprise between Michael Bublé, baritone part, and Barbra Streisand, lead part	6
Interlude orchestral feel revisited in the tag	7

Figure 12.23 shows where each of these elements were captured in the roadmap:

Figure 12.23

Elements used in "It Had to Be You," arranged by Steve Tramack.

Key events	Set up two features: lead first, with key change...	... passing the melody to the baritone	Key change from bari melody; introduce rhythmic themed element	Title; start journey	Emotional words - highlight	Feature lead	First climax; ramp down, and then ramp up into the real heart of the song	**Key moment:** Feature bari melody and lead resposne	Climax - nobody **ELSE**. Most touching moment: **I love you still (always will)**	**Call/response vamping feel.** Enjoy the lead/bari relationship. Fading to black...	Final line features lead as top voice, walking up to the high root
Harmonic highlights	**Use major seventh (melodic feature in chorus) and voicings to create a sense of melancholy past**	**Key change with melodic pass to baritone; create excitement into chorus (past to present)**	"Power V7" chords in middle - create impact to match present joyous feelings	Major seventh, aug "crunch" at title - implies intimacy and love despite faults. Dom 9ths provide excitement	Use **colorful chords** to emphasize difference between "true" and "blue". Glad - use triad, not seventh. Climactic V7 at end	**Lead solo at improvised melody.** Tighter chords at responses to start building sooner toward first climax	Higher tessitura at **first climax**; use tessitura and voicings to create symmetry with first A; ramp with key change into reprise	iv6 power chords transition to C	**Highest voice chord at climax.** Use spread harmony at "always will" echo.	Use the orchestration to land the 2nd inversion V7 (tenor root); with a feeling of ebb and flow	Use the major seventh one more time (deceptive cadence-type feel)
Melodic highlights	Opening line sets up repeated motif	Improvised melody at the end of the verse to create excitement into the chorus.	Motif from Buble/Streisand version; revisit in tag	**Major seventh! Ascending conjunct motion, building anticipation**	More **leaps** (ascending, descending). Hits highest note at end	Improved melody at first line (a la Streisand) to major seventh - **feature this**	Melodic climax at "nobody else" - sets up final climax in reprise. Repeated motif from beginning of chorus	Bari melody with lead (often times in tenor line) responses. Don't lose melody!	**Melodic climax - nobody ELSE.** Improvised melody after climax leading to intimate moment	None	**Improvised melodic riffs (from original); Walk up to high root**
Texture	**Homorhythmic to feature lyrics,** and start to set up the lead/bari feature with a duet (could be, should be). Embellish in transitions.		**Instrumental feel, matching original**	Introduce easy swing features to support lyric and melodic highlights	More embellished, **more rhythm** - feeling of the band building toward a first climactic event at the end of B	Start to build in **call/response** feel (melody with harmony part echoes). Use bass downbeats to create feeling of deep brass pulses	**Homorhythmic - focus on lyrics** (first time through C section). These lyrics are the point of the song.	**Call / response (from original). Bari melody, lead responses.** Bass/tenor reinforce bari/lead	Homorythmic. Use bari echo for intimate moment. Reinforce duet one more time at the title	Bring back into the **interlude orchestration feel** with call and response extension	Embellished, winding down feeling (similar to original)
3 **Lyrics**	*Seems like dreams that I always had, could be, should be making me glad. Why am I blue? It's up to you to explain.*	*I'm thinking maybe, baby, you'll go away. Someday, some way, you'll come and say: "it's you I need", and you'll be pleading in vain.*	*Big band Scat*	*It had to be you, just had to be you. I wandered around and finally found the somebody who*	*Could make me be true, could make me be blue. Or even be glad, just to be sad thinking of you.*	*Some others I've seen might never be mean. Might never be cross, or try to be boss, but they wouldn't do.*	*For nobody else gave me a thrill. With all your faults, I love you still. It had to be you, marvelous you, It had to be you.*	*It had to be you, just had to be you. I wandered around and finally found the somebody who*	*For nobody else gave me a thrill. With all your faults, I love you still* ***(always will)****. Had to be you, wonderful you, no one but you.*	*Repeated call / response*	*Repeated lyrics*
F	1st half	2nd half	Interlude	A	B	A	C	A	C	C ext	Final riff
	Verse			Chorus 1				Reprise		Tag	
Key	Db	E	Db	Db				D		D	
	Tell 'em what you'll tell 'em		Tell 'em							Tell 'em what you told 'em	

Song: It Had to Be You

Group: Sweet and Sour

Key approach / theme(s): Duet between lead and baritone; lyric theme with strong melodic and rhythmic themed support.

Notes: Inspired by the Michael Buble / Barbra Streisand version. Feature lead/bari melody passing. Contestable

Keep the bass part in the staff (lowest note = Ab) and leverage lead voice for features (above and below teno

By starting with these elements, developing the arrangement becomes a much more attainable prospect.

Let's look at how some of these choices and planning elements translated into the arrangement. We're not going to explore the actual process of creating the arrangement; that will be covered in more depth in other places within the book. Further examples of this kind will be featured as we explore the different facets of arranging at different levels of expertise and complexity in *Arranging Barbershop,* Vol. 2.

Embark on the Journey

Ask ten arrangers how they approach the actual process of capturing and developing the chart, and you're likely to get ten different answers. These are covered in more depth in Vol. 3 of *Arranging Barbershop*, Visions of Excellence, and scattered throughout the book in the various use cases and example sections. Kevin Keller provided a great overview of his step-by-step process in Chapter 10 of this book. The rest of this chapter is dedicated to applied specific thoughts and goals in arrangement. Here's a quick overview of my process of arriving at the result:

> *Next Thing Next.* Once you have the blueprint, write out the melody line and the lyrics. Realize that, once you've done this, you're 25% done! (Well, not always, but it makes me feel better). Note that I specified the melody. If you're passing the melody during a section, write the melody in the appropriate voice parts.
>
> *Lay the Foundation.* The arrangement's bass line is always a good place to go next. Often, in a solid barbershop arrangement, the bass is going to be singing the root or the fifth of the chord, unless the voice leading dictates otherwise. Listen to your source material inspiration; the instrumental bass line is probably serving those same purposes. This is often a good place to start, particularly if your arranging is driven by your ear more so than being strictly theory driven. One note for arrangers from other styles: on triads, the bass part is almost always on the root. If the melody is low, consider passing it to the bass singer for short passages rather than write the bass line down only where a low bass like Dan Walz[51] or Brett Littlefield[52] is going to be able to sing it.
>
> *Complete the First Pass.* Next, write in the tenor and/or baritone harmony, paying attention to voice leading. Don't worry if the chord isn't perfect. I had a great conversation about arranging with Kevin Keller, and he gave me some advice which helped cut my hours/arrangement in half: don't obsess over individual chords. Focus on texture and voice leading, and let the chords fall where they may. This made a dramatic difference both on the amount time spent per chart, the amount of frustration incurred, and more singable voice parts. Ideally, all the voice parts will sing like their own melodies, though the baritone melody will likely seem the most avant-garde of the bunch. There's nothing in the rest of the musical world quite like the barbershop baritone line.

---

[51] Bass of the 2019 BHS Champion quartet, Signature. YouTube

[52] Bass of the 1996 BHS Champion quartet, Nightlife and 2013 Champions, Masterpiece. YouTube

Unsticking. Use your knowledge of theory to help you a) identify what harmonies are implied by a given melody for a given measure, b) ensure that you're writing complete chords (if you're just starting out arranging, it's a good idea to avoid passing tones, suspensions, and incomplete chords), and c) figure out where to go if you arrange yourself into a corner. Arranger and music teacher Kirk Young gave me some great advice when I first started arranging and found myself stuck based on some alternate harmonization choices that I made: Arrange the end of a section first (it probably ends on a V7, leading to I at the beginning of the next section), and then arrange backwards through the chart.

Considerations for Developing the Chart

As the song progresses and sections repeat—AABA or verse, chorus, verse, chorus, bridge, chorus—consider carefully whether you're going to modify repeated source material. Little changes for seemingly no reason other than the arranger not being able to decide what voicing or progression or embellishment they like best simply confuse and frustrate an ensemble (particularly choruses). If you're going to change the arrangement from A to A, or chorus to chorus, make sure there's a good reason, such as development of prior material and overall development of the chart, a different texture, melody passing to other voices. Make sure the changes are dramatic enough that they won't confuse singers or audiences; otherwise, leave it alone. It also means fewer measures that you must arrange!

The Next Step

The cleanup process can take as long as the entire creative and editing processes. This can include making sure you include all lyrics, spelling chords correctly, and adding any performance hints, such as dynamic markings, tempo markings, accents, etc. At some point, iterating through the process, you'll have a complete arrangement. Determine when the arrangement is complete, or at least is complete enough. Otherwise, in the pursuit of finding the ultimate chord, voicing or progression, it'll never be done. Sometimes, it is best to give the ensemble and have them sing it. Find out what works, what doesn't, and learn from them.

So, with that overview, here's a detailed look inside the results of this process, tied back to the blueprint from the planning process.

Verse: 1st Half

The blueprint highlights the use of chords and voicings to create a sense of melancholy past. I did this by having the lead and tenor crossing, placing the melody frequently above the tenor. When the listener is used to hearing the melody in an inside voice, having the lead exposed creates a sense of vulnerability. This also leveraged the ranges and similar voices of sisters, who are both alto singers classically. As shown in Figure 11.24, the I13 in measure 2 on "always" adds to the sense of melancholy.

Figure 12.24

Excerpt from "It Had to Be You," arranged by Steve Tramack.

I also wanted to set up the two features, the lead and baritone. The happy couple-to-be is first introduced and featured on the "could be, should be" in measure 3, as shown in Figure 12.25. However, the lyrics in the verse highlight relationship challenges and uncertain outcomes. The ♭VI9 on "glad" in measure 4 highlights this tension.

Figure 12.25

Excerpt from "It Had to Be You," arrangement by Steve Tramack.

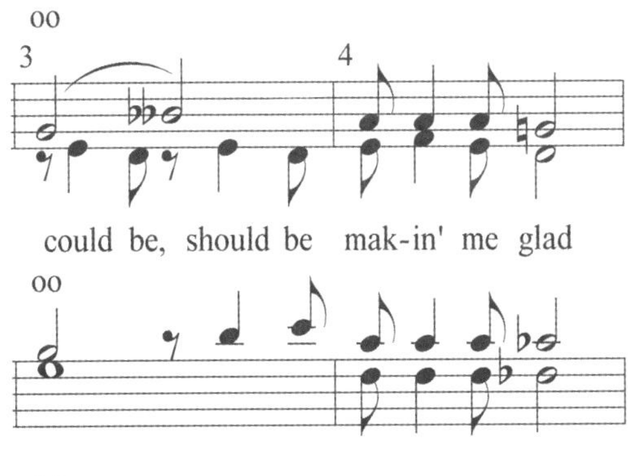

Embellishment is a focus, leading to the first key musical event (the key change and melody passing in measures 8–9) of the arrangement. The embellishments highlighted in figure 12.26 serve four purposes:

1. Provide fill over the sustained melody note, leveraging the melodic motif from the first line, this time sung by the tenor in measure 7 ("exPLAIN, oh please, EXplain").
2. Allow the lead to introduce the major seventh flavor, which is such an important part of the melody line in the chorus, beat 3 in measure 7.
3. Introduce the baritone, co-featured in the duet. The chart pleads for the baritone to tell their story, which occurs on the baritone melody in the second half of the verse.

4. Change the key from D♭ to E, tertian movement, which is where the baritone melody will be centered.

To get there, we use a descending full step motion from the D♭maj7 (Imaj7) to a C♭9 (the ♭VII dominant 9th of the D♭ tonic). The voicing of this dominant ninth, missing the 5th, is known in barbershop circles as the *Moon 9th.* This tonic to♭VII7 / dominant ninth is an often-used progression in the style, sharing common tones with a iv6, which also progresses to I.

Figure 12.26

Excerpt from "It Had to Be You," arrangement by Steve Tramack.

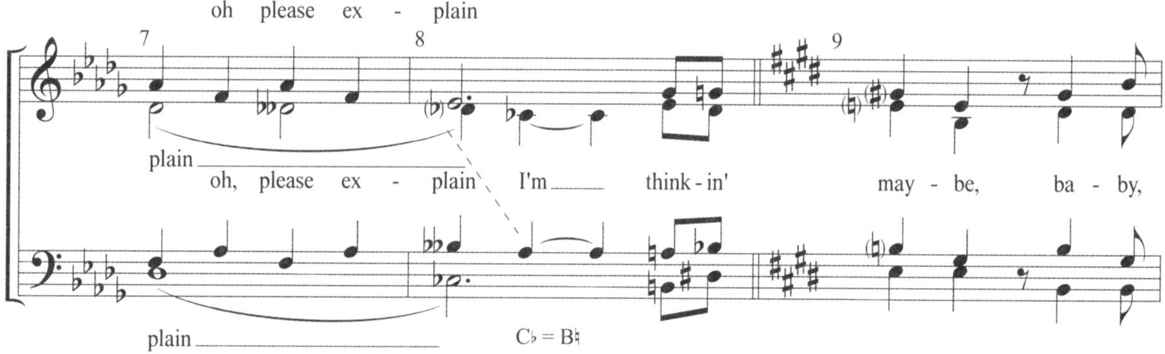

The C♭9 in beat 1 of measure 8 is the enharmonic of the dominant (B7) of the target key, E, which creates for an easy transition, as well as a nice voice leading ramp for the baritone melody.

Verse: 2nd Half

In measure 12, shown in Figure 12.27, to keep the voices in their best range and keep the focus on the baritone as a key actor in this play, the baritone dips below the bass for the "say" chord.

Figure 12.27

Excerpt from "It Had to Be You," arrangement by Steve Tramack.

This voicing, with the bass above the baritone, provides some additional character, mirroring the lead being outside the quartet, above rather than below. It's also a choice that was made specifically based on the voices in the quartet and playing to their strengths.

The improvised melody in measure 14, shown in Figure 12.28, also provides an opportunity to head toward our first climactic moment in the song. Often, each primary section of form, the verse, chorus, etc., will have its own climactic moments, which is the case here.

Figure 12.28

Excerpt from "It Had to Be You," arrangement by Steve Tramack.

The end of the verse (measures 15–16, shown in Figure 12.29) needed to serve three purposes, highlighted in the blueprint:

1. Create a climactic moment for the verse and a sense of completion
2. Transition back to the key of D♭
3. Create a logical handoff of the melody back to the lead

I used another common tone progression from the B7 to a D7 on beats 3 and 4 ("vain, oh,") in measure 16, which allowed for a half-step progression to return to the D♭. The voice leading for all four parts should allow for easy transitioning between keys.

Figure 12.29

Excerpt from "It Had to Be You," arrangement by Steve Tramack.

Interlude

The goal here was to emulate the big band backing Michael Bublé and Barbra Streisand, providing a peak power chord (A♭7) on the syncopated second beat in measure 18, and leveraging this as a passage of time transition from the melancholy-tinged past to the wonderful present and future.

Figure 12.30

Excerpt from "It Had to Be You," arrangement by Steve Tramack.

First Chorus

1A

The blueprint highlights a couple of factors: feature the melodic hook (major seventh) at the title and introduce the easy swing rhythmic features. The chart does this with the lead solo leading into the Imaj7 chord at measure 21. Figure 12.31 highlights the bass and bari downbeats in measures 22 and 23 against the push beats, reinforcing the swing:

Figure 12.31

Excerpt from "It Had to Be You," arrangement by Steve Tramack.

The duet between lead and bari help to reinforce that this is their song—a texture which is used throughout the piece. See Figure 12.32.

Figure 12.32

Excerpt from "It Had to Be You," arrangement by Steve Tramack.

1B

The melody begins heading toward a more climactic event, and the tessitura reflects the emotional differences between true and blue. The planned approach was both more rhythmic while using chord choices and voicings to convey emotions.

I used the strengths of the lead and tenor ranges, due to their similarities, and the jazz sense of the quartet in measures 29 and 30 with the voicing and embellishment choices.

Figure 12.33

Excerpt from "It Had to Be You," arrangement by Steve Tramack.

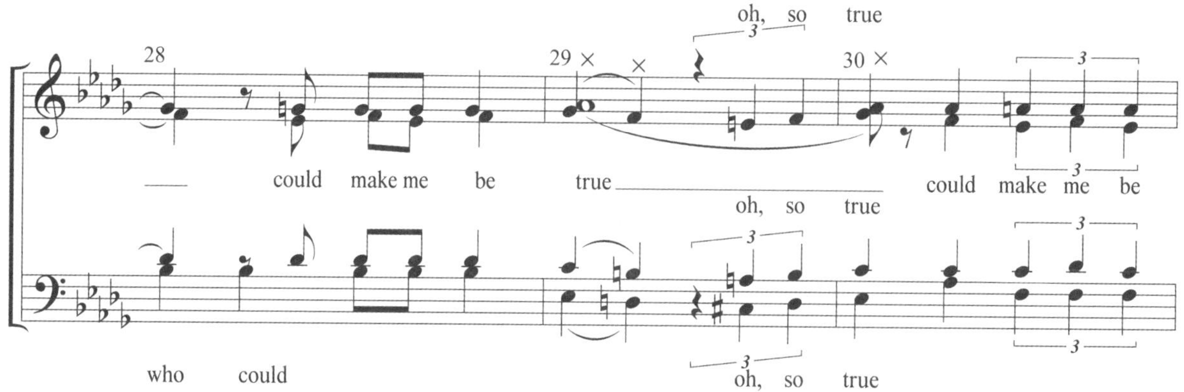

Figure 12.34 shows the tension in the "so" chord, which features the bari, and both adds emotion while highlighting the lead/bari relationship. The similar motion in the swipes for the lead (beat 1) and bari (beat 3) in measure 31 subtly highlights their connection, demonstrating a similar range of emotions.

Figure 12.34

Excerpt from "It Had to Be You," arrangement by Steve Tramack.

I used the II major triad (instead of the II7) to create a sense of purity and clarity on "glad." This chord is also lower voiced, allowing for building anticipation through the rest of the phrase:

Figure 12.35

Excerpt from "It Had to Be You," arrangement by Steve Tramack.

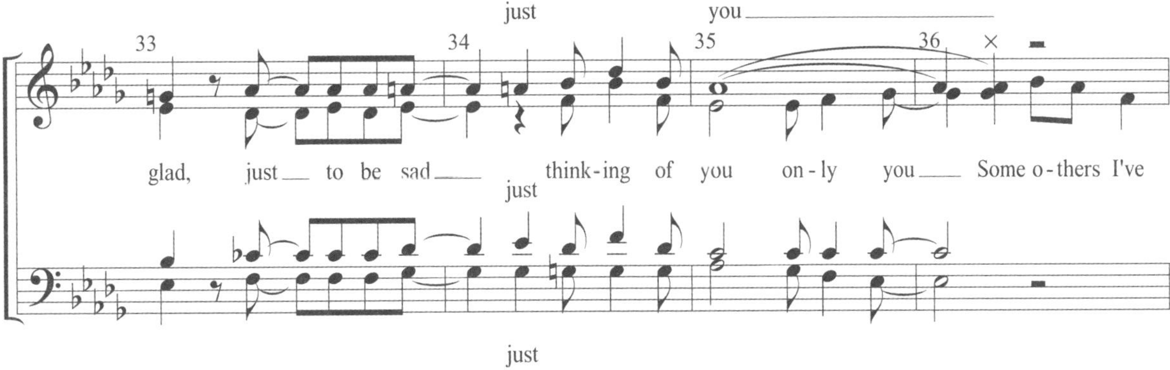

2A

Figure 12.36 shows the improved melody in the transition back to the second A section is highlighted by allowing the lead to solo.

Figure 12.36

Excerpt from "It Had to Be You," arrangement by Steve Tramack.

The lead entrance as a solo also allows for a call and response texture:

Figure 12.37

Excerpt from "It Had to Be You," arrangement by Steve Tramack

.

Stronger rhythmic pulses are enabled through the trio entrance and bass accented entrance on the second beats of measures 41 and 42.

Figure 12.38

Excerpt from "It Had to Be You," arrangement by Steve Tramack.

1C

The blueprint highlights three aspects:

1. Higher tessitura to support the first climax on "nobody else."
2. Homorhythmic texture to focus on the lyrics, often important in the C section of an ABAC form. The C section is often the point of an ABAC form chorus, delivering the key message and, in this case, providing a sense of closure by ending exactly as the chorus started: with the title of the song.
3. Create a feeling of symmetry, coming off the climax, returning to a similar tessitura as the beginning of the chorus.

I used both the higher tessitura and closer voiced 9th chords to demonstrate the excitement of "else" and "thrill." See Figure 12.39.

Figure 12.39

Excerpt from "It Had to Be You," arrangement by Steve Tramack.

Note that the homorhythmic texture, with limited embellishment, allows focus on the lyrics but keeps the sense of motion. The first chorus ends in roughly the same tessitura as it began (in measure 52, shown in Figure 12.40), then quickly ramps into the key change:

Figure 12.40

Excerpt from "It Had to Be You," arrangement by Steve Tramack.

Second Chorus (Half Chorus)

1A

This is a key moment in the chart with featured moments for both the baritone on the melody and the lead with improvised responses. This was already in the original Bublé/Streisand performance, so I simply captured that in the chart. The role of the bass and tenor is to stay out of the way by reinforcing either the bari melody or the lead response in respective duets and trying to not call attention to either line.

Figure 12.41

Excerpt from "It Had to Be You," arrangement by Steve Tramack.

Additional features of the lead and baritone occur in measure 56 and 57, with the bass and tenor providing a strong harmonic foundation while staying in the background. See Figure 12.42.

Figure 12.42

Excerpt from "It Had to Be You," arrangement by Steve Tramack.

1C

The final C section in this half chorus sets up the focus by the melodic peak occurring on "else."

Figure 12.43

Excerpt from "It Had to Be You," arrangement by Steve Tramack.

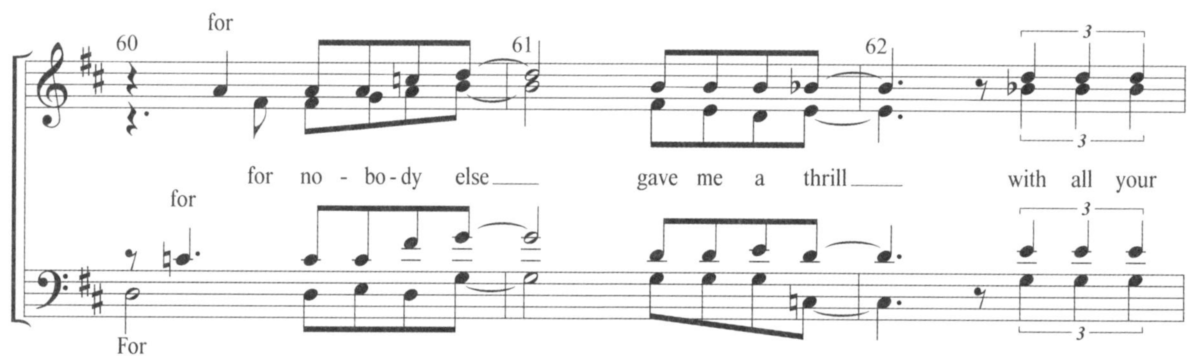

While this is the musical climax, the emotional climax directly follows in measures 62–64, as shown in Figure 12.44. Because this was written specifically for the lead and bari to sing at their wedding, I wanted to provide the groom (bari) the chance to profess their love for their bride (lead). Their musical relationship in the arrangement has been set up via multiple duets, melody passing and call and response at this point, so any time either part does something outside of a homorhythmic texture, it's going to be recognized. The arrangement helps the quartet set up this heartfelt moment:

Figure 12.44

Excerpt from "It Had to Be You," arrangement by Steve Tramack.

This followed with one final duet in measure 65, as shown in Figure 12.45:

Figure 12.45

Excerpt from "It Had to Be You," arrangement by Steve Tramack.

Tag

The tag truly functions in a "tell 'em what you told 'em" fashion. As highlighted in the plan and shown in Figure 12.46, drawing upon inspiration from the original performance, it reprises:

- The orchestral interlude in between the verse and first chorus (taken directly from the Bublé/Streisand piece) in measures 67–73
- The melody passing from lead to bari throughout the tag
- The call and response texture
- The melodic featured major seventh in measure 75
- Leveraging the vocal strengths of the lead in a higher head voice range in measures 75–76

Figure 12.46

Tag from "It Had to Be You," arrangement by Steve Tramack.

Finished Product

Figure 12.47 shows the arrangement in completion.

Figure 12.47

"It Had to Be You," arrangement by Steve Tramack.

IT HAD TO BE YOU

Words by GUS KAHN

Music by ISHAM JONES
Arranged by STEVE TRAMACK
For ***Sweet & Sour***

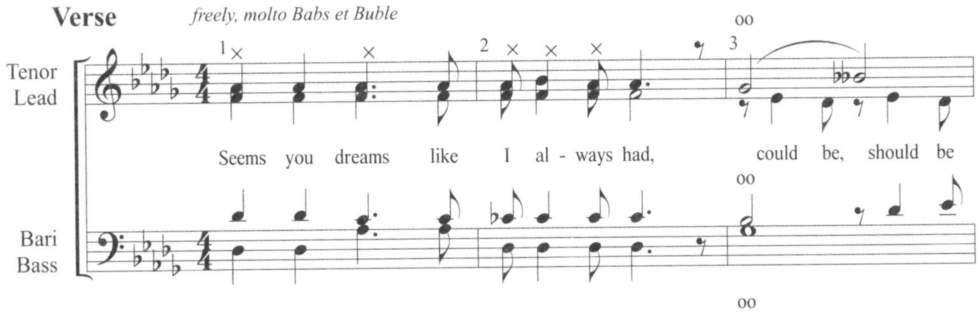

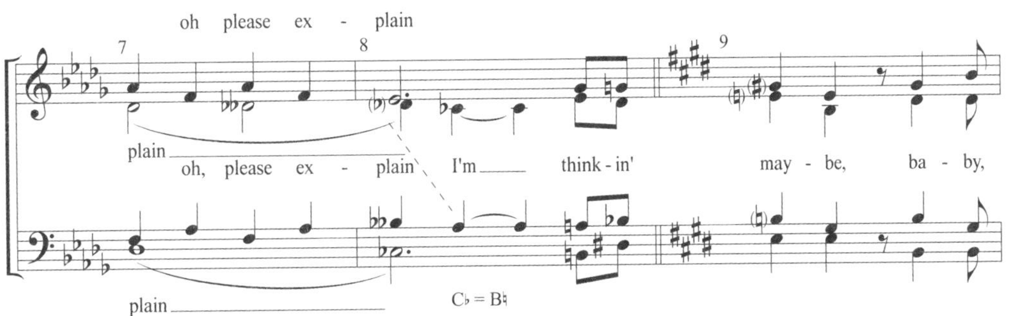

IT HAD TO BE YOU, p. 2

IT HAD TO BE YOU, p. 3
just you
round
just had to be you
I wan-dered a - round
just you
Just
just you
round
and fin - al - ly found
the some - bo - dy
who
the
the some - bo - dy
oh, so true
could make me be
true
could make me be
oh, so true
who could
oh, so true
so blue
blue
so blue
or ev - en be
glad,
just to be sad
so blue

IT HAD TO BE YOU, p. 4

IT HAD TO BE YOU, p. 5

IT HAD TO BE YOU, p. 6
whoa
for nobody else
gave me a thrill
for
For
freely
with all your faults
I love you still
Had to be
Sammy
always will
a tempo
Tag
you wonderful you,
no one but
you
da ba dat dat
dm dm dm dm
da ba just me and you
da ba dat dat
da ba no one but
da ba dat dat
dm dm ba ba dm
dm dm dm dm
dm dm ba dm

IT HAD TO BE YOU, p. 7

Conclusion

In conclusion, here's the process I followed for this arrangement:

1. I found a song to arrange (It Had to Be You).
2. I closely considered the performer and their strengths and weaknesses in developing the plan and the arrangement.
3. I took the time to plan the journey in a fair amount of detail by building a blueprint, which factored aspects from an iconic performance along with the preferences of the quartet.
4. Only then did I embark on what turned out to be an exceedingly fulfilling journey.

Visit YouTube to view a performance by Sweet & Sour.

Now it's time for you to do the same. And enjoy the journey, as well as the results! A new work of art—introduced into the world from your imagination, coupled with the original inspiration of the composer and lyricist, brought to life by the performer, and shared with an entirely new audience—can be thrilling. You will have also done your part in helping to make sure that the barbershop harmony artform continues to be preserved.

Tag

By Steve Tramack

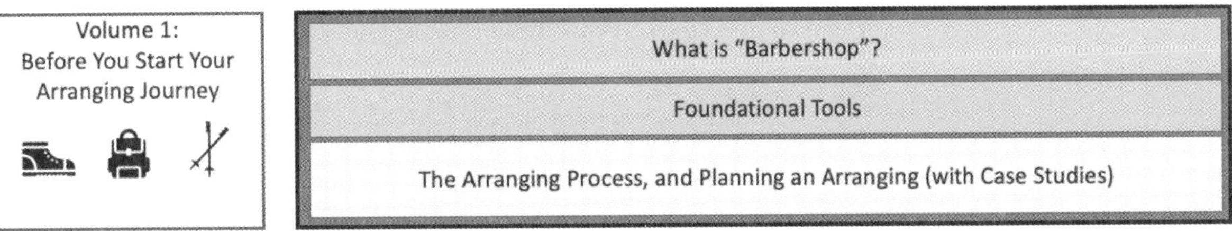

Congratulations on completing the first leg of your arranging journey! Hopefully, by taking the journey before the journey, you feel more prepared to embark on your next arranging process. Let's review what we've discussed in Vol. 1:

- We began with a historical perspective, exploring both the roots of the style and a comparison of some of the earliest guidelines for arranging barbershop with today's standards.
- We dissected a definition of the style, as defined by the Barbershop Harmony Society in 2018, and provided examples of the elements of the style in action. We explored how some of the core, fundamental aspects (the immutable laws of barbershop) could be applied to songs from multiple genres of music.
- Adding to our arranging toolbox, we reviewed the ranges for all voices, and reviewed music theory as applied to barbershop harmony. This included some comparison and contrast of concepts (e.g., *consonance* and *dissonance*) which have stylistic implications that differ from other genres of Western music.
- We explored the arranging process and discussed the importance of planning before embarking on an arranging journey. This included discussion about different roles and personas during the arranging process, different types of arrangement, and a methodology for planning an arrangement.
- To demonstrate these processes in action, we included three different case studies: an end-to-end, view-from-30,000-feet arranging process from Kevin Keller, the basics of harmonizing of an Irving Berlin melody by Steve Armstrong, and the process put into action by me, following an arrangement of "It Had to Be You" from concept to completion.

Vol. 2 of *Arranging Barbershop* now dives into the arranging journey itself. Volume 2 is divided into three parts: Beginning, Intermediate and Advanced. It includes end-to-end case studies at each level from master arrangers such as Steve Armstrong and Clay Hine and provides deeper dives into concepts pertinent to each level of skill and expertise. As with any journey and skilled skier/hiker/climber, even advanced arrangers may find new ways of thinking about fundamental concepts in the beginning and intermediate arranging sections of Vol. 2. You may also want to dive right into one of the more advanced experiences. It is structured to allow for either path as you proceed along your journey. Happy travels and see you in Vol. 2!

Permissions

A Nightingale Sang in Berkeley Square (1940)
Words and Music by Manning Sherwin, Eric Maschwitz
Copyright © 1940 The Peter Maurice Music Co., Ltd., London, England Copyright Renewed and Assigned to Shapiro, Bernstein & Co., Inc., New York for U.S.A. and Canada International Copyright Secured All Rights Reserved Used by Permission
Reprinted by permission of Hal Leonard Corporation

Annie Laurie (1834)
Words and Music by William Douglas and Alicia Scott
Public Domain

Aura Lee (1864)
Words and music by W. W. Fosdick and George R. Poulton
Arrangement by Barbershop Harmony Society
Public Domain
Reprinted by permission of the Barbershop Harmony Society

Bicycle Built for Two (1892)
Words and music by Harry Ducre
Public Domain

California, Here I Come (1924)
Words and music by Bud DeSylva, Joseph Meyer, and Al Jolson
Arrangement by David Wright
Public Domain
Reprinted by permission of David Wright

Come On, Let's Have Some Fun (2021)
Words and music by Tom Gentry
Arrangement by Tom Gentry
Reprinted by permission of Tom Gentry

Dear Old Girl (1903)
Words and music by Morse, Theodore F. and Buck, Richard H.
Arrangement by Tom Gentry
Public Domain
Reprinted by permission of Tom Gentry

Donna
Words and music by Ritchie Valens
Copyright © 1958 EMI Longitude Music Copyright Renewed All Rights Administered by Sony Music Publishing LLC, 424 Church Street, Suite 1200, Nashville, TN 37219
International Copyright Secured All Rights Reserved
Reprinted by permission of Hal Leonard Corporation

Five Foot Two
Words and music by Ray Henderson, Sam M. Lewis and Joseph Widow Young
Arrangement by Joe Liles

Reprinted by permission of Hal Leonard Corporation

Georgia on My Mind
Words and music by Stuart Gorrell and Hoagy Carmichael
Arrangement by David Harrington

Reprinted by permission of Hal Leonard Corporation

Gimme a Little Kiss (1926)
Words and music by Maceo Pinkard, Whispering Jack Smith, Roy Turk
Arrangement by Mel Knight
Public Domain
Reprinted by permission of the Barbershop Harmony Society

Hello, Mary Lou
Words and music by C. Mangiaracina, Gene Pitney
Arrangement by David Wright

Reprinted by permission of Hal Leonard Corporation

How Could You Believe Me
Words and music by Burton Lane and Alan Jay Lerner
Arrangement by Renee Craig

Reprinted by permission of Hal Leonard Corporation

I Am the Walrus
Words and music by John Lennon and Paul McCartney

Reprinted by permission of Hal Leonard Corporation

I'm Into Something Good
Words and music by Gerry Goffin and Carole King
Arrangement by John Fortino

Reprinted by permission of Hal Leonard Corporation

If I Had My Way (1913)
Words and music by James Kendis and Lou Klein
Arrangement by Tom Gentry
Public Domain
Reprinted by permission of Tom Gentry

It Had to Be You (1927)
Words and music by Isham Jones and Gus Kahn
Arrangement by Steve Tramack
Public Domain
Reprinted by permission of Steve Tramack

Jeannie with the Light Brown Hair
Words and music by Stephen Foster
Arrangement by Ed Waesche
Public Domain
Reprinted by permission of the Barbershop Harmony Society

Lida Rose / Will I Ever Tell You
Words and music by Meredith Willson
Arrangement by Mo Rector and Joni Bescos
© 1957 (Renewed) FRANK MUSIC CORP. and MEREDITH WILLSON MUSIC
International Copyright Secured All Rights Reserved
Reprinted by permission of Hal Leonard Corporation

Mama's Black Baby Boy (1893)
Words and music by the Unique Quartet
Arrangement by the Unique Quartet
Public Domain

Manhattan (1925)
Words and music by Lorenz Hart and Richard Rodgers
Arrangement by Adam Bock
Public Domain
Reprinted by permission of Adam Bock

Mean to Me
Words and music by Roy Turk and Fred E. Ahlert
Arrangement by David Wright
TRO - © Copyright 1929 (Renewed) Cromwell Music, Inc., New York, NY, Pencil Mark Music, Inc., Bronxville, NY, Azure Pearl Music, Beeping Good Music and David Ahlert Music All Rights for Pencil Mark Music Administered by BMG Rights Management (US) LLC All Rights for Azure Pearl Music, Beeping Good Music and David Ahlert Music Administered by Bluewater Music Services Corp.
International Copyright Secured All Rights Reserved Including Public Performance For Profit Used by Permission
Reprinted by permission of Hal Leonard Corporation

My Mother's Eyes
Words and music by Abel Baer and L. Wolfe Gilbert
Arrangement by Renee Craig

Reprinted by permission of Hal Leonard Corporation

My Wild Irish Rose (1899)
Words and music by Chauncey Olcott
Arrangement by the Barbershop Harmony Society
Public Domain
Reprinted by permission of the Barbershop Harmony Society

Night and Day
Words and music by Cole Porter

Reprinted by permission of Hal Leonard Corporation

Oh When the Saints Go Marching In (Traditional)
Public Domain

Oh, How I Miss You Tonight (1925)
Words and music by Benny Davis, Joe Burke, and Mark Fisher.
Arrangement by Renee Craig and Bill Wyatt
Public Domain
Reprinted by permission of the Barbershop Harmony Society

Rainbow Connection
Words and music by Paul Williams and Kenneth Ascher
Arrangement by Steve Tramack

Reprinted by permission of Hal Leonard Corporation

School Days (1907)
Words and music by Will Cobb and Gus Edwards
Public Domain

Shine
Original Verse: Words, Music and Arrangement by David Wright

Reprinted by permission of David Wright

Shine On, Harvest Moon (1908)
Words and music by Nora Bayes and Jack Norworth
Arrangement by Val Hicks and Earl Moon
Public Domain
Reprinted by permission of the Barbershop Harmony Society

Something Good
Words and music by Richard Rodgers
Arrangement by David Wright

Reprinted by permission of Hal Leonard Corporation

Where the Southern Roses Grow (1904)
Words and music by Richard Henry Buck and Theodore F. Morse
Arrangement by Dave Stevens
Public Domain
Reprinted by permission of the Barbershop Harmony Society

Sweet Adeline (1903)
Words and music by Richard Husch Gerard and Harry Armstrong
Arrangement by the Barbershop Harmony Society
Public Domain
Reprinted by permission of the Barbershop Harmony Society

The Chordbuster's March
Words and music by W. A. Wyatt
Arrangement by W. A. Wyatt

Reprinted by permission of the Barbershop Harmony Society

The Story of the Rose (Heart of My Heart) (1899)
Words and music by Andrew Mack and "Alice"
Arrangement by the Barbershop Harmony Society
Public Domain
Reprinted by permission of the Barbershop Harmony Society

There'll Be Some Changes Made
Words and music by Benton Overstreet, Billy Higgins
Arrangement by Tom Gentry

Reprinted by permission of Hal Leonard Corporation

Too Marvelous for Words
Words and music by Johnny Mercer, Richard Whiting

Reprinted by permission of Hal Leonard Corporation

Was willst du dich, o meine Seele
Words, Music and Arrangement by J S Bach
Public Domain

We Will Rest Awhile (1911)
Words, Music and Arrangement by Scott Joplin
Public Domain

When I Lost You (1912)
Words and music by Irving Berlin
Arrangement by Steven Armstrong
Public Domain
Reprinted by permission of Steven Armstrong

When I Lost You (1912)
Words and music by Irving Berlin
Arrangement by Steve Tramack
Public Domain
Reprinted by permission of Steve Tramack

When You and I Were Young, Maggie (1908)
Words and music by George Johnson and James Butterfield
Public Domain

Yesterday
Words and music by John Lennon and Paul McCartney
Copyright © 1965 Sony/ATV Music Publishing LLC Copyright Renewed All Rights Administered by Sony/ATV Music Publishing LLC, 8 Music Square West, Nashville, TN 37203
International Copyright Secured All Rights Reserved
Reprinted by permission of Hal Leonard Corporation

You Are My Sunshine
Words and music by Jimmie Davis
Arrangement by Vicki Uhr
Copyright © 1940 by Peer International Corporation Copyright Renewed
International Copyright Secured All Rights Reserved
Reprinted by permission of Hal Leonard Corporation

You Make Me Feel So Young
Words and music by Mack Gordon, Josef Myrow
Arrangement by Mark Hale
© 1946 (Renewed) WB MUSIC CORP.
International Copyright Secured All Rights Reserved
Reprinted by permission of Hal Leonard Corporation

You Tell Me Your Dream (1899)
Words and music by by Albert H. Brown, Charles N. Daniels, Seymour Rice
Arrangement by Phil Embury
Public Domain
Reprinted by permission of the Barbershop Harmony Society

You Were Only Fooling
Words and music by Larry Fotine, Ben Gordon, Billy Faber
Arrangement by Steve Tramack
Words by Billy Faber and Fred Meadows Music by Larry Fotine Copyright © 1946, 1948 Shapiro, Bernstein & Co., Inc., New York Copyright Renewed
International Copyright Secured All Rights Reserved Used by Permission
Reprinted by permission of Hal Leonard Corporation

Glossary of Terms

A Cappella – A term applied to vocal music which is performed without accompaniment.

A tempo – A musical direction indicating a return to a previously established tempo.

Absolute pitch – See *perfect pitch.*

Accelerando – A musical direction indicating a gradual speeding up of the tempo.

Accidentals – The signs (sharp (♯), flat (♭), natural (♮), double sharp (𝄪) and double flat (𝄫) used in musical notation to indicate chromatic alterations of pitches or to cancel them.

Ad lib – Ad libitum. Tempo and rhythm may be altered at the discretion of the performer.

Added ninth – The major ninth (see *ninth*) added to a triad (see *triad*). The chord so obtained, such as C–E–G–D.

Added second – See *Added ninth.*

Added sixth – The major sixth (see *sixth*) added to a triad (see *triad*). The chord so obtained, such as C–E–G–A.

Amen (plagal) cadence – The cadence (see *Cadence*) with the subdominant preceding the tonic: IV–I. Known as the *amen* or *plagal cadence* because of its traditional use for "amen" at the close of the hymn.

Arrangement – An adaptation in vocal harmony of a composed song using principles of voicing, voice leading, and harmonization which reveal variety and unity.

Augmentation – A form of rhythmic alteration which lengthens the original note values, usually doubling those values.

Augmented interval – An interval which is a chromatic ½-step larger than a major second, a major sixth, a perfect fourth, or a perfect fifth. Other intervals may be augmented but are impractical in ordinary musical usage.

Augmented seventh chord – A seventh chord whose characteristic interval is the augmented fifth; a seventh chord consisting of root, the major third above, the augmented fifth above, and the minor seventh above, as: C–E–G#–Bb, or F–A–C#–Eb.

Augmented triad – A chord consisting of root, the major third above and the augmented fifth above, as C–E–G# (or Eb–G–B).

Back time – An arranging device which lengthens the duration of syllables or words in the harmony parts as they support the melody.

Balance – The effect achieved through proper voice volume on each note of a chord.

Bar – A vertical line across the staff, dividing it into measures; sometimes called bar line; a measure (see *measure*).

Barbershop ninth chord – A ninth chord consisting of root, the major third above, the perfect fifth above, the minor seventh above and the major ninth above, as C–E–G–B♭–D. Because there are only four parts in barbershop music, either the fifth or the root is omitted. See *dominant ninth chord.*

Barbershop seventh chord – A seventh chord consisting of root, the major third above, the perfect fifth above, and the minor seventh above, as: D–F#–A–C, or F–A–C–Eb.

Baritone – the inside harmony voice. Similar range to the lead.

Beat – The unit of measurement in music, the pulse in music. Most music beats are organized in groups of 2, 3, or 4 per measure; See *pulse.*

Beats – A pulsation in sound intensity produced by the combination of two or more tones of slightly different frequency. The beat frequency is equal to the difference in frequency between any pair of tones. In a different musical context, a beat refers to the time duration of accented and unaccented pulsations which convey the sense of tempo of a song.

Bell chord – An arranging device by which a chord is constructed by a succession of notes sung by each voice in turn.

Blossom effect – An arranging device in which the four voices start in unison and, in contrary motion, expand to a four-part chord.

Blues style – A jazz style characterized using *blue notes*, that is, the lowered third, seventh, and sometimes fifth degrees of the major scale.

Break – an outdated vocal pedagogy term referring to the span of notes in a given singer's range indicating a register transition. Modern, acceptable terms are *passaggio*, *register event,* and *area of transition*

Bridge – The middle section of the traditional American Tin Pan Alley song. The B (middle) section of the ABA form of such songs; also called release.

Cadence – A melodic harmonic progression that occurs at the end of a composition, section or phrase, con-veying the impression of a momentary or permanent conclusion. See *amen cadence.* Also *deceptive cadence.*

Caesura – This sign (//). indicates that a rather long breath should be taken. Under certain conditions, it may indicate a grand pause, a longer breath taken for dramatic effect.

Cascade effect – An arranging device in which the four voices start in unison and, while the top voice sustains his tone, the three lower voices move downward to the notes of a chord. Opposite of *pyramid.*

Chart – Colloquial term for an arrangement.

Chest Voice – A historical vocal pedagogy term for notes primarily used by a singer that correspond to their speaking voice

Chord – A musical sound consisting of three or more notes sounded together.

Chord progression – A succession or series of chords.

Chorus of a song – That part of a song which normally follows the verse; also called refrain. While there may be more than one verse to a song, there is generally only one chorus which is repeated after each verse. The term refers to either melody or lyrics, or to both together.

Chromatic note – A note which has been raised or lowered by an accidental from its normal position in the scale.

Chromatic scale – A twelve-tone scale with ½-steps between all successive notes.

Circle of Fifths – The twelve tones of the chromatic scale arranged in a sequence of ascending or descending perfect fifths. The circular, clockwise arrangement of the twelve keys in an order of ascending fifths (C, G, D, A, etc.); Of greater concern is its importance as a generator of harmonic progressions, since roots of chords most commonly move to roots of other chords which lie a perfect fifth below, as in the counterclock-wise progression: C7–F7 to B♭7, etc.

Clef – A musical sign placed at the beginning of each line of music to give precise pitch meaning to the staff.

Climax – The high point of a song, toward which both music and words build.

Clock system – A chord nomenclature system devised in the early 1940s by veteran Barbershopper Maurice "Molly" Reagan. The system is based on the circle of fifths which places the twelve chromatic notes found within the octave and their enharmonic equivalents on the face of a clock. The 12 o'clock position is the tonic, the 1 o'clock position is the dominant, etc.

Close position voicing – The distribution of notes in a chord so that all four voices fall on consecutive notes of the chord, and the interval from highest to lowest is an octave or less.

Coda – See *tag.*

Combination tones – Tones perceived by a listener when two or more tones of different frequency are sounded simultaneously to produce a beat rate fast enough to be recognized as a tone of a given pitch. Also called coincident partials. Combination tones contribute significantly to the expansion of sound.

Comma – This sign (,) indicates that a short, quick breath should be taken at the point where it appears in the music.

Common time – Same as four-four meter. Four beats to the measure.

Consonance – A smooth sound resulting from the combination of two or more tones whose frequencies are related as the ratios of small whole numbers where-by the roughness related to the beat phenomenon is reduced to a minimum. See *dissonance.*

Consonant – Harmonious. Also, one of a class of speech sounds (as p, k, m, d, s) characterized by constriction or closure at one or more points in the breath channel.

Contrapuntal – Having two or more simultaneous melodies.

Contrary motion – Involving melodic movement by two voices, usually the tenor and bass, in opposite directions.

Crossed voices – Pertaining to the situation where the lead is above the tenor or below the bass or where the baritone is above the tenor or below the bass, or where the bass is above any of the other three parts. The lead below the baritone does not constitute crossed voices as this voicing commonly exists in barbershop music.

Cut time – A meter signature indicating two beats per measure.

Deceptive cadence – The delaying of final harmonic repose by a harmonic progression to an unexpected chord at the point of cadence, as V7–VI.

Decrescendo – A musical direction indicating a gradual decrease in loudness.

Di – The solmization syllable for raised *do*, as C# in the scale of C. See *solmization*; *Sol-Fa.*

Diatonic – The seven tones of the natural major scale.

Diction – The pronunciation and enunciation of words in singing.

Difference tone – A very faint note resulting from the difference of the frequencies of two notes sounded simultaneously.

Diminished interval – An interval which is a chromatic ½-step smaller than a minor third, a minor seventh, a perfect fourth, or a perfect fifth. Other intervals may be diminished but are impractical in ordinary musical usage.

Diminished seventh chord – A seventh chord whose characteristic interval is the diminished seventh; a seventh chord consisting of root, the minor third above, the diminished fifth above and the diminished seventh above, as F#–A–C–E♭, or B–D–F–A♭, etc.

Diminished triad – A chord consisting of root, the minor third above and the diminished fifth above: as C–E♭–G♭, or G#–B–D, etc.

Diminution – A form of rhythmic alteration which shortens the original note values, usually halving those values.

Diphthong – A combination of two vowel sounds that form a single word syllable, such as "a" in "way"—[we] (ay-ee)—or "I" in "mine"—[mɑ: in] (ah-ih)—etc.

Dissonance – The absence of consonance characterized by a rough sound resulting from the beat produced by two or more tones whose frequencies are not simply related. See *consonance.*

Dissonant – Inharmonious. Also, a combination of tones (chord) that requires resolution such as a barbershop seventh chord.

Divorced voicing – The distribution of notes in a chord so that either the tenor or the bass is distantly removed from the other three voices.

Do – The solmization syllable for the first degree of the major scale. See *Solmization*, *Sol-Fa.*

Dominant – The fifth degree of either a major or a minor scale. Also, a chord whose root is on that scale degree.

Dominant ninth chord – A ninth chord built on the fifth scale degree consisting of root, the major third above, the perfect fifth above, the minor seventh above and the major ninth above as G–B–D–F–A in the key of C. Because there are only four parts in barbershop music, either the fifth or the root is omitted. See *barbershop ninth chord.*

Dominant seventh chord – The barbershop seventh chord built on the fifth scale degree consisting of root, the major third above, the perfect fifth above and the minor seventh above, as G–B–D–F in the key of C. See *Barbershop seventh chord*

Double – A condition existing when two voices sing the same letter-named pitch in unison, at the octave or at the double octave.

Doubling – Creating a double.

Double time – At double speed; a tempo twice as fast as the preceding tempo.

Downbeat – The first beat of a measure, so called because the director's motion is made in a downward direction.

Duet – A composition or part of a composition or arrangement for two performers only. In barbershop music it refers also to three or four voices singing only two parts.

Duration – The length of a musical tone. In musical notation duration is indicated using varying note values-half notes, quarter notes, etc.

Diminuendo – A musical direction indicating a gradual decrease in loudness. Same as decrescendo.

Dynamics – Degree of loudness or softness in a musical performance, indicated by the musical directions piano (*p*), pianissimo (*pp*), mezzoforte (*mf*), forte (*f*), and fortissimo (*ff*).

Echo – An arranging device used as harmonic and/or durational fill-in which repeats a word or group of words.

Embellishment – Any arranging device such as a swipe, key change, echo, bell chord, etc., designed to add interest and variety to harmonizations of songs.

Enharmonic – Sounding the same but written differently, as: C# and D♭.

Equal temperament – A system of tuning in which the octave is divided into 12 equal semitones (½-steps), as with a piano, to permit such instruments to be played in any key with only small harmonic inaccuracies.

Expanded sound – One of the hallmarks of barbershop singing is the presence of expanded sound, or the auditory perception of additional notes generated by the energetic interaction between overtones (see combination tones), particularly when harmonics coincide with formants.

Expression – The elements of rubato tempo, phrasing, dynamics, accents, fermatas, and tenutos which are used by performers in interpreting music.

Fa – The solmization syllable for the fourth degree of the major scale, as E♭ in the scale of B♭ Major. See *solmization, Sol-Fa.*

False cadence – Same as *deceptive cadence.*

False relation – See *cross relation*

Falsetto – A historical vocal pedagogy term for notes above chest and head voice in male-presenting voices.

Fermata – A hold or pause, indicated by the sign "𝄐"

Fi – The solmization syllable for raised *fa* as F# in the scale of C Major.

Fifth – The note of a chord lying an interval of a fifth above the root, as G in the chord C–E–G. See *perfect fifth; interval.*

Fifth, interval of a – An interval covering five scale degrees. See *perfect fifth.*

First inversion – The distribution of the notes of a chord so that the third of the chord is the lowest sounding note.

Fine (fee-nay) – The end.

Flat – The musical symbol (♭) that lowers the pitch of a piano white key note ½-step. Also, below pitch, as to sing flat.

Folk song style – A style of harmonization characterized by generally limited harmonic interest, avoidance of chromatic notes, and lack of full four-part chords.

Form – The order of the component parts of an arrangement (introduction, verse, chorus, tag, etc.). Also, the architectural division of the musical material into phrases and sub-phrases.

Formants – A series of broad resonant frequency bands that correspond to the natural resonant frequencies of the vocal tract. The character of distinct vowel and sung consonant sounds is determined by the positioning of the jaw, tongue, lips, etc., during singing whereby unique patterns of resonant formant frequencies are established.

Forte (f) – Dynamic marking meaning loud.

Fortissimo (ff) – Dynamic marking meaning very loud.

Fourth, interval of a – An interval covering four scale degrees. See *perfect fourth.*

Four-three chord – A musical term which indicates a seventh chord in the second inversion. See *second inversion.*

Four-two chord – A musical term which indicates a seventh chord in the third inversion. See *third inversion.*

Free style – See *Ad lib*; free tempo.

Free tempo – Performed without a regularly recurring beat or pulse. Also called free style. See *Ad lib.*

Frequency – The number of periodic vibrations or cycles occurring per second. See *Hertz.*

From the top – Colloquial term for start at the beginning; from the first measure. Barbershoppers will also say "from the edge" and "upper left."

Fundamental – The lowest tone, or generator, of a series of harmonies and overtones. It is the first harmonic. See *overtones* and *harmonics.*

Glee club style – A style of harmonization characterized by melody mostly in the top voice, and consisting primarily of diatonic harmony, often using incomplete chords and unnecessary doublings.

Glissando – See *portamento.*

Grand pause – This sign (//) indicates a long pause, often for dramatic effect. See *caesura.*

Half-diminished seventh chord – A seventh chord whose characteristic interval is the diminished fifth; a seventh chord consisting of root, the minor third above, the diminished fifth above, and the minor seventh above, as B–D–F–A, or D–F–A♭–C . In popular sheet music, m7♭5.

Half-time – At half speed; a tempo half as fast as the preceding tempo. See *stomp time.*

Harmonic anticipation – The premature appearance of a harmony in a chord progression. A chord which appears before the implied harmony requires it.

Harmonic rhythm – The rhythmic pattern with which harmonies change within any given portion of music.

Harmonic series – See *overtones.*

Harmonics – Tones of higher pitch that are present in a regular series in nearly every musical sound, and whose presence and relative intensity determine the timbre of the musical sound. The term also includes the fundamental. See *overtones.*

Harmonization – The basic setting of the melody with three harmonizing parts, faithful to the composer's melody and to the implied harmony.

Harmony – The sounding together of tones. Also, the study of chords and chord progressions.

Head voice – A historical vocal pedagogy term for notes above what is typically called chest voice. When referring to a male-presenting voice, head voice is a lighter chest voice and not falsetto. When referring to female-presenting voice, head voice is analogous to falsetto in male-presenting voices.

Hertz – This term has replaced the older understanding of vibrations per second in honor of Heinrich Hertz, German physicist, 1857–1894. Abbreviation Hz.

High baritone voicing – The distribution of the tones of a chord so that the usual tenor note is given to the baritone and the tenor sings the baritone note an octave higher.

Homorhythmic – One of the hallmarks of the barbershop style and differentiating aspects from other a cappella styles, homorhythm is a texture having a similarity of rhythm in all parts, such as all voices parts singing the same word sounds at the same time. Homorhythm is a condition of homophony, which is a blocked chordal texture. Homorhythmic textures deliver lyrics with clarity and emphasis. Textures in which parts have different rhythms are defined as *heterorhythmic.*

Hz. – See *Hertz.*

Implied harmony – A succession of harmonies and chord progressions suggested by the composer's melody.

Inflection – A musical direction indicating a slight accent on a note, chord, or syllable.

In tempo – See *a tempo.*

Interlude – A section, generally newly composed, added to an arrangement to separate or to connect larger sections of the arrangement

Interpolation – The insertion of a small portion of one song into an arrangement of another song.

Interpretation – The personal and creative delivery by a performer of a song's message and emotional content. See *expression.*

Interval – The difference in pitch between two tones.

Intonation – The degree to which the tonal center appropriate to any point in a song remains invariant, and/or the degree to which consonant interval relationships between the harmony parts and the projected melodic line are maintained.

Introduction – A musical phrase preceding the first main portion (verse or chorus) of a song.

Just diatonic scale – The scale of just intonation. A musical scale containing exact intervals in the harmonic series of a given fundamental tone. It may be constructed by tuning the subdominant, tonic, and dominant triads with true major thirds and fifths in the ratio 4:5:6.

Just intonation – A system of tuning based on acoustically pure perfect fifths and major thirds. The natural tuning preferred for barbershop singing. See *perfect fifth; major third*; see *equal temperament*; see *just diatonic scale.*

Just temperament – Same as *just intonation.* See *just diatonic scale.*

Just tuning – Same as *just intonation.* See *just diatonic scale.*

Key – The prevailing tonal center as expressed by a key signature. Also, the scale and all relationships embodied in it.

Key change – A modulation. A change of key during a composition or arrangement

Keynote – The first note of the scale and the central tone of the key. Also called tonic or *do.*

Key signature – Sharps or flats placed at the beginning of each line of music to indicate the key.

La – The solmization syllable for the sixth degree of the major scale, as: A in the scale of C Major; G in the scale of B♭ Major, etc. See *solmization, Sol-Fa.*

Le (lay) – The solmization syllable for lowered *la*, as: A♭ in scale of C Major.

Lead – The melody in a barbershop song. Also, the one who sings this part.

Lead-in notes – See *pick-up notes.*

Leading tone – The seventh degree of the scale lying a ½-step below the tonic.

Legato – A manner of performance in which successive notes are joined smoothly without separation.

Li (lee) – The solmization syllable for raised *la*, as: A# in the scale of C Major.

Lyric – The words of a song.

Major – A qualifying term denoting specific kinds of intervals, scales, triads, and keys.

Major interval – An interval ½-step larger than a minor interval.

Major key – Having the qualities and relationships of the tones of a major scale and the chords built on those scale tones.

Major scale – A scale with the whole and ½-step pattern of the white keys from C–C on a piano.

Major seventh chord – A seventh chord whose characteristic interval is the major seventh. A seventh chord consisting of root, the major third above, the perfect fifth above and the major seventh above, as C–E–G–B; or B♭-D–F–A.

Major third, interval of a – An interval covering exactly two whole steps, as: C–E; F–A; and B♭–D.

Major triad – A chord consisting of root, the major third above and the perfect fifth above, as C–E–G, D–F#–A, etc.

Me (pronounced may) – The solmization syllable for lowered *mi*, as E♭ in the scale of C Major.

Measure – A metric unit consisting of a specific number of beats delineated by bar lines.

Mediant – The third degree of either a major or minor scale. Also, a chord whose root is on that scale degree.

Medley – An arrangement containing all or major parts of two or more songs having a unified theme or idea.

Meter – The basic, prevailing pattern of beats and accents in a song, or section of a song; indicated by the meter signature, such as 2/4, 3/4, 6/8, etc.

Meter change – A change of meter during a composition or arrangement

Meter signature – Arabic numerals placed at the beginning of a piece of music to indicate the meter.

Mezze forte (mf) – Dynamic marking meaning moderately loud but not as loud as forte (f).

Mezze piano (mp) – Dynamic marking meaning moderately soft but not as soft as piano (p).

Mi (mee) – The solmization syllable for the third degree of the major scale, as D in the scale of B♭ Major; or B in the scale of G Major. See *solmization, Sol-Fa.*

Middle C – The C near the middle of the piano keyboard. In the notation of TTBB barbershop music, it is the note on the third space of the treble staff (with the 8 underneath the clef) and the note on the first ledger line above the bass staff. For SSAA barbershop notation, it is the note on the first ledger line below the treble staff and the note on the second space of the bass clef (with the 8 above the clef).

Minor – A qualifying term denoting specific kinds of intervals, scales, triads, and keys.

Minor key – Having the qualities and relationships of the tones of a minor scale and the chords built on those tones.

Minor scale – A scale with the whole and ½-step pattern of the piano white keys from A–A. In actual usage the seventh tone of this scale is almost always raised a ½-step to a pitch a ½-step below the tonic. In addition, the sixth scale degree is also sometimes raised.

Minor seventh chord – A seventh chord whose characteristic intervals are the minor third and the minor seventh. A seventh chord consisting of root, the minor third above, the perfect fifth above, and the minor seventh above, as: D–F–A–C, and G–B♭–D–F.

Minor sixth chord – A minor triad with an added major sixth, such as: C–E♭–G–A, or E–G–B–C#.

Minor triad – A chord consisting of root, the minor third above and the perfect fifth above, such as D–F–A, E–G–B, or G–B♭–D.

Mode – A scale form, such as major or minor.

Modern style – A style of harmonization characterized by melody usually in the top voice, and harmonies of sixth chords, major seventh chords, ninth, eleventh, and thirteenth chords, plus other, more dissonant chords. Also considered Jazz style.

Modulation – See *key change.*

Music theory – That part of the study of music consisting of all the elements of harmony and notation.

Natural – The musical symbol (♮) that cancels a sharp, flat, double sharp or double flat.

Neutral vowel – A sound such as "oh" or "ah" which is sung usually by three voices as an accompaniment to a solo, or solo passage, in a barbershop arrangement.

Neutral syllable – A sound such as "bum bum" or "doo wah" which is sung by one or more voices in a barbershop arrangement

Ninth chord – Any chord whose largest interval above the root is a ninth. See dominant ninth chord.

Ninth, interval of a – An interval covering nine scale degrees. It may be a major ninth, that is, an octave plus a whole step, such as C–D, or E–F#; it may be a minor ninth, that is, an octave plus a ½-step, such as C–D♭, or E–F. See *dominant ninth chord.*

Non-chord tone – A tone which is not part of the prevailing harmony. See *suspension, passing tone and pedal tone.*

Notation – The technique of placing musical symbols on manuscript paper.

Octave, interval of an – An interval covering eight scale degrees, as C–C, F#–F#, etc.

Octet – A group of eight performers. In barbershop music, there are two singers on each voice part.

Open position voicing – The distribution of the notes in a chord so that the interval from the lowest to the highest note is more than one octave.

Over arranged – Colloquial term referring to an arrangement embellished to the extent that the melodic and lyric interest are obscured or lost.

Overtones – Any frequency produced by an acoustical instrument, including the voice, that is higher in frequency than the fundamental. It is customary to refer to the first overtone as the second harmonic, the second overtone as the third harmonic, etc. They are present in a regular series in every musical sound, and the presence, absence, and relative strengths of them determine the quality of musical sound. See *harmonics.*

Parallel harmony – A succession of chords in which all or most of the voices move in parallel melodic lines. Generally undesirable in barbershop music except for special effects or when specifically required by the implied harmony.

Parallel motion – Involving melodic movement by two or more voices in the same direction and maintaining the same basic interval relationship between the voices.

Parody – A satirical imitation, such as may be created in music by replacing the original lyric with a comic one, or by changing the composition itself in a comic manner.

Passing tone – A non-chord tone which occurs in an ascending or descending scale pattern. Not typically characteristic of the barbershop style.

Patter – An arranging device featuring the adaptation or composition of lyrics which are sung in more rapid rhythmic pattern than the melody and lyric which they support. There are several variations of this device.

Pedal tone – A tone which is held by one voice while other voices move freely over, under, or around it. Consonant pedal tones are acceptable in the barbershop style.

Perfect fifth – An interval covering five scale degrees and containing exactly seven ½-steps, as C–G, B♭–F, etc.

Perfect fourth – An interval coveting four scale degrees and containing exactly five half steps, as G–C, F–B♭, etc.

Perfect octave – An internal covering eight scale degrees, as C–C, F–F, etc.

Perfect pitch – The ability or capacity of an individual to identify a pitch immediately by letter name, without reference to a previously sounded note of different pitch. See *relative pitch.*

Piano (p) – Dynamic marking meaning softly.

Pianissimo (pp) – Dynamic marking meaning very softly.

Pick-up note(s) – A note or series of notes preceding the downbeat of a musical phrase.

Pitch – The sensation of relative highness or lowness of a sound, determined primarily by the frequency of vibration of the sound-producing medium.

Precision – The area of a performance which refers to attacks, releases, and synchronization.

Pop style – A style of harmonization characterized by frequent unison singing and much use of the solo voice with a vocal background consisting of singing neutral vowels or syllables.

Portamento – Sliding smoothly from one tone to another, continuously changing pitch.

Pulse – A rhythmic recurrence of beats; a single beat; a slight emphasis to a syllable or note.

Pyramid – An arranging device which incorporates the gradual expansion of a harmonic texture from a single pitch, sung solo or in unison by two or more voices, to a full chord, by the addition of chord tones above the starting pitch. Opposite of cascade.

Ra (rah) – The solmization syllable for lowered *re*, as D♭ in C Major.

Range – The pitches a voice can produce, from lowest to highest Also the span of pitches, from lowest to highest, in a particular song or arrangement

Re (ray) – The solmization syllable for the second degree of a Major scale, as D in the scale of C Major, or C in the scale of B♭ Major. See *solmization, Sol-Fa.*

Refrain of a song – See *chorus of a song.*

Register – A series of tones of similar quality within the range of a voice which are produced by a particular adjustment of the vocal folds.

Relative pitch – The ability to recognize or identify the interval relationship between two different pitches.

Release – The termination or cessation of sound. Also see *bridge.*

Resolution – The process in which a note or chord of lesser consonance (e.g., a barbershop seventh chord) moves to another note or chord of greater consonance.

Resonance – The intensification and enrichment of a musical tone by the acoustical amplification of those harmonic frequencies which lie within the format frequency bands.

Rhythm – The organization of music in respect to time. It is expressed by using notes of various durational values. See *meter, beat, measure, syncopation, meter signature, duration.*

Rhythmic propellant – Any of several arrangement devices (echoes; pick-up notes, backtime, swipes, etc.) whose primary purpose is to help maintain the ongoing rhythmic motion in a song.

Ri (ree) – The solmization syllable for raised *re*, as D# in the scale of C Major. See *solmization, Sol-Fa.*

Ritard – Abbreviation for ritardando. Also abbreviated rit. A musical direction indicating a gradual slowing down of the tempo.

Root – The note upon which a chord is built and from which it takes its name.

Root position – The distribution of the tones of a chord so that the root of the chord is the lowest sounding note.

Rubato – A controlled flexibility of tempo within a phrase or measure, characterized by a slight quickening and/or slight slowing of tempo. Not as free as ad lib.

Scale – A pattern of pitches arranged in ascending or descending order. See *major scale, minor scale.*

Scat – Derived from vocal jazz, scat is a vocal improvisational style using wordless vocables or nonsense syllables, using the voice as an instrument rather than a lyrical singing mechanism.

Second, interval of a – An interval covering two scale degrees. It may be a major second, that is, a whole step, such as C—D, or E–F#, or it may be a minor second, that is, a ½-step, such as B– C, or F#–G.

Second inversion – The distribution of the tones of a chord so that the fifth of the chord is the lowest sounding tone.

Secondary dominant ninth chord – A chord with the same interval structure as the dominant ninth chord, but whose root is not the fifth degree of the scale. See *dominant ninth chord.* See *barbershop ninth chord.*

Secondary dominant seventh chord – A chord with the same interval structure as the dominant seventh chord, but whose root is not the fifth degree of the scale. See *dominant seventh chord.* See *barbershop seventh chord.*

Seventh, interval of a – An interval covering seven scale degrees. It may be a major seventh, such as C–B, or G–F#; a minor seventh, such as C–B♭, or G–F; or a diminished seventh, such as C#–B♭.

Seventh chord – Any chord whose largest interval above the root is a seventh. See *dominant seventh chord, major seventh chord, augmented seventh chord, minor seventh chord, barbershop seventh chord, diminished seventh chord.*

Sforzando (Sfor-tsahnd'-oh) – A musical direction indicating a strong accent on a note or chord. (sfz or >)

Sharp – The musical symbol (#) that raises the pitch of a white key on a piano by ½-step. Also, the high side of a pitch, as in "sing sharp."

Six-five chord – A musical term which indicates a seventh chord in first inversion.

Six-four chord – A musical term which indicates a triad in second inversion.

Si (see) – The solmization syllable for raised *sol*, such as G# in the scale of C Major.

Sixth, interval of a – An interval covering six scale degrees. It may be a major sixth, such as: C–A, or E–C#, or a minor sixth, such as C–A♭, or E–C.

Sixth chord – Any chord whose largest interval above the root is a sixth. See added *sixth, interval of a sixth.*

Sol – The solmization syllable for the fifth degree of a major scale, such as F in scale of B♭ Major. See *solmization, Sol-Fa.*

Sol-Fa – A system of ear training and sight singing in which the notes are sung to syllables and the ear is trained to recognize and reproduce, through the syllables, the notes on the printed page. Also called Solfege.

Solmization – The use of syllables to designate the tones of the scale. See *Sol-Fa.* Also *Do, Re, Mi, Fa, Sol, La, Ti.* Also, *Di, Ri, Fi, Si, Li*, ascending; and *Te, Le, Se, Me, Ra*, descending.

Solo – Alone. A composition or part of a composition or arrangement for one performer with or without accompaniment. In barbershop music, the soloist is often accompanied by the remaining three voices.

Song theme – That component of the song (lyric, melody, harmony, rhythm, or parody) which gives it its entertainment value.

Sound flow – A continuous uninterrupted execution of word sounds except where staccato or stress is inten-tionally used for interpretive purposes.

Spread chord – A chord whose tones are distributed in extreme open position voicing. See *open position voicing.*

Staccato – A manner of performance in which successive notes are detached or separated from one another.

Staff – The set of five lines and four spaces, each representing a different pitch, on which music is written.

Stomp time – A manner of performance characterized by a slow, heavily accented beat, generally performed at half the tempo of the major portion of the performance. Used for contrast and/or climactic effect

Subdominant – The fourth degree of either a major or minor scale. Also, a chord whose root is on that scale degree.

Submediant – The sixth degree of either a major or minor scale. Also, a chord whose root is on that scale degree.

Sub-climax – A point of emphasis in a song, which may be melodic and/or lyric, that does not take away from the climax (high point); but may enhance it.

Summation tone – A very faint note resulting from the sum of the frequencies of two notes sounded simultaneously.

Supertonic – The second degree of either a major or minor scale. Also, a chord whose root is on that scale degree.

Suspension – The sustaining of one of the notes of a chord while the other notes move so that it demands resolution, usually downward to the next chord tone. Non-chord suspensions are not characteristic of the barbershop style.

Syllables – The component parts of words. In solmization the words *do, re, mi*, etc. See *solmization, Sol-Fa.*

Synchronization – The degree of coordination achieved in the execution for chord progressions and word sounds.

Syncopation – A rhythm having accents which do not agree with the normal metrical accents.

Swipe – A progression of two or more chords sung on a single word or syllable. A characteristic feature of the barbershop style of music.

Tag – The coda or special ending added to a song or to an arrangement

Target vowel – The primary sustained vowel sound of the word being sung.

Te (tay) – The solmization syllable for the lowered below the tonic.

Temperament – See *system of tuning.* See *equal temperament, just intonation.*

Tempered tuning – See *equal temperament.*

Tempo – The speed of a composition determined by the speed of the beat to which it is performed.

Tempo ad lib – A musical direction indicating variable tempo. See *rubato, ad lib.*

Tenor – The top voice in a barbershop quartet or chorus.

Tenuto – Usual definition: to hold a note for its full value. In actual practice it involves a slight lengthening of the note.

Tessitura – From the Italian for "texture," tessitura refers to the general lie of a vocal part, whether it is high or low in average pitch. From *A Cappella Arranging,* "a vocal part may cover two octaves: if most of that time is spent in the upper octave, the part has a *high* tessitura. If it's all over the place, it's a *wide* tessitura."[53]

Third, interval of a – An interval covering three scale degrees. It may be a major third consisting of two whole steps, such as C–E, or D–F#, or a minor third consisting of a step and a half, such as C–E♭, or D–F.

Third inversion – The distribution of the tones of a seventh chord so that the seventh is the lowest sounding note.

Thirteenth chord – Any chord whose largest interval above the root is a thirteenth. In barbershop usage, four tones of this seven-note chord are omitted (the root usually doubled), leading to some confusion with the sixth chord.

Ti (tee) – The solmization syllable for the seventh degree of a major scale. It lies ½-step below the tonic. See *tonic.*

Timbre – A result of the presence and relative strength of overtones which makes one voice resemble, or differ from, another.

Time signature – See *meter signature.*

Tone – A musical sound of definite pitch.

Tonic – The key note. The first note of the scale and the central note of the key.

Transpose – To write or to perform in a different key from the original.

Tremolo – An excessive vibrato that leads to deviation from exact pitch. See *vibrato.*

Triad – A three-note chord composed of alternating scale tones, as C–E–G, F–A–C, etc.

---

[53] A Cappella Arranging, Deke Sharon and Dylan Bell, page 332

Trio – A composition or part of a composition or arrangement for three performers only. In barbershop music, trio refers to the three parts singing an accompaniment to a solo.

Tritone Substitution – From *A Cappella Arranging*: "A jazz harmonic progression wherein a dominant seventh chord is swapped for a dominant seventh chord a tritone away. That means that a Dm7–G7–C progression would become a Dm7–D♭7–C. The reason this works is that the third and the seventh of the G7 chord (B and F) are the seventh and the third of the D♭ chord, and they will still resolve inward (provided there is good voice leading) to C and E."[54]

True scale – A scale with intervals tuned in just intonation. See *just intonation.*

Tune-up chord – The tonic chord of the key in its characteristic voicing used to tune the quartet or chorus preparatory to singing. Oftentimes, the leads sing the root, basses also the root but an octave lower, baritones sing the fifth of the chord between the leads and basses, and the tenors sing the third of the chord above the lead note.

Tuning – Adjusting pitch to obtain desirable tonal relationships. See *intonation, overtones, just intonation.*

Undertone – See *difference tone.*

Unison – The combined sound of two or more notes at the same pitch.

Upbeat – The final beat of a measure; the beat immediately preceding the downbeat. Sometimes confused with the term pick-up notes. See *downbeat, pick-up notes.*

Verse – The part of a song which normally precedes the chorus or refrain.

Vibrato – A method of giving expressive quality to the sound of a note by means of rapid and minute fluctuations of pitch.

Voice – A part, such as tenor, lead, baritone, or bass. Also, the music written for that part.

Voice leading – The principles governing the progression of the various voice parts in an arrangement, especially in terms of the singability of the individual lines.

Voicing – The manner of distribution of the tones of a chord among the four voice parts. See *close position voicing, open position voicing, spread chord.*

Volume – The degree of loudness or softness.

Volume relationship – See balance.

Vowel – One of a class of speech sounds (a, e, i, o, u) in the articulation of which the oral part of the breath channel is not blocked or constricted.

Walking bass – From *A Cappella Arranging*: "A bass line that moves in a scaler and/or chromatic fashion from chord to chord. Frequently found in jazz."[55] This technique is used in barbershop arranging in a 3-against-1 texture with the bass frequently providing the beats in the measure while the trio is syncopating.

Waltz time – 3/4 meter. Having a meter signature indicating three beats per measure.

---

[54] A Cappella Arranging, Deke Sharon and Dylan Bell, page 332
[55] A Cappella Arranging, Deke Sharon and Dylan Bell, page 332

Woodshedding – Impromptu four-part singing without benefit of printed arrangements. A form of creativity in harmonizing.

Contributors

	**Steve Armstrong** has been involved in barbershop singing for nearly 50 years, joining the Oshawa Horseless Carriagemen when he was just 13 years of age. Steve began his early directing career at the age of 19, and by the age of 32 Steve had directed both the Scarborough Dukes of Harmony and the East York Barbershoppers into international competitions. Following that, Steve was a co-founder of the Toronto Northern Lights and directed them to 14 International medals, including the International Chorus Championship in 2013. He earned his Bachelor's Degree in Music Education from the University of Toronto in 1984. Steve has been a member of three Ontario District Championship Quartets (1988 "Flipside", 1996 "Jukebox" and 2022 "Detour"), all of which have competed at the Barbershop Harmony Society's international competitions. In addition, Steve has been a society judge for over 36 years, served as Music Category Specialist from 2017-2019 and has been the Chair of the Society's Contest and Judging program since 2020. He has served on the judging panel of several International competitions as well as many overseas contests. An accomplished barbershop arranger, coach and instructor, Steve's skill and experience have been sought after by many quartets and choruses. He has coached throughout the barbershop world, and he has taught at the society's Harmony University as well as schools for other barbershop organizations. Steve lives in Oshawa, ONT with his wife Lori and son Joel where they attend the local Salvation Army church.
	**Dylan Bell** is a world-renowned vocal arranger, performer, producer, and instructor. His award-winning arrangements have been sung around the world by vocal groups from Ann Arbor to Zurich. Bell has written for some of the finest a cappella groups in the world, including the Nylons (Canada) and the Swingle Singers (UK). Bell also regularly contributes articles to the Contemporary A Cappella Society of America. He lives in Toronto. Visit Dylan at www.dylanbell.ca.

Adam Bock is an arranger and singer based in New York City. After graduating with his bachelor's in music composition and joining the BHS in 2010, he spent two wonderful years in his hometown of St. Louis with the Ambassadors of Harmony before moving to NYC to sing with Voices of Gotham and forge a career. He joined a rock band and toured the country and world until the pandemic brought public performance to a screeching halt. He is now pursuing his master's in music education and plans to teach vocal and general music in NYC's public schools.

Mo Field is a musician, composer, arranger, artistic director, Barbershop Harmony Society certified judge and international coach of barbershop and a cappella performing ensembles. She was the director of Stockholm City Voices from 2003 through their rise to international acclaim. A multi-instrumentalist and published songwriter (ASCAP), her craft spans multiple genres. Mo is a seasoned musician and performer with a passion and curiosity for the creative and all creative people. She is regularly on faculty of Harmony University and currently is the Artistic Director of the Great Northern Union. Mo lives in Toronto with her partner and kittens.

Tom Gentry's barbershop career began with The Music Man quartet in high school, and he loved the harmony instantly. Since then, he has arranged roughly 800 songs, worked at the Barbershop Harmony Society in a staff position (1985–1992), sang with two international medalist choruses (Houston Tidelanders and San Diego Sun Harbor Chorus) and many quartets, directed the Akron (Ohio) Derbytown Chorus, and has traveled around the barbershop world.

A charter member (1977) of the woodshedding organization AHSOW and former Arrangement judge (1979–92), he has served as a Music judge (1993–2023), having once served as the category specialist. He is a 35-year faculty member of Harmony University. In 2006, Tom was inducted into the Johnny Appleseed District Hall of Fame and in 2022 attended my 51st consecutive international convention. Tom is an Honorary Member of BinG! (Barbershop in Germany) and an Honorary Life Member of Harmony, Incorporated.

Rafi Hasib is a software engineer and musician based in New York City. Born in Dhaka, Bangladesh, he immigrated to the US at a young age, where music and art helped him connect with his peers when words alone could not.

As long as he can remember, Rafi enjoyed exploring how different instruments work and blend together, often improvising vocal harmonies with the radio. While studying engineering at the University of Pennsylvania, Rafi was hired as a teaching assistant who embraced the value of making complex concepts understandable in the simplest terms. Inspired by the late composer Dr. Bruce Montgomery, he spent his free time arranging for his university glee club, a cappella group, and barbershop quartet, culminating with scoring an original musical, "The Glee of Clubs," complete with a pit orchestra.

Today, Rafi is a lifelong member of the Barbershop Harmony Society, who has sung in multiple award-winning choruses and served in various administrative roles, focused on the human connection behind technical ideas. He sees this book as the quintessential opportunity to enrich our community through a deeper understanding of the music that draws us together.

Clay Hine, in his own words: "Growing up around folks who were great barbershoppers and even more importantly, great people, was the best kind of brouhaha. That really kicked into full fun fracas mode for me when, at 14 years old, I was finally able to join the chorus my dad directed in Detroit, Michigan. Over the years since then, I've sung with a few quartets: with my dad in Atlanta Forum (1987 Dixie District Quartet Champs), FRED (1999 SPEBSQSA International Quartet Champs), A Mighty Wind (earning a few medals along the way), and most recently, Category 4 (7th place international finalists—for 3 years in a row—there should be a consistency award). I've also directed the Big Chicken Chorus (described as 'poultry in motion' by some— well, just me—on our way to earning 3 medals in international competition) and am currently the director of the award-winning Atlanta Vocal Project. I've also written over 400 vocal arrangements for many male, female, and mixed ensembles and some of those have created a whole new style of brouhaha. My amazingly patient wife Becki is also very involved in Sweet Adelines International as a judge, coach, and chorus director—her Song of Atlanta Chorus has ballyhooed their way into finishing as high as 4th in the SAI international competition. My daughter, Melody sings with the 2019 Harmony Incorporated quartet champions, Hot Pursuit. Melody also causes quite the entertaining kerfuffle with her arranging brouhaha. When my son, Camden, is not too busy earning college degrees, he also enjoys the brouhaha of singing barbershop."

Kevin Keller has been a barbershopper since 1978. In addition to being a performer, coach, teacher, and judge, he has been arranging for top level groups since the late 1990s. He has arranged over 300 songs in the barbershop style as well as SATB and other a cappella styles. In 2020, he was inducted into the Barbershop Hall of Fame.

"The song has ended, but the melody lingers on…" for beloved Barbershopper **Joe Liles**. There are no words, no notes, no harmonies large enough to encompass the breadth of Joe's influence on the Barbershop Harmony Society, and on the barbershop art form. In addition to hundreds of original songs, and hundreds of arrangements, his fingerprints are on untold more works that he brought to print as Music Publications Editor, as a teacher, mentor, and colleague to other arrangers.

A member of the BHS Hall of Fame, a seniors quartet champ, a past Society Executive Director— any list of accomplishments falls woefully short of describing the man, whose quick wit and groan-worthy puns fired at maximum intensity right up to his final days. Joe's friends around the globe (numbering in the tens of thousands) will remember him for being keenly interested in each life, each person he met. Because although he loved barbershop, he loved Barbershoppers even more. Joe passionately, devoutly, with every breath, wanted more people singing, in every combination—men's, women's mixed—in every style. He directed SPEBSQSA choruses and Sweet Adelines Choruses. He created music for church groups, for high school groups, for people he'd never met but who had found him. Joe joined the great choir in the sky in August of 2021 at the age of 90.

Adam Scott works as a music editor for The Church of Jesus Christ of Latter-Day Saints. He holds a M.M. in choral conducting and a B.A. in music composition. Before this he worked as music educator and editor of music publications for the Barbershop Harmony Society. He has collaborated with composers and arrangers including Dr. Kirby Shaw and Deke Sharon. He has been a certified Musicality judge since 2016.

Adam has written/arranged over a thousand pieces of music, composing everything from piano pieces to major works. He specializes in writing custom works to suit individual ensembles. His classical music is sung by various middle / high schools and colleges. He is published by MusicSpoke, Music House Publications, Sheet Music Plus, Hal Leonard, and his own private studio.

Adam lives in Nashville, TN with his wife, Bethany, and four (loud) boys.

	**Steve Scott** is the Director of Harmony University and Education Services for the Barbershop Harmony Society. A barbershopper for over thirty years, Steve taught voice and choir at the college level before joining the BHS staff. His research interests include the biophysiology of the barbershop singing voice, barbershop acoustics, and barbershop history. He is a certified Singing judge, a frequent faculty member for harmony colleges around the world where he teaches voice techniques and vocal pedagogy, a voice teacher, and coach. Steve also serves as the assistant director and principal vocal coach of the 2022 international champion chorus, the Music City Chorus, both in Nashville TN. He enjoys living in the Nashville area with his wife and two children.
	**Deke Sharon** is known colloquially as "the father of contemporary a cappella." Arguably one of the best-known and most prolific a cappella arrangers in the world, with over 2,000 arrangements to his credit, Sharon has been a vocal (pun intended) exponent of contemporary a cappella music through his founding of the Contemporary A Cappella Society of America, now a worldwide presence with members in dozens of countries. He has written 6 books: A Cappella Arranging (2012), A Cappella (2015), The Heart of Vocal Harmony (2016), A Cappella Warmups for Pop and Jazz Choir (2017) and So You Want to Sing A Cappella (2017) and Teaching Music Through Performance in Contemporary A Cappella (2020). He vocally produced five seasons of The Sing Off for NBC in the US as well as international versions in the Netherlands, South Africa and China, and served as music director for Disney+ Best in Snow. He was arranger, on-site music director and vocal producer for all three of Universal's hit films in the Pitch Perfect franchise as well as the spinoff TV show Bumper in Berlin. He was featured on camera in Lifetime Television's Pitch Slapped, coaching the group Stay Tuned and on BBC1's Pitch Battle as music director and guest judge and has arranged music for the Oscar-winning film *The Social Network*. He is also the vocal orchestrator for and producer of Broadway's first a cappella musical: *In Transit* (2016). He lives in San Francisco.
	**Steve Tramack** joined the Barbershop Harmony Society in 1983 and proves the adage that barbershopping runs in the blood. Great-grandfather Frank Barker started a chapter in 1946; his father, Dave, was a 40+ year member, and his son Joshua, wife Renee, and daughters Christina and Samantha are all BHS members. Renee, a member of Harmony Inc. since 1982, co-directs New England Voices in Harmony (2014 and 2018 International champions) with Samantha. Renee, Christina and Samantha sing in Taken 4 Granite (2016 Harmony Inc Queens), and Samantha, Christina and Joshua sing in Sweet & Sour (2022 BHS District quartet champions and International quartet quarterfinalist) Steve is actively involved in several facets of barbershopping, including (as of 2022): 10-time International chorus director; 5-time International quartet competitor; Certified Musicality judge (2010), and BHS Musicality Category Specialist (2020–2024); Over 300 commissioned arrangements, ranging from International champions (BHS, Harmony Inc, SAI) to chapter quartets and choruses; Active coach of male, female and mixed

	ensembles worldwide; 19-year Harmony University faculty member and chair of the Arranging Track.
	**Andrew Wittenberg** is a PhD Candidate in Music Theory at the University of Cincinnati, College-Conservatory of Music. He has sung in a wide variety of choral and vocal ensembles throughout his undergraduate and graduate degrees in music, and since joining the BHS in 2020, he has sung with the Southern Gateway Chorus and joined its music leadership team. He teaches classes in music theory, sight-singing, and ear training while he works on his dissertation on barbershop harmony. Andrew lives in Cincinnati, OH with his wife, Janie, and his two miniature schnauzers, Dorian and Lydian.
	**David Wright**, from St. Louis, Missouri, is a mathematician, professor, arranger, composer, director, coach, judge (since 1981), Harmony University faculty member, historian, baritone, and member of the Barbershop Harmony Hall of Fame. He helped design the Musicality Category and served as its first Category Specialist. He is Associate Director of the St. Charles Ambassadors of Harmony, four-time International Chorus Champions. He is a prolific arranger, having arranged for many top quartets and choruses. About 90 of his arrangements have been sung in gold medal performances.